THE EASTERN ENLARGEMENT OF THE EU

THE EASTERN ENLARGEMENT OF THE EU

edited by

Marek Dabrowski
Center for Social and Economic Research, Poland

and

Jacek Rostowski
Center for Social and Economic Research, Poland

KLUWER ACADEMIC PUBLISHERS
Boston / Dordrecht / London

Distributors for North, Central and South America:
Kluwer Academic Publishers
101 Philip Drive
Assinippi Park
Norwell, Massachusetts 02061 USA
Telephone (781) 871-6600
Fax (781) 871-6528
E-Mail <kluwer@wkap.com>

Distributors for all other countries:
Kluwer Academic Publishers Group
P.O. Box 322
3300 AH Dordrecht, THE NETHERLANDS
Telephone 31 (0) 78 6576 000
Fax 31 (0) 78 6576 254
E-Mail services@wkap.nl>

Electronic Services <http://www.wkap.nl>

Library of Congress Cataloging-in-Publication Data
The eastern enlargement of the EU / edited by Marek Dabrowski and Jacek Rostowski.
p.cm.
Includes bibliographical references and index.
ISBN 0-7923-7828-8
1. Fiscal policy--Europe, Eastern. 2. Fiscal policy--Europe, Central. 3. European Union--Europe, Central. 4. European Union--Europe, Eastern. 5. Europe, Eastern--Economic policy--1989- 6. Europe, Central--Economic policy. 7. Europe--Economic integration. I. Dabrowski, Marek, 1951- II. Rostowski, Jacek.

HJ1000.7 .E2 2001
339.5'2'0943--dc21 00-049319

Printed on acid-free paper.

Printed in the United States of America

This printing is a digital duplication of the original edition.

Contents

List of Figures

List of Tables

Contributors

Marek Dąbrowski is Professor of Economics and V-Chairman of the Board of Trustees of CASE – the Center for Social and Economic Research in Warsaw, economic consultant to a number of governments in transition countries, and a Member of the Monetary Policy Council of the National Bank of Poland. He has served as First Deputy Minister of Finance and as a Member of Parliament. He is the author of a number of publications on the political economy of transition and the macroeconomics of transition.

Max Gillman is Associate Professor of Economics at the Central European University, Budapest, Hungary. He obtained his Ph.D. from Chicago University. He has published a number of articles on monetary theory and macroeconomics.

Stanisław Gomułka is Reader in Economics at the London School of Economics. He has been at the heart of Polish economic policy making since 1989 as adviser to successive Ministers of Finance and to the National Bank of Poland. He is the author of a number of books on economic growth and a large number of papers on the economics of the transition from communism.

Michał Gorzelak is a Researcher at CASE, Warsaw, and at the Research Institute of the Polish Academy of Sciences and the Central Statistical Office, Warsaw.

Wojciech Maliszewski is a Researcher at CASE, Warsaw, and a PhD student at the London School of Economics

Peter Mihalyi is Professor of Economics at the University of Veszprem, Hungary and also teaches at the Central European University, Budapest. He has served as Chief Economist of the Privatization Agency and as Deputy Minister of Finance in Hungary.

Ryszard Petru is a Researcher at CASE, Warsaw, and an Economist at the Word Bank Regional Office, Warsaw. He has served as Advisor to Minister of Finance on pension and health-care reforms in Poland.

Jacek Rostowski is Professor of Economics at the Central European University, Budapest, a Trustee of the CASE Institute, Warsaw, and also Chairman of the Macroeconomic Policy Council at the Ministry of Finance, Warsaw. He has published widely on the macroeconomics of transition.

Ondřej Schneider is Chief Economist at Patria Finance, Prague. He obtained his PhD from the CERGE at Charles University, Prague.

Joanna Siwińska is a Researcher at CASE, Warsaw, and a PhD student at Warsaw University

Pavel Štepanek is Chief Executive Director and a Member of the Board of the Czech National Bank. He has served as Deputy Minister of Finance of the Czech Republic.

Mateusz Walewski is a Researcher at CASE, Warsaw

Katarzyna Zawalińska is a Researcher at CASE, Warsaw.

Acknowledgements

This volume contains part of the results of ACE PHARE Research Project No. P96-6089-R on: "The Medium and Long-term Perspectives of Fiscal Adjustment of Selected Central European Countries" undertaken between June 1997 until July 1999 by CASE – the Center for Social and Economic Research in Warsaw. The project team consisted of Marek Dabrowski (project coordinator), Stanislaw Gomulka, Urszula Kosterna, Georges de Menil, Peter Mihalyi, Jacek Rostowski, and Pavel Stepanek (research partners), Magdalena Tomczynska (project secretary), Max Gillman, Michal Gorzelak, Atilla Hajos, Monica Iosif, Piotr Jaworski, Wojciech Maliszewski, Jaroslaw Neneman, Ryszard Petru, Ondrej Schneider, Joanna Siwinska, Marek Styczen, Magdalena Tomczynska, Zoltan Vajda, Mateusz Walewski, and Katarzyna Zawalinska (research assistants). Participants of the project prepared 22 research papers and background studies, partly presenting country cases and partly comparative analyses. Most of these were published preliminarily as working papers in the CASE-CEU Working Papers, CASE Studies and Analyses, and CASE Reports series. This volume presents a selection of the comparative papers which mainly concentrate on basic macroeconomic and fiscal problems. Original papers were revised and updated as necessary. Katarzyna Wilary helped with the technical editing of this volume.

Marek Dabrowski
Jacek Rostowski

Chapter 1

MACROECONOMIC AND FISCAL CHALLENGES DURING THE EU ACCESSION PROSESS: AN OVERVIEW

Marek Dąbrowski

INTRODUCTION

At the end of 1997 five transition countries – the Czech Republic, Estonia, Hungary, Poland, and Slovenia – were invited to start negotiations on their accession to the EU. In December 1999 five other countries – Bulgaria, Latvia, Lithuania, Romania and Slovakia joined the first group.

Until now (i.e. the summer of 2000), accession negotiations have concentrated on various institutional, legal, and microeconomic issues. The macroeconomic problems of candidate countries have not been discussed extensively as yet, and it is not clear what kind of macroeconomic criteria will be finally applied as conditions of membership. Most researchers and analysts while discussing the macroeconomic perspectives of candidate countries traditionally refer to the five criteria set by the Maastricht Treaty. However, these were formally binding only on the first group of EMU candidates and will not be automatically applied to the new EU members (see Kosterna, 1998, p. 10). Moreover, as we shall see below, these criteria are not necessarily always suitable, given the specificities of the macroeconomic situation of candidate countries.

The above does not mean that the candidate countries will not face serious macroeconomic and fiscal challenges or that these problems will not complicate the accession process. Assessing the macroeconomic situation of candidate countries using the Maastricht criteria gives the erroneous impression that they are already close to fulfilling the requirements of EMU membership, and will not experience serious problems with macroeconomic convergence. In addition, too frequent acknowledgement of the leading position of some countries in the transition process (particularly of Hungary or Poland) does not also help them face the scale and nature of possible difficulties.

The purpose of this chapter is to present an overview of the main macroeconomic challenges that may appear during the accession process, and indeed post-accession.[1] The analytical part of the chapter is based on statistical data ending in 1997 or 1998, hence, it cannot reflect the macroeconomic developments of 1999-2000, which may have influenced some of our assessments and conclusions.

Our analysis will start from the differences in GDP per capita between the CEECs and EU member countries, relative growth performance, and growth prospects (Section 1). Then we will turn to problems of financing growth, i.e. the savings-investment gap, capital inflows, and current account deficits (Section 2). This will be followed by an analysis of monetary and exchange rate policies and inflation performance (Section 3). Fiscal policy may play an important role in supporting the disinflation process, mitigating excessive current account deficits, and creating favorable conditions for economic growth. At first glance, the current fiscal situation of the countries analyzed does not look bad (though it is differentiated), but there are a number of problems that are not reflected in the standard cash-basis fiscal statistics. Examples are the implicit pension debt or contingent liabilities in the banking system. Moreover, the medium and long-term fiscal perspectives of the countries analyzed depend strongly on the expected rate of GDP growth, and under a low growth scenario, they are very bad indeed (Section 4). Candidate countries also represent too high a level of fiscal redistribution of GDP (Section 5). Finally, I will try to specify possible strategies for dealing with the problems identified (Section 6).

1. IS CATCHING-UP TO EU NATIONAL INCOME LEVELS LIKELY?

Former communist countries have lost out on at least a half-century of normal economic development. The nature of their growth built serious structural distortions into their economies, which made them highly inefficient, compared to the rest of the world. This led to an unavoidable output decline after the collapse of communism (see Winiecki, 1990; Gomulka, 1998). According to the simulation of Fischer, Sahay, and Vegh

(1998a), GDP per capita in the six Central and East European countries, i.e., Bulgaria, former Czechoslovakia, Hungary, Poland, Romania, and former Yugoslavia, would have been at least three times higher on average by 1992, if they had continued the capitalist way of development after World War II. Making up for this lost time will take at least 15 years in the case of the Czech Republic, 20 years in the case of Hungary and Poland, and 30 years in the case of Romania.

Table 1.1 illustrates the 1995 per capita GDP level of the candidate countries calculated in PPP terms and compares it with the average GDP per capita level of the three lowest income countries in the EU, i.e. Greece, Portugal, and Spain. The gap ranges from 74% of the average EU level in the case of Lithuania to 30.1% in the case of the Czech Republic.

Table 1.1. EU candidate countries: per capita GDP in US dollars, PPP based

Country	GDP per capita	% of average for 3 low-income EU countries
Bulgaria	5132	43.9
Czech Republic	8173	69.9
Estonia	7203	61.6
Hungary	6211	53.1
Latvia	5002	42.8
Lithuania	3035	26.0
Poland	6364	54.4
Romania	3542	30.3
Slovakia	6671	57.1
Slovenia	6342	54.3
Average for 3 low-income EU countries	11690	x

Source: Fischer, Sahay, and Vegh (1998a) based on the World Economic Outlook Database.

After a few years of output decline, the countries that were more advanced in the transition process returned to economic growth, when their initial market reforms began to bear fruit. However, the rate of growth has been uneven, as is demonstrated in Table 1.2.

Table 1.2. Real GDP growth in candidate countries, 1990-1998.

Country	1990	1991	1992	1993	1994	1995	1996	1997	1998
Bulgaria	-9.1	-11.7	-7.3	-1.5	1.8	2.9	-10.1	-6.9	4.0
Czech Rep.	-1.2	-14.3	-3.3	0.6	2.7	6.4	3.9	1.0	-2.2
Estonia	-8.1	-7.9	-21.6	-8.2	-1.8	4.3	4.0	11.4	4.0
Hungary	-3.5	-11.9	-3.1	-0.6	2.9	1.5	1.3	4.6	5.0
Latvia	2.9	-10.4	-35.2	-16.1	2.1	0.3	3.3	6.5	3.8
Lithuania	-5.0	-13.4	-21.3	-16.2	-9.8	3.3	4.7	6.1	4.4
Poland	-11.6	-7.0	2.6	3.8	5.2	7.0	6.1	6.9	4.8
Romania	-5.6	-12.9	-8.8	1.5	3.9	7.1	3.9	-6.6	-5.5
Slovakia	-2.5	-14.6	-6.5	-3.7	4.9	6.9	6.6	6.5	4.4
Slovenia	-8.1	-8.9	-5.5	2.8	5.3	4.1	3.1	3.8	3.9

Source: Havrylyshyn, Izvorski, and Rooden (1998, tabl. 1), WEO (1999, table 1.3).

So far, Poland has presented the best cumulative growth record. However, one must take into consideration that Poland was the first country to start comprehensive economic reforms (at the end of 1989) and the first to overcome the output decline (in 1992). Among countries which began transition somewhat later Slovakia, Slovenia, and the three Baltic countries can also be classified as fast growing countries. Hungary, starting its transition very early, but was surprisingly a slow growing country until 1996, partly as a result of the 1994-1995 macroeconomic crisis. The Czech Republic, another reform leader recorded only one year of fast growth (1995), while 1998-1999 has brought a return of output decline. Again, the macroeconomic crisis of 1997 seems to be at least a partial explanation for this phenomenon. Romania started its economic growth relatively early (1993), in spite of very limited progress in macroeconomic stabilization and microeconomic restructuring at that time. This "premature recovery" led to a macroeconomic crisis in 1996-1997, which turned into a serious recession in 1997-1999. The same happened with the Bulgarian growth experience of 1994-1995, which ended with one of the most severe financial crises in the whole transition and a deep output decline in 1996-1997. Due to a very tough reform program, Bulgaria seems to have returned to economic growth, as is reflected by its 1998 results.

Explaining the "transformation recession" and the subsequent recovery and growth, as well as their differentiation across countries is no easy task (see Gomulka, 1998). Relatively short time series, not necessarily of good quality, and inherent difficulties in measuring various qualitative factors influencing growth behavior make any econometric analysis quite risky. However, most attempts [2] have come to the following conclusions:

1. The size and length of the initial transformation output decline[3] was determined both by the size of accumulated macro- and microeconomic distortions, and by the transition policy pursued by governments.
2. During the recovery, the conventional determinants, i.e. investment, labor, and human capital accumulation, played only a limited role. The

reallocation of existing resources as result of elimination of previous distortions (e.g. price and trade liberalization) seems to have been much more important. Thus, uncharacteristically of other depressions, macroeconomic stabilization, and progress in structural and institutional reforms usually emerge as the most important factors determining growth performance.

3. External trade shocks and political shocks also seriously influenced growth, at least in the short run. Among many such impulses, one can mention the succession of Balkan conflicts or the financial crisis in Russia and other CIS countries in 1998 (which affected Poland and the Baltics in 1998-1999).
4. Once the initial recovery is completed, further growth will probably be determined, to a greater extent than before, by conventional determinants, i.e. investment, labor, and human capital.

This last conclusion brings us to the problem of the growth prospects of the candidate countries. There is a widespread expectation that these economies will grow faster than the current EU members, gradually closing the development gap. The first obvious argument supporting such an expectation is based on the well know convergence hypothesis: countries with lower initial GDP per capita usually grow faster, other things being equal, than countries with higher GDP per capita level (see – Barro and Sala-I-Martin, 1992; Sachs and Warner, 1996).

Rostowski (Chapter 2) gives a number of additional arguments connected with the expected continuation of economic reforms. EU candidate countries will probably be fast growing for the following reasons:

1. They have stopped pursuing the very bad economic policies, which they had in the past under central planning (pervasive government control, extensive subsidies, massive foreign trade distortions, etc.).
2. The existence of considerable gains from learning by doing within the institutional infrastructure of the market economy, which was initially non-existent (e.g. the bankruptcy courts, customs services, and financial institutions), which can be expected to continue for some time to come.
3. New structural reforms which are coming on stream (e.g. pensions' reform, privatization of utilities);
4. Expected benefits of EU and EMU membership.

In the light of the earlier discussion of the sources of early post-transition recovery, one needs to ask to what extent these potential sources of growth have already been used up (particularly the first two factors). Visual inspection of Table 1.2 does confirm the feasibility of the fast growth hypothesis (at a rate of at least 4-5%) though there is no guarantee that such a high rate will be sustained through the whole of the next decade. Among the first group of candidates, the Czech Republic seems the most problematic. Among the remaining five countries, Romania appears to be in the most dramatic situation.

Using 1995 PPP based per capita GDP data, Fischer, Sahay and Vegh (1998a) tried to forecast future average rates of growth of the CEE countries using the Barro (1991) and Levine and Renelt (1992) growth equations. They also estimated the number of years needed by each country to converge to the average level of per capita GDP of the three lowest income EU countries (Greece, Portugal and Spain), assuming that the latter will grow at an average annual rate of 2%. Results are presented in Table 1.3.

Table 1.3. Simulation of average GDP per capita growth rates and number of years needed by the EU candidate countries for convergence to GDP per capita level of low-income EU countries.

Country	Barro equation		Levine-Renelt equation	
	rate of growth	number of years	Rate of growth	number of years
Bulgaria	4.92	29	5.01	28
Czech Rep.	5.44	11	4.40	15
Estonia	5.23	16	4.93	17
Hungary	5.28	20	5.02	22
Latvia	5.50	25	5.79	23
Lithuania	6.10	34	6.22	33
Poland	5.42	18	4.75	23
Romania	5.47	36	5.64	34
Slovakia	5.86	15	5.00	19
Slovenia	5.31	19	4.58	24

Source: Fischer, Sahay, and Vegh (1998a)

Two important conclusions can be drawn from this simulation. First, growth rates in the range of 5-7% seem to be a realistic forecast.[4] Thus, the fast growth hypothesis may be taken as a reasonable assumption for projecting other macroeconomic and fiscal variables. However, such an optimistic scenario depends strongly on further progress in economic reforms and sound economic policy. Second, even the fast growth scenario does not give prospects of fast convergence, even to the level of the lowest-income EU countries. In the best case (that of the Czech Republic), according to the Barro equation, catch-up will take 11 years, in the worst cases (Lithuania, Romania) - more than 30 years. Such a long lasting convergence period may create economic, social, and political problems, which may themselves complicate the accession process.

Growth prospects have important implications for other macroeconomic variables and policies. The fast growth hypothesis implies, for example, strong pressure for real appreciation and expanding current account deficits on the one hand (see next section), but on the other it also gives much more room for maneuver in fiscal policy (see Section 4). A slow growth scenario makes balance of payments problems less acute, but seriously challenges the sustainability of the long-term fiscal position of candidate countries.

2. BALANCE OF PAYMENTS PROBLEMS

A fast growth scenario in the candidate countries (far faster than in the EU itself) will lead to sustained real appreciation of national currencies and widening current account deficits. These phenomena can be explained from at least three theoretical points of view:

1. the investment-saving imbalance (and the balance of payments identity);
2. consumption smoothing models;
3. real appreciation coming from the Harrod-Balassa-Samuelson (H-B-S) effect.

Focussing on the investment-saving imbalance, a high growth scenario may require an increasing investment to GDP ratio as non-investment sources of growth (improving X-efficiency and the efficiency of factor allocation) have been substantially exploited in the first stage of the post-transition recovery in a number of countries. Table 1.4 presents the investment and savings data for eight candidate countries: Bulgaria, the Czech Republic, Estonia, Hungary, Poland, Romania, Slovakia, and Slovenia. Both indicators are highly differentiated across the countries, which may partly reflect measurement problems. However, some interesting observations can be drawn from this table as well as from Table 1.5, which records the current account balances of the ten candidate countries.

Table 1.4. Selected transition economies: gross saving and investment ratios as % of GDP, 1991-1997

Country / Indicator	1991	1992	1993	1994	1995	1996	1997
First group of candidates							
Czech Republic:							
gross domestic saving rate [c]	36.84	27.45	20.23	20.11	23.31	26.91	
gross investment rate [c]	29.89	27.07	18.39	20.37	27.81	34.52	
Estonia:							
gross domestic saving rate [c]	34.48	32.75	22.18	18.29	18.19	14.08	
gross investment rate [c]	20.93	21.03	23.93	26.59	25.62	24.81	
Hungary:							
gross domestic saving rate[b]	18.1	15.3	10.6	14.4	20.4	22.4	23.4*
gross investment rate[b]	20.6	16.1	20.0	22.2	24.1	24.5	25.4*
Poland:							
Gross domestic saving rate[a]	15.86	15.44	15.77	17.29	18.31	17.1	
Gross investment rate[a]	19.9	15.2	15.6	15.9	18.0	20.2	
Slovenia:							
gross domestic saving rate [c]	26.42	24.73	20.61	23.16	21.89	22.24	
gross investment rate [c]	20.61	18.41	18.73	19.75	21.20	22.09	
Other candidate countries							
Bulgaria:							
gross domestic saving rate [e]	18.4	4.5	2.0	4.5	10.8	7.5	13.6
gross domestic investment rate [e]	25.2	19.9	15.3	9.4	15.7	8.4	11.8
Romania							
gross national saving rate [e]	24.8	22.9	24.2	25.4	21.0	23.0	19.6
gross domestic investment rate [e]	28.0	31.4	29.0	26.9	25.7	31.3	28.3
Slovakia							
gross domestic saving rate [e]	28.3	24.9	22.1	27.7	30.8	28.0	28.4
gross domestic investment rate [e]	31.2	28.8	27.6	22.2	27.5	39.9	35.5

Source: Jakubiak (1999) based on: a: GUS: SNA, b: IMF Staff Country Report No. 97/104, c: World Development Indicators, d: own calculations based on IFS and WDI databases; *IMF estimates. Author's estimate based on: e – IIF (1998, tables S305, S315).

Table 1.5. Current account deficit as % of GDP in candidate countries, 1991-1997.

Country	1991	1992	1993	1994	1995	1996	1997	1998
Bulgaria	-7.2	-9.3	-12.8	-2.1	-1.0	-0.8	4.1	-2.6
Czech Republic	..	-1.7	2.2	-0.1	-2.9	-8.7	-6.0	-1.5
Estonia	..	-1.0	1.3	-7.1	-4.4	-9.1	-12.0	-8.7
Hungary	0.8	0.9	-9.0	-9.5	-5.6	-3.7	-2.1	-4.8
Latvia	..	15.2	19.7	5.5	-0.4	-5.5	-6.1	-11.0
Lithuania	..	5.4	-3.1	-2.1	-10.2	-9.2	-10.2	-12.1
Poland	-1.0	-0.3	-0.1	2.3	3.3	-1.0	-3.1	-4.5
Romania	-4.5	-7.5	-4.7	-1.7	-5.6	-7.8	-6.7	-7.9
Slovakia	..	0.4	-5.0	4.8	2.3	-11.1	-6.9	-9.7
Slovenia	1.5	7.4	1.5	3.8	-0.1	0.2	0.2	0.0

Source: Linn (1999).

Apart from Bulgaria and Slovenia, in 1997 the candidate countries recorded insufficient savings (relatively to investment) and, as a result, they experienced current account deficits. Moreover, in almost all countries significant deterioration of the current account balance can be observed from the mid-1990s. In 1997 in the Czech Republic, Estonia, Latvia, Lithuania, Romania, and Slovakia, current account deficits exceeded 5% of GDP, the level that is usually considered as the threshold indicating external vulnerability.

Apart from the Czech Republic, Romania, and Slovakia, the gross domestic investment to GDP ratio seems to be too low to permit the fast growth scenario.[5] The mediterranean countries (Greece, Portugal and Spain) recorded gross investment rates of about 30-35% of GDP during their accession process to the EU and just after accession (Jakubiak, 1999). This may indicate the scale of investment growth to be expected in the candidate countries in the coming decade.

The current investment boom in some candidate countries may support the above hypothesis. For example, in both Poland and Slovakia real gross fixed investment has increased at an average annual rate of 20% during 1995-1997, and in Poland the rate of increase has accelerated in each successive year (EBRD, 1998, p. 223).

Increasing gross domestic investment to GDP will need increases in either gross domestic saving or in the current account deficit. Gross domestic saving rates are determined by a number of policy and institutional factors, many of them historical (for example, high inflation episodes, or financial crises in the past).[6] One may expect that continuing disinflation, further development of the financial sector, and the introduction of funded pension systems, will push up the savings rate. Nevertheless, increasing the savings rate is likely to be a very gradual process, conditional on a number of developments (Liberda and Tokarski, 1999, for Poland). Thus, further widening of current account deficits due to the import of foreign savings seems to be unavoidable in most countries.

Importing foreign savings, i.e. capital inflow, has its own supply side dynamics. There are a number of "supply factors" inducing capital inflows, which are likely to be present in the applicant countries (Rostowski, Chapter 2):

- Consequences of H-B-S effect (see below). Increased productivity in the tradable goods sector and increased prices of non-tradables, lead to an increased return on capital in both sectors in the fast growing country.
- Progressive liberalization of capital flows in candidate countries.
- Increased maturity of the institutional infrastructure will strengthen creditors' property rights and exit possibilities for shareholders.[7] The prospect of imminent EU membership can be expected to raise foreign investors' awareness of the progress that has been made in this regard.

However, massive inflows of foreign savings, even if provoked by supply side factors, may crowd out part of domestic savings. This can happen through the interest rate channel: other things being equal, capital inflows put downward pressure on interest rates discouraging domestic savings.

Saving behavior can be also assessed from the inter-temporal consumption smoothing perspective. People who expect to be richer in the future than they are at present will behave rationally if they smooth their consumption path by borrowing today in order to consume more now, and repaying their debts later. At the level of a whole country this leads to foreign borrowing (capital inflow) and a current account deficit (Rostowski, Chapter 2; Rybinski and Szczurek, 1998).

Finally, the H-B-S effect leading to continuous real appreciation of candidate countries' currencies should be discussed. Although the H-B-S effect itself does not lead to worsening current account positions, as real appreciation of the domestic currency is matched by productivity gains[8], it can provoke other phenomena causing increased saving-investment imbalance (Rostowski, Chapter 2). First, real appreciation means that national income measured in foreign currency rises faster than when it is measured in domestic currency. As a result, the command of domestic residents over foreign resources increases faster than indicated by the growth of real GDP at domestic prices (in which the inflation in the non-tradables sector is discounted). This higher than conventionally measured real growth justifies more smoothing of consumption, and a higher current account deficit than otherwise. Second, if a large part of the government's debt is denominated in foreign currency (as is the case in many transition countries) then real appreciation leads to a decline in the ratio of public debt to GDP, and therefore of the ratio of public debt to the potential tax base (Siwinska, 1999a). Even if Ricardian equivalence is only partial, residents can be supposed to expect a lower share of taxes in national income will be needed to service the existing public debt. This raises future disposable income and the desire to smooth consumption (and raise the current account deficit) along with it. Third, from the perspective of foreign investors, high expected growth rates and real appreciation in applicant countries means increasing asset values. This may induce a further inflow of capital to buy while the assets are still relatively cheap, worsening the current account balance.

Why is the problem of avoiding "excessive" current account deficits so important for the macroeconomic policy of candidate countries? If transition economies have the possibility of importing additional savings that contribute to a higher rate of economic growth, why reject such an opportunity by restricting the current account deficit? Part of the answer has been already given: the "appreciation – capital inflow" bubble. Secondly there is possible inefficient use of imported saving if domestic absorption capacities are inadequate. The history both of the former communist countries and of developing countries gives many examples of the wasteful use of imported savings. The availability of cheap foreign financing can also discourage some countries from the fiscal adjustment effort required (a negative political economy effect). However, the potential un-sustainability of a large current account deficit, and the unpleasant consequences of a sudden reversal of capital flows, is the most serious problem.

Rostowski (Chapter 2) points out the danger of a "capital inflow - real appreciation" bubble, with the real exchange rate and current account deficit rising ever more above its medium term equilibrium level until, finally, the bubble bursts, causing a currency crisis and sometimes also a banking crisis. Sudden capital outflows and thus sharp pressure for devaluation can also be caused by external factors, such as a financial crisis in a neighboring country or rapidly worsening sentiment on the international financial markets. In any case, sharp devaluation may have serious negative consequences: it can undermine the solvency of the domestic banking and corporate sectors, increase the burden of external debt service (both public and private), provoke a new wave of inflation, stop economic growth for a number of years, and seriously hurt a government's credibility. Any of these could reduce the EU accession prospects of the country affected.

What kind of policies can help avoid "excessive" current account deficits and the danger of balance of payments crises? The answer is not easy. First, deciding on what is the sustainable level of the current account deficit seems an impossible task, particularly for very small open economies. Second, there is the problem of a shortage of effective policy tools for keeping the current account deficit at the desired level.

In some of the transition economies (Hungary, Poland, and Slovenia) monetary and exchange rate policies have been used to try to prevent excessive real appreciation and deterioration of the current account balance (see next section). However, this has led to a softening anti-inflationary policy and has involved significant fiscal costs (see – Dabrowski et al., 1999), while the positive effects on the current account are doubtful. Defending the exchange rate against nominal appreciation (or alternatively a reluctance to slow down the pace of nominal depreciation) could not prevent real appreciation through higher inflation or solve the problem of the fundamental saving-investment imbalance. As capital accounts of transition countries are being progressively liberalized, monetary policy will become even less effective for targeting the current account position (Rostowski, Chapter 2).

Fiscal tightening seems at first sight to be the other available measure for keeping the current account position under control (Rybinski and Szczurek, 1998). Although fiscal adjustment is, without doubt, very desirable from the point of view of the medium and long term fiscal sustainability of candidate countries (see Section 4), it may not improve their current account positions, as a "crowding in" phenomenon may take place (Rostowski, Chapter 2). Improving fiscal balances will improve candidate countries' financial rating (decreasing country risk) and encourage more private capital inflows, which have to be balanced by a larger deficit on the current account.

Continuation of microeconomic and regulatory reforms may contribute to marginally decreasing demand for external financing on the part of financial and corporate sectors not exposed sufficiently until now to hard budget constraints.[9] Again, though positive from the point of view of avoiding the insolvency of part of the banking and corporate sectors (and the possible contingent fiscal consequences), it is unlikely that such developments will improve current account positions significantly.

All the above arguments lead to the conclusion that the danger of balance of payment crises could be eliminated only through a radical change of the monetary regime, i.e. by the country's giving up its independent monetary policy. This can either take the form of a currency board, or full substitution of the national currency by one of the main world currencies (in the case of EU applicant countries the euro is the most natural choice).

So far, three of the EU candidate countries, i.e. Estonia, Lithuania, and Bulgaria have introduced currency board arrangements, and have accomplished remarkable macroeconomic stabilizations. The very high current account deficits of Estonia and Lithuania (see Table 1.5), with no signs of serious speculative attacks against their currencies even during the August 1998 Russian crisis, show how effective currency boards can be in resolving the problem of balance of payments vulnerability.

A currency board regime has a fiscal advantage over the adoption of another country's currency: it allows the retention of seigniorage revenue. However, it can be still subject to speculative attacks, which is no longer the case once the domestic currency has been abolished (a *new* domestic currency would have to be created if the country concerned wished to leave the eurozone). Experience of economically costly attacks against the Argentinian peso after the Mexican and Asian crisis show that this is not a merely hypothetical danger.

This is the reason why recently the idea of the total substitution of the domestic currency by one of the major international currencies has enjoyed increasing popularity. A "dollarization" proposal for Argentina (see Hanke and Schuler, 1999) got the biggest publicity. Bratkowski and Rostowski (1999a, 1999b) proposed unilateral "euroization" for Poland, even before membership of the EU. Robert Mundell (1999) suggests either unilateral euroization or a currency board based on the euro as an attractive option for all the EU candidate countries. The authors concerned stress the following benefits: (i) importing low inflation, (ii) importing low interest rates, and (iii) importing relative prices from the EU countries.

Certainly, giving up monetary independence will not totally eliminate the problem of sudden capital outflow provoked, for example, by bad economic policy such as deterioration of the fiscal position or unfavorable political developments. Such an outflow may cause, among other things, a stock market crash, contraction in the real sector and increased unemployment. However, some of the reasons for possible sudden capital outflow (a current account deficit perceived as "excessive", expectation of changes in exchange rates, limited credibility of domestic monetary policy, etc.) will no longer exist, and the country concerned should be able to enjoy the benefits of greater macroeconomic predictability and stability, as well as lower international transaction costs.

On the other hand, the exchange rate will no longer be available to serve as a shock absorber, or as a mechanism compensating for various microeconomic rigidities, particularly in the field of incomes policy. This may create pressure for the real sector to increase its flexibility. Since such a change in microeconomic behavior needs time, moving to a fixed exchange rate regime will probably cause some temporary output and employment costs. However, there are at least three serious arguments in favor of moving in this direction. First, the macroeconomic performance of Estonia shows that giving up independent monetary policy combined with tough fiscal discipline and fast microeconomic reforms can create very good foundations for sustainable economic growth. Second, and more fundamentally, the relation between macroeconomic policy and microeconomic reforms is that *"...the former shifts around the burden of the problem while the latter solves the problem."* (Gillman, Chapter 4). If an economy suffers microeconomic distortions (e.g. labor market rigidities), the first best solution is to eliminate these distortions, while attempts to compensate for them through macroeconomic policy amounts to a second best solution at best. Thus, the complete elimination of the exchange rate mechanism as an accommodative mechanism may force agents into greater flexibility (as they cannot expect accommodative devaluation anymore), and may force governments to accelerate microeconomic reforms. Third, the first group of five candidate countries can be expected to join the third stage of EMU (adoption of the euro) in the relatively near future (at the latest by 2010), so the adjustment discussed above is unavoidable. Speeding up accession to the eurozone can bring them not only efficiency gains in the medium and long run, and eliminate the risk of balance of payments crisis in the meantime, but it also helps them avoid what is likely to be a very difficult and painful period of ERM-II membership (Bratkowski, and Rostowski, 1999a and 1999b).

3. DISINFLATION, MONETARY AND EXCHANGE RATE POLICIES.

In 1998, eight of the ten candidate countries found themselves with single digit inflation, while Hungary was a bit above the 10% threshold and Romania remained still in the zone of high inflation (see Table 1.6). Only Bulgaria, Lithuania and Latvia were close to the euro zone countries recent performance (1-1.5% in 1998) while Estonia and Slovenia were next in this ranking. All other countries have still quite a long way to go to converge to the eurozone inflation level and to meet Maastricht inflation criterion (i.e. inflation not exceeding the average of the three best performers within EMU +1.5 percentage points). In addition, it is necessary to note that strong deflationary trends on the international oil and other commodities markets in 1997-1998, which have now been reversed, contributed significantly to the impressive progress with disinflation in all countries recorded in Table 1.6.

Table 1.6. Selected transition countries: end-of year inflation, 1991-1998.

Country	1991	1992	1993	1994	1995	1996	1997	1998
Bulgaria	338,7	79,4	63,8	121,9	32,9	310,8	578,6	0,9
Czech Republic	52,0	12,6	18,8	9,7	7,9	8,6	10,1	6,8
Estonia	...	942,2	35,7	41,6	28,8	15,0	12,5	4,5
Hungary	32,0	24,7	21,1	21,2	28,3	19,8	18,4	10,3
Latvia	...	958,2	34,8	26,2	23,3	13,2	7,0	2,8
Lithuania	...	1162,5	188,8	45,0	35,5	13,1	8,5	2,4
Poland	60,3	44,5	37,7	29,5	21,6	18,5	13,2	8,6
Romania	223,0	199,2	295,5	61,7	27,8	56,9	151,6	43,8
Slovakia	58,3	9,1	25,0	11,7	7,2	5,4	6,4	5,6
Slovenia	247,0	88,2	22,9	18,3	8,6	8,8	9,4	5,7

Source: IMF, EBRD and PlanEcon data

Looking back at the whole transition period, only the three Baltic countries show a fast and continuous trend of disinflation, from the hyperinflation of 1992 to the low one digit level, close to that of the EU. Poland also started from near-hyperinflation in the second half of 1989 and followed a continuous disinflation path (apart from 1999 and 2000, which have brought a modest reversal of the disinflation). However, the speed of Polish disinflation has not been as impressive and its current level is higher than that of the Baltic countries. At the other extreme, Hungary never had 12 consecutive months' inflation higher than 35% but it had not manage to decrease CPI inflation below 18% by the end of 1997. The Czech Republic and Slovakia experienced relatively limited and short lived inflation jumps resulting from price liberalization (in 1991 end of year inflation reached 52% in the Czech Republic and of 58.3% in Slovakia). From 1994 until the end of 1997, the 12-month inflation rate stabilized around 8-10% in the Czech Republic and 6-7% in Slovakia. A similar situation can be observed in

Slovenia. Only 1998 brought more substantial disinflation in these four countries, but it is not yet clear whether the low inflation level be sustained given the reversal of price trends on the world commodities markets. Bulgaria and Romania have become examples of several stabilization failures due to weak monetary and fiscal policies, and an inability to impose hard budget constraints on large enterprises and commercial banks. Bulgaria seems to have finally learned from its mistakes, has introduced a currency board regime in 1997, balanced its budget and accelerated the pace of microeconomic reforms, while Romania continues balancing on the verge of financial crisis.

The slow pace of disinflation in the Central European countries, which are the most advanced in the transition process, can be explained by the generally accommodative character of their monetary policies. In Hungary and Poland (until the end of 1997) central banks have regularly financed fiscal deficits (Table 1.7). This has also happened, at least occasionally, in the Czech Republic and Slovakia. Additionally, the National Bank of Hungary was deeply involved in quasi-fiscal operations, connected mainly with servicing public foreign debt on behalf of government (Markiewicz, 1998).

Table 1.7. Central Bank Credit to Government, 1992-7 (in % of GDP).

Country	1992	1993	1994	1995	1996	1997
Bulgaria	6.0	11.0	5.5	4.9	14.5	-0.1
Czech Rep.	...	-2.1	-2.4	-1.0	-0.8	0.7
Estonia	...	0.0	0.0	0.0	0.0	0.0
Hungary	16.5	13.2	11.2	7.5	7.3	1.7
Latvia	0.0	0.0	0.0	0.0	0.0	0.0
Lithuania	0.0	0.0	0.0	0.0	0.0	0.0
Poland	5.2	1.5	1.5	0.1	0.1	0.5
Slovakia	...	...	...	...	...	1.5
Slovenia	0.0	0.0	0.0	0.0	0.0	0.0

Source: IMF (1998b, table 5)

Exchange rate policies oriented towards export promotion and current account targeting, rather than supporting disinflation have been another part of the same story of accommodation. This has been the case formally in Poland and Hungary, which have used a pre-announced crawling peg devaluation regime and in Slovenia, which has done the same in a less formal way. Such an orientation of exchange rate policy not only deprives a small open economy of its most effective anti-inflationary anchor (see: Dabrowski et al., 1999, Antczak and Gorski, 1998) but also causes serious complications in controlling the money supply. Struggling against market pressure for nominal appreciation (or at least for slower depreciation than induced by the crawling peg/crawling band mechanism) the central bank must regularly purchase foreign exchange. In order to avoid uncontrolled growth of money aggregates central bank interventions on the forex market must be heavily sterilized by decreases in the net domestic assets of the central bank (i.e. by central bank borrowing). This reduces the level of reserve money but involves significant fiscal and quasi-fiscal costs.

The slow and opportunistic disinflation policies we have noted in most CEE countries have given hardly any benefits in terms of better growth performance. On the contrary, empirical research related to transition economies (see e.g. Christoffersen and Doyle, 1998; Gillman, Chapter 4) confirms the negative correlation between inflation and growth, which is found in research conducted on broader groups of countries (see e.g. Gosh, and Phillips, 1998).

In the light of the above analysis, the monetary policy of some of the candidate countries should be seriously modified. The crawling peg/ crawling band mechanisms which have been used for such a long time in Hungary and Poland are evidently inconsistent with the expected EMU membership criteria. They also delay the moment of inflation convergence, as they multiply the inflationary consequences of the H-B-S effect. In Poland the wide crawling band was finally abolished in April 2000 in favor of free floating. In Hungary a narrow crawling band (+/- 2%) is still in operation.

However, even an abandonment of crawling devaluation mechanisms does not solve the problem of the internal inconsistency of the Maastricht convergence criteria. A fixed exchange rate (or early adoption of euro in the candidate countries as suggested in the previous section) remains in conflict with the inflation criterion (i.e. inflation not exceeding 1.5 percentage points above the average of the three best EMU performers), as a result of the much faster growth rate expected in the candidate countries than in the core EU countries (see Section 1) and the H-B-S effect (Rostowski, Chapter 2; see also Halpern and Nemenyi, 1999, for Hungary).[10] In fact, this kind of inconsistency is already observed in the case of fast growing EMU members (Ireland, Spain).

Solving this dilemma can go in one of two opposite directions. The <u>first</u> would give priority to inflation convergence, delaying the date of the ultimate fixing the exchange rates of the candidate countries in relation to euro and, therefore, their EMU membership (and interest rate convergence). This variant implies nominal exchange rate appreciation with all the political costs and balance of payment risks connected with such a scenario (Rostowski, Chapter 2). Moving in this direction will require a truly independent central bank able both politically and technically to pursue consistent disinflation targeting and build a strong anti-inflationary reputation. The <u>second</u> solution would be to go ahead with EMU membership, giving up the inflation convergence criterion after the ultimate fixing of candidate countries' exchange rates to the euro. Taking into consideration all the arguments, including the balance of payment challenges discussed in the previous section, the second option seems to be more promising for the candidate countries growth prospects and overall macroeconomic stability. A slightly higher inflation in some regions of the common currency area, if caused only by productivity differentials (the H-B-S effect), should not undermine the credibility of macroeconomic policy, the propensity of the population of these regions to save (here the introduction of the euro may have a much bigger positive importance than any possible negative impact of a modest inflation differential), or investment / growth prospects.

4. PRESENT AND FUTURE FISCAL IMBALANCES

The fiscal situation of the candidate countries is quite differentiated (see Table 1.8). Estonia and Slovenia record general government balances fluctuating around zero. Latvia recorded a substantial fiscal deficit early on, and subsequently improved its fiscal position achieving general government surplus in 1997. The Czech Republic and Poland represented moderate, stable levels of general government deficits in the range of 1-3% of GDP. Slovakia, generally belonging to the moderate deficit group, recorded more volatility and deteriorating fiscal balances in 1997-1998. Hungary, Bulgaria, Lithuania, and Romania[11] represented high general government deficits, reflecting serious difficulties with fiscal adjustment. The first two have improved their fiscal performance in 1997-1998[12], while Romanian fiscal disequilibrium remains severe. Lithuania, after improving its general government fiscal position in 1997, saw it deteriorate again in 1998.

Table 1.8. Revenues, expenditures, and general government balance in transition economies on a disbursement basis, 1994-1997 (in % of GDP).

Country	Indicator	1994	1995	1996	1997
Bulgaria	Revenues	39.9	36.6	34.3	31.5
	Expenditures	45.7	43.0	47.6	34.1
	Balance	-5.8	-6.4	-13.4	-2.6
Czech Rep.	Revenue	44.9	43.8	42.7	40.7
	Expenditure	46.0	45.7	43.9	42.8
	Balance	-1.2	-1.8	-1.2	-2.1
Estonia	Revenue	41.3	39.9	39.0	39.4
	Expenditure	39.9	41.1	40.5	37.0
	Balance	1.3	-1.2	-1.5	2.4
Hungary	Revenue	51.4	48.1	46.8	44.9
	Expenditure	59.7	53.2	49.9	49.5
	Balance	-8.3	-7.1	-3.1	-4.6
Latvia	Revenue	36.5	35.5	36.5	39.0
	Expenditure	40.5	38.8	37.8	37.6
	Balance	-4.0	-3.3	-1.3	1.4
Lithuania	Revenue	32.7	32.8	30.1	33.5
	Expenditure	37.5	37.3	34.7	35.4
	Balance	-4.8	-4.5	-4.6	-1.9
Poland	Revenue	47.5	45.7	45.1	44.1
	Expenditure	49.5	48.4	47.5	45.8
	Balance	-2.0	-2.7	-2.5	-1.7
Romania	Revenues	32.1	31.9	29.8	27.0
	Expenditures	33.9	34.5	33.7	31.5
	Balance	-1.8	-2.6	-3.9	-4.5
Slovakia	Revenue	46.4	47.1	46.9	41.5
	Expenditure	47.7	46.9	48.3	46.4
	Balance	-1.3	0.2	-1.3	-4.9
Slovenia	Revenue	45.9	45.7	45.2	45.0
	Expenditure	46.1	45.7	44.9	46.2
	Balance	-0.2	-0.0	0.3	-1.2

Source: WEO (1998), tables 17-19.

While the fiscal position of general government illustrates current flow imbalances, public debt statistics (Table 1.9) show the extent to which past imbalances have accumulated and what the room for maneuver for fiscal policy is in the future.

Table 1.9. Public debt to GDP ratio in selected transition countries, in %, 1994-1997

Country	1994	1995	1996	1997
Czech Republic	14.1	11.5	10.1	10.5
Estonia [a]	2.1	3.2	4.2	3.8
Hungary	87.1	86.0	72.4	68.0
Latvia [a]	3.3	5.1	5.5	1.1
Lithuania [a]	3.3	5.6	9.9	10.7
Poland	72.3	57.9	51.1	48.0
Romania	17.0	18.0	23.0	33.0
Slovenia	15.4	16.8	22.2	24.1

Note: a – Long-term public and publicly guaranteed external debt to GDP

Sources: Gillman (1999); Siwinska (1999a); Siwinska (1999b); Stepanek and Schneider (Chapter 7).

Individual countries started the transition with very different levels of public debt. Romania and the former Czechoslovakia had practically none. Bulgaria, Hungary, the former Yugoslavia, and Poland were heavily indebted, while the former USSR had a moderate level of indebtedness. After the collapse of the USRR, all of its foreign assets and liabilities were taken over by Russia (the so-called zero option). All other FSU countries, including the Baltic states started their independent existence with no debt. Poland and Bulgaria have been beneficiaries of large foreign debt reductions.

Hence, individual countries have differing scope for further expansion of public debt. Bulgaria presents the most dramatic case. Despite a 46% debt reduction from the London Club in July 1994, its total public debt still exceeded 100% of GDP. Although Romania started the transition process with zero public debt, it increased quite dramatically, particularly in 1996-1997, as result of high fiscal deficits combined with a contraction of measured GDP. Latvia and Estonia have managed to keep their public debt close to zero. Lithuania, on the other hand, shows a strong upward trend in public debt/GDP, though the level remains as yet relatively low. Slovenia has a moderate, though steadily growing level of public indebtedness.

Hungary and Poland, which entered the transition period with the largest debt burden, have managed to substantially lower their debt to GDP ratios. The improvement in the Hungarian debt ratio can be attributed to (i) primary fiscal surpluses, (ii) an inflow of non-debt deficit financing, mainly privatization receipts, and (iii) a high nominal growth rate of GDP which was greater than the interest rate on public debt, which resulted in the economy „outgrowing" the debt. In the case of Poland the improvement can be assigned mainly to external debt reduction, which was the result of agreements with the Paris and London Clubs. Other important factors were also the high rate of real GDP growth and the real appreciation of the zloty (Siwinska, 1999a).

Although the Czech Republic seems to be in a relatively good fiscal position, the decline in its debt/GDP ratio has been reversed since 1997 due to devaluation of the *koruna*, GDP decline, and a significant loosening of fiscal policy (see Stepanek and Schneider, Chapter 7). Additionally, the Czech Republic, unlike Poland and Hungary, has not as yet resolved the problem of bad debts in its banking sector, so that its true public indebtedness is significantly underestimated.

Superficial inspection of Tables 1.8 and 1.9 may suggest an optimistic assessment of the prospects for the convergence of the candidate countries on the EMU fiscal criteria as specified by the Maastricht and Amsterdam Treaties (the so-called Stability and Growth Pact). Apart from Hungary, the other "first wave applicant" countries formally meet both the deficit and the debt criteria for EMU membership. However, such optimism may be premature for a number of reasons.

First, some countries recently recorded a deterioration of their current fiscal balances (for example, the Czech Republic and Slovakia).

Second, the same ratio of the budget deficit and public debt to GDP that is easily financed in developed countries is not necessarily equally easily financed in transition economies, due to their lower level of monetization, less developed domestic financial markets and lower international financial ratings (Kosterna, 1998). These drawbacks can be probably eliminated only once applicant countries become members of the EMU.

Third, official fiscal statistics on a disbursement basis do not necessarily cover all fiscal activities or show the whole fiscal disequilibrium of a country. An example is the restructuring of bank and enterprise debt by issuing special government bonds, as has occurred in Bulgaria, Hungary, Poland, and some other countries in the first half of 1990s. This increased public debt and future fiscal burdens though it was not reflected in the current budget composed on a disbursement basis.

So-called contingent fiscal liabilities, in the form of explicit and implicit public guarantees, constitute another form of potential fiscal burden reflected neither in budget deficits, nor in public debt statistics. As mentioned earlier, this is particularly important in the Czech Republic. Contingent fiscal liabilities in that country are estimated by Stepanek and Schneider (Chapter 7) at 12.7% of GDP in 1998, i.e. higher than the officially recorded public debt. Furthermore, these liabilities are expected to expand rapidly in future.

Last, but far from least, implicit pension debt (i.e. unfunded pension liabilities) should be added to the overall specification of fiscal liabilities (Table 1.10). Total implicit pension debt corresponds to more than 200% of GDP in Romania. The equivalent figures for Poland and Hungary before the pension reforms in these two countries were more than 300% of GDP in Poland, and more than 400% GDP in Hungary (see Gomulka and Styczen

1999, and Vajda 1999). The implicit debt for those already retired turns out to be close to 100% of GDP in the Czech Republic, Hungary and Romania, and close to 200% of GDP in Poland. [13]

Table 1.10. Size of implicit1 pension debt in % of GDP

Implicit pension debt	Total	already retired	Presently working	All – old age	all – disability
Czech Rep. (1998)	284	81	203	53 [2]	19 [2]
Hungary –WB (1994) [4]	231	100	131	147	64
Hungary –Vajda –(1995)	407	..	..	..	..
Poland (1996)	302	197 (165) [3]	105 (87) [3]	108[3] (81) [2]	104[3] (63) [2]
Romania (1997)	211	100	111	68	17
Germany (1992)	221	106	115	..	..
France (1992)	264	128	136	..	..
Italy (1990)	358	171	187	..	..
Japan (1990)	166	68	98	..	..
USA (1990)	109	32	77	..	..

Notes: 1)Assumes 2% rate of growth of real pensions and 3% discount rate.2) Current beneficiaries only. 3) Outside agriculture. 4) The World Bank estimates relate to the start of 1994. They exclude agricultural pensions and any other benefits financed from the central government budget.

Source: Gomulka (1999).

Comparison with the developed countries at the beginning of 1990s[14] shows that the four Central European countries analyzed are closer to the situation in the continental EU, rather than to that of the UK, US and Japan, where the level of implicit pension debt is much lower. Before their pension reforms, Poland and Hungary with their extraordinary high pension liabilities were close to Italy in 1990, while the obligations of the Czech Republic and Romania are similar to those of France and Germany.

Apart from existing fiscal imbalances and tensions, all the transition countries face new challenges to their public finances in the coming decade. These can be grouped into three broad categories: (i) the fiscal consequences of unfavorable demographic trends, (ii) costs of pension, health and other reforms, (iii) costs and benefits connected with the EU accession.

Unfavorable demographic trends in all of Europe, including most European transition countries, will push up the dependency ratio causing, other things being equal, further financial deterioration of the PAYG pension systems in existence, and therefore further increases in public pension expenditure as a proportion of GDP.

The same concerns health care expenditures. Assuming that most health expenditures are directed to the oldest, and financing comes from contributions paid by those currently employed, the logic of financing public health care does not differ much from that of the PAYG pension system. Hence, the expected aging of the population will put enormous pressure on public health finances. As in the case of the public pension system, health care problems create a convenient issue for populist politicians, which makes expenditure-cutting reforms very difficult. In addition, information asymmetry and supplier induced demand for medical services are serious obstacles in establishing effective cost control mechanisms in any type of health system financed from public sources (see Mihalyi and Petru, Chapter 9). Fast technical progress also induces demand for new medical equipment, technologies and medicines, which are usually more expensive (though more effective) than the traditional ones.

The prospect of a demographically induced crisis of the PAYG system has pushed most European countries to initiate different types of pension reform to cushion the negative fiscal impact of increasing dependency ratios. Among the candidate countries, the Czech Republic, Hungary, Latvia, Poland, and Slovenia increased retirement age explicitly or implicitly, and have corrected their formulas for indexation of pensions so as to decrease the replacement rate. Additionally, Hungary and Poland have already initiated a multi-pillar system, including fully funded components, while Croatia, Latvia, Estonia, Romania, and Macedonia are in various stages of preparation of such reforms (Rutkowski, 1999).

Moving towards a multi-pillar pension system involves substantial fiscal costs in the next decade connected with converting a part of the implicit pension debt into an explicit one. These transition costs are estimated to be 1.7% of GDP per annum on average for Poland (Gomulka and Styczeń, 1999). For Hungary, they will amount to 0.35% of GDP in 2000, increasing to 1.05% of GDP in 2002, and then gradually decreasing to zero in the end of the next decade (Vajda, 1999).

However, the long term fiscal advantages of these reforms are indubitable, as the PAYG pillar will be downsized. According to Gomulka and Styczen's (1999) estimates, the replacement rate in Poland under the old system (i.e. in the absence of the 1999 reform) would decline, but would nevertheless remain high, varying between 53% to 60% depending on the indexation rule. The reform will push this rate down to between 39% and 46% in 2040 (for the first and second pillars together), again depending on the indexation rule. For the first pillar (and it is this which is important for public finances) the replacement rate will go down to 30% by 2050.

Under the reform, an initial fiscal deterioration in the first pillar, by some 2% of GDP annually, is followed by a gradual improvement, amounting to about 3% of GDP by 2050. In the absence of any reform, an initial deterioration, also by about 2% of GDP, is followed by a further gradual deterioration, amounting approximately to an additional 2% of GDP by 2050. This deterioration, by some 4% of GDP during the first half of the 21st century, would bring the deficit of the public pension system outside agriculture to about 5% of GDP by the end of that period. As the deficit of the agricultural pension fund is about 2.5% of GDP, the total pension related deficit in Poland would increase during next 50 year from 3% to about 7.5% of GDP.

In Hungary, reduction of pension expenditures in the first pillar will be visible soon, mainly due to up-front elimination of various pension privileges. Assuming zero contracting out from the first to the second pillar (the least beneficial assumption from the point of view of the public finances), the financial balance of the PAYG system will gradually improve from a small deficit at the end of the 1990s to a surplus exceeding 2% of GDP around the year 2014. Later on this surplus will gradually diminish, moving again into deficit after 2038, due to unfavorable demographics. However, the deficit will be much smaller than in the absence of reform. In the latter case it would reach close to 6% of GDP in 2050 (Palacios and Rocha, 1998). When we add the costs of partial transition from the first to the second pillar, the first pillar will record a deficit of 1% of GDP at the start of reform (1998-1999) with a continuous improvement in the next decade and surplus around the year 2008 (Vajda, 1999).

The Czech response to the expected demographic challenge has concentrated on changes in the PAYG system: a gradual increase in the retirement age, linking benefits more directly to contributions, and adopting a price indexation formula for pensions in order to lower the replacement rate (Gomulka, Chapter 5). The threat of making explicit a substantial part of the implicit pension debt accumulated under the present system has served as the main argument against embarking on a Hungarian-Polish type of reform in the Czech Republic (Schneider, 1999).

This partial pension reform in the Czech Republic seems to be quite inadequate, and the deficit of the PAYG system is expected to deteriorate from 0.7% of GDP in 1999 to 1.5% of GDP in 2010 with further deterioration after this date (Schneider, 1999). Gomulka (Chapter 5) additionally points to the effects of the 1997-1999 recession and delayed enterprise restructuring which may bring a sharp increase in the unemployment rate and the dependency ratio.

As regards health care reform, at the beginning of the 1990s the Czech Republic and Hungary moved from a tax financed government controlled system (involving also government responsibility for the provision of medical services) to a Bismarckian mandatory public health insurance system. Poland followed in 1999 (Mihalyi and Petru, Chapter 9). This was done mainly under pressure from the doctors' lobby. There are serious doubts also whether this is the best choice from the fiscal point of view, as the system of mandatory health insurance is usually more expensive than the

British type tax-financed system with additional private provision of medical services on a competitive basis.

As the Czech Republic and Hungary noted an increase in health care expenditures, one can expect that a similar expenditure increase will occur in Poland. Gorzelak (1999) has assumed that in the first 4 years of the health-care reform expenditures will increase by 0.5% of GDP each year, after which a stable additional burden of 2% of GDP must be added to budget expenditures annually.

Unfortunately, EU accession does not offer any relaxation of fiscal constraints on the candidate countries. On the contrary, future EU membership seems an expensive investment. Candidate countries will have to increase their environmental and infrastructure expenditures in order to fulfil EU directives. Additional expenditures will also be needed in public investment (transportation and energy infrastructure), public administration (for example, strengthening border and customs controls on the new external EU borders, improving the administration of justice, etc.). According to World Bank (1997) estimates, Poland will have to spend an additional 1.5% of GDP annually on infrastructure and energy security purposes already in 1998-2000. In addition, the Czech Republic, Hungary and Poland have to bear new costs connected with their NATO membership.

On the other hand, EU transfers to the candidate countries will probably have a very limited cushioning impact on their fiscal situation. According to Tomczynska's (1999b) and Gorzelak's (1999) very rough estimates based on the decisions of the Berlin EU summit in March 1999, the expected net EU transfers[15] in the pre-accession period will not exceed 0.2% of GDP annually in the case of the Czech Republic and Hungary, and 0.6% of GDP in the case of Poland. After accession, they may gradually increase to 0.7% of GDP in the Czech Republic and Hungary and to 2% of GDP in Poland towards the end of the next decade. This is much less than transfers received by the Mediterranean countries fifteen or twenty years ago and below the expenditures connected with accession (see above).

Finally, fiscal prospects will strongly depend on future growth performance. The rate of economic growth influences the fiscal situation at least in two ways. First, a higher growth rate enables an economy to "outgrow" its public debt, increasing the probability that the rate of growth of nominal GDP will be higher than the nominal interest rate. A high growth rate also means faster real appreciation of domestic currency (due to the H-B-S effect), which decreases the ratio of the foreign debt to GDP. Thus, under the high growth scenario the primary fiscal balance needed to stabilize a given debt to GDP ratio will be less than that under a low growth scenario.

Second, achieving a given primary fiscal balance is much easier under high growth scenario than in the case of low or negative growth. In the short term, nominal revenues usually depend on nominal GDP, while expenditures tend to stay at some constant real level.[16] In other words, government cannot reduce its costs below some minimum level, while its revenues may fall rapidly when the economy gets into crisis. During years of growth, an increase in production shifts up revenue (via taxes) while expenditures do not necessarily have to be increased.

The results of Maliszewski, Gorzelak and Siwinska's fiscal projections for the Czech Republic, Hungary, Poland and Romania (Chapter 3) show great differences in the public debt to GDP ratios in the year 2010, between the high growth (5% per annum) and the low grpwth (2% per annum) scenarios. The differences are of the order of 15-30 percentage points in the debt/GDP ratio. In the Czech Republic and Poland even the high growth scenario does not prevent the debt to GDP ratio from growing unless these countries adopt additional fiscal adjustment measures.

5. HIGH LEVELS OF FISCAL REDISTRIBUTION

Table 1.8 illustrates the generally high level of fiscal redistribution of GDP in CEE transition countries. Looking at the ratio of general government expenditure to GDP in 1997 one can distinguish:

- A group of high spending countries (between 40 and 50% of GDP), which contains all of Central Europe – Hungary, Slovenia, Slovakia, Poland, and the Czech Republic.
- A group of medium spending countries (between 30 and 40% of GDP), which contains the three Baltic countries (Estonia, Latvia, and Lithuania), Bulgaria[17] and Romania.

According to "Wagner's law", the level of fiscal redistribution is positively related to the level of development. However, the general level of fiscal redistribution in the EU candidate countries is too high, in fact, it is comparable with that in current EU members, which have a much higher GDP per capita. When Western European countries had the same level of economic development as the most developed Central European countries do today (some 30 years ago) their general government expenditure to GDP ratio did not exceed 30-35% (see Kosterna, 1998). Similar (or even lower) levels of fiscal redistribution can be observed at present in Latin America, which has GDP per capita levels close to those of Central Europe.

A high share of government expenditure in GDP does not stimulate economic growth in the long run, as it reduces the rate of private saving available for investment financing. This effect is particularly adverse in transition economies where the rate of saving is rather low and government expenditure is strongly dominated by consumption spending (see below).

The high tax rates needed to finance such large public expenditures[18] hamper private business activity and stimulate its outflow abroad (or to the shadow economy). In effect, high taxes lead to the erosion of the tax base. High social spending usually discourages legal employment and distorts the labor market. High government expenditure and revenues also create the temptation of discretionary fiscal redistribution. This, in turn, leads to distortions in resource allocation, tax evasion, intensive rent seeking, corruption, etc. Finally, the microeconomic effectiveness of government spending is generally lower than that of private spending. This relates both to consumption and investment expenditures.

Analyzing the structure of general government expenditure one must note the role of overly generous social programs, particularly pension systems that are responsible for the general over-expansion of government expenditures in transition countries and the crowding out of such items as investment on public infrastructure. Table 1.11 shows the level of social security transfers and Table 1.12 – the size of public pension expenditures, which represent a major component of social transfers.[19] According to these data, only Lithuania and Romania can still avoid the trap of becoming a "premature post-communist welfare state".

Table 1.11. Social security transfers in selected transition countries, 1996 (in % of GDP).

Country	Social transfers in % of GDP
Czech Republic	12.2
Estonia	11.0
Hungary	14.4
Latvia	16.1
Lithuania	8.8
Poland	20.8
Slovakia	14.5
Slovenia	20.2

Source: WEO (1998), p. 112, table 24.

Table 1.12. Public pension expenditures in transition countries, 1996 (in percent of GDP).

Country	Pension expenditures in % of GDP
Bulgaria	9.5
Czech Republic	8.4
Estonia	7.6
Hungary	9.7
Latvia	10.8
Lithuania	6.2
Poland	14.4
Romania	5.8
Slovakia	8.3

Source: WEO (1998), p. 115, box 10.

6. CONCLUDING REMARKS

Central European and Baltic countries applying for EU membership will face several serious macroeconomic and fiscal challenges in the coming decade. Some of these result from an unfortunate past: Central and Eastern Europe lost half a century of normal capitalist development and must now catch up with Western Europe. Intensive catching up will create huge investment needs, and thus an investment-saving imbalance, high current account deficits, and pressure for appreciation of domestic currencies. The situation is further complicated by an unfinished transition agenda and an imperfect transition record in many countries. For example, fiscal deficits additionally worsen investment-saving imbalances, particularly in Hungary, Romania and Lithuania. The financial sector is underdeveloped and in some countries and burdened with contingent liabilities, which hampers mobilization of domestic savings (e.g. the Czech Republic). Inflation still exceeds the Western European level, in some countries by a substantial margin (e.g. Hungary, Poland). Monetary and exchange rate policies in most countries in the first group of candidates (apart from Estonia) have been oriented towards accommodating fiscal imbalances, fine tuning growth, and export promotion rather than to fighting inflation consistently. Privatization, restructuring and market oriented institutional reforms are far from being completed (apart from Hungary, which has mostly finished its privatization agenda). The unfinished microeconomic agenda limits the flexibility of the supply side response to shocks and creates additional sources of macroeconomic risk (for example, the excessive borrowing of large state and formerly state enterprises not exposed to hard budget constraints).

Some contemporary challenges are common to all European countries or even to all countries around the world. Globalization is the first on this list and it has far reaching consequences for all aspects of life. Continuously increasing competition relates not only to markets for goods and services, but also to capital markets and (to a smaller extent) to labor markets. Widespread liberalization of financial flows enables economic agents to arbitrage between currencies, tax and regulatory systems, various levels of property rights' protection, legal infrastructure, and levels of macroeconomic and political risk by moving business activity, investments and assets between countries or between currencies. This seriously limits national sovereignty in all spheres, not only those of economic policy but also of political life, raising the minimum acceptable criteria of economic and political responsibility. These developments also have implications for the ability of small countries to run their own independent monetary systems and independent monetary policies.

Another long term challenge, common to most developed and transition countries is connected with population aging, which has a serious negative impact on the financial balance of PAYG pension systems, health insurance systems, and some forms of social aid. In the much longer-term population aging will also negatively influence the rate of private saving and growth prospects. Only a radical liberalization of immigration policies will be able to limit these adverse consequences of population aging in developed countries, but at present, such liberalization does not seem to be very probable for political reasons.

Environmental needs will also create pressure for increased spending (including spending by government), particularly in less developed countries, including the EU candidates from Central and Eastern Europe. This pressure will exist irrespective of their EU membership, though accession conditions may call for faster adjustment in this field.

The accession process itself means another major package of reforms for the candidate countries with a complexity similar to that of the first stage of transition at the beginning of the 1990s. Many of these reforms will cost candidate countries money and will be only partly compensated by net official EU transfers. In fact, looking at accession from the fiscal point of view, it is a kind of investment, which should be recoverable thanks to a more stable economic, legal and political environment, better infrastructure and institutions, and therefore better growth prospects. However, how quickly this additional spending will pay off remains an open question and depends on the economic policy of the EU itself and of its future members (as well as the quality of the economic systems of the latter).

The prospect of EU membership offers, however, a unique chance for importing stable institutions, the new common European currency, and credibility of economic policies. The macroeconomic convergence criteria can also help governments to carry out the necessary fiscal adjustment measures, particularly those relating to excessive social transfers. All these factors should facilitate the elimination of a significant part of the macroeconomic fragility and external risk connected with: (1) high current account deficits - as after EMU accession or unilateral euroization these will merely represent interregional flows inside the common currency area); (2) unstable domestic currencies (as these will cease to exist); (3) high fiscal deficits (brought under control by the Stability and Growth Pact), etc. The new institutional and macroeconomic environment should facilitate stable and macro-economically safe capital inflows, high investment rates, and rapid growth.

ENDNOTES

[1] This chapter is a shortened and revised version of an earlier study of the same title prepared as the Summary Report of the ACE-PHARE research project on "Medium and Long-Term Perspectives of Fiscal Adjustment of Selected Central European Countries", grant no. P96-6089-R, and published in the CASE Reports series (No. 26). In the above mentioned report, I drew extensively on the contributions of the following project participants: Georges de Menil, Max Gillman, Stanislaw Gomulka, Michal Gorzelak, Piotr Jaworski, Urszula Kosterna, Wojciech Maliszewski, Peter Mihalyi, Jaroslaw Neneman, Ryszard Petru, Jacek Rostowski, Ondrej Schneider, Joanna Siwinska, Pavel Stepanek, Marek Styczeń, Magdalena Tomczynska, Zoltan Vajda, Mateusz Walewski, and Katarzyna Zawalinska. This means that they also helped me indirectly to prepare this chapter and I want to acknowledge their role. However, I accept sole responsibility for the content and quality of the text.

[2] Among the latest see e.g. De Melo, Denizer, Gelb and Tenev (1997), Fischer, Sahay and Vegh (1998b), Havrylyshyn, Izvorski, and van Rooden (1998), IMF (1998a). All these exercises are based on endogenous growth theory.

[3] It should be noted that, for a variety of methodological reasons, the size of this decline has been usually overestimated. These include: overestimation of the initial GDP level, underestimation of the rapidly expanding unofficial sector during transition, and difficulties with estimating quality changes are the most frequent statistical problems observed in individual countries.

[4] Table 1.3 contains forecasted rates of growth of GDP per capita. If we assume some population growth it will give higher GDP growth rates.

[5] We do not have the ability to analyze the effectiveness of existing investment spending. We can only suspect that in countries less advanced in transition, and particularly those delayed in microeconomic restructuring, at least part of estimated investment spending may be of very low effectiveness.

[6] They can be also determined by the demographic structure of population (see – Bloom and Malaney, 1999).

[7] In the presence of limited liability and asymmetric information in the provision of finance, there is increased risk to lenders as leverage increases, so that only part of the current account deficit can be financed through the accumulation of foreign debt by the private sector. The rest is financed by foreign direct investment (FDI).

[8] The H-B-S in transition economies was empirically analyzed by Halpern and Wyplosz (1995). For other empirical research see also Halpern (1996) and Maliszewska (1998).

[9] This relates, for example, to big state owned banks or big infrastructural monopolies such as railways, energy producers and suppliers, etc.

[10] Assuming that real appreciation will come from the H-B-S effect only and that the share of tradables to GDP will be ca. 50%, the danger of violating the inflation convergence criterion becomes real if the growth rate difference is higher than 3 percentage points.

[11] In the case of Romania, official fiscal statistics do not cover the quasi-fiscal operations which the National Bank of Romania actively conducted until 1996. For example, in 1996 the general government deficit on a cash basis, augmented by the fiscal deficit, amounted to 6.5% of GDP instead of the officially recorded 3.9% of GDP (Daianu, 1999).

[12] Bulgaria moved from a high fiscal deficit (until 1996) to a fiscal surplus in 1998.

[13] The main reason for this difference is the unusually large number and size of disability and survivors' pensions in Poland.

[14] Since that time a number of OECD countries, for example Italy, have also carried out pension reforms that decreased the implicit pension debt recorded in Table 1.10.

[15] Net of the expected contribution of the future members to the EU budget.

[16] Sometimes this dependence is even negative, as a low or negative growth rate means higher unemployment and higher pressure for other social expenditure.

[17] From 1997 only. Earlier Bulgaria belonged to the high spending group.

[18] We assume that a high expenditure level must eventually be financed by taxpayers. If a country runs a fiscal deficit, it will have to be covered either by the inflation tax (immediately or with a certain time lag), or by a higher tax burden in the future (to finance public debt servicing).

[19] It is important to note, however, that data presented in Table 1.12 may not be fully comparable due to different tax treatment of pension benefits. For example, in the Czech Republic pensions are not subject to personal income tax (Tomczynska, 1999a), and this distorts comparison with other countries. If taxes were applied and compensated for in gross pensions, pension expenditure would be some 1.5% of GDP higher than officially reported (Gomulka, 1999).

REFERENCES:

Antczak, Małgorzata, and Urban Górski (1998): *The Influence of the Exchange Rate Stability on Inflation: A Comparative Analysis*, CASE - Center for Social and Economic Research, Warsaw, Studies and Analyses, No. 137.

Barro, Robert J. (1991): *Economic Growth in a Cross-Section of Countries*, Quarterly Journal of Economics, Vol. 106, pp. 407-443.

Barro, Robert J. and Xavier Sala-I-Martin (1992): *Convergence*, Journal of Political Economy, Vol. 100, pp. 223-51.

Bloom, David E., and Pia Malaney (1999): *Population Change and Economic Development: The Great Debate Revisited*, Harvard Institute for International Development, Consulting Assistance on Economic Reform II Policy Study, September.

Bratkowski, Andrzej S., and Jacek Rostowski (1999a): *Zlikwidowac zlotego (Abolish zloty)*, Rzeczpospolita, March 6, Warsaw.

Bratkowski, Andrzej S., and Jacek Rostowski (1999b): *Wierzymy w euro (We believe in euro)*, Rzeczpospolita, April 26, Warsaw.

Christoffersen, Peter, and Peter Doyle (1998): *From Inflation to Growth: Eight Years of Transition*, IMF Working Paper, WP/98/100.

Dabrowski, Marek et al. (1999): *Disinflation, Monetary Policy and Fiscal Constraints, Experience of the Economies in Transition*, CASE – Center for Social and Economic Research, Warsaw, Reports, No. 16, March.

Daianu, Daniel (1999): *Strain and Economic Adjustment. Romania's Travails and Pains*, paper prepared for the 5th Dubrovnik Conference on Transition Economies: *Ten Years of Transition: What Have We Learned and What Lies Ahead*, June 23-25, Dubrovnik, Croatia.

De Melo, Martha, Cevdet Denizer, Alan Gelb, and Stoyan Tenev (1997): *Circumstance and Chice: The role of Initial Conditions and Policies in Transition Economies*, International Finance Corporation, Washington D.C.

Fischer, Stanley, Ratna Sahay, and Carlos A. Vegh (1998a): *How Far Is Eastern Europe from Brussels?* IMF Working Paper, WP/98/53, April.

Fischer, Stanley, Ratna Sahay, and Carlos A. Vegh (1998b): *From Transition to Market: Evidence and Growth Prospects*, IMF Working Paper, WP/98/52, April.

Ghosh, Atish R., and Steven Phillips (1998): *Inflation, Disinflation, and Growth*, IMF Working Paper, WP/98/68.

Gomulka, Stanislaw (1998): *Output: Causes of the Decline and the Recovery*, CASE-CEU Working Papers Series, No. 8.

Gomulka, Stanislaw (1999): *Comparative Notes on Pension Developments and Reforms in the Czech Republic, Hungary, Poland and Romania*, CASE - Center for Social and Economic Research, Warsaw, Studies and Analyses, No. 182.

Gomulka, Stanislaw and Marek Styczeń (1999): *Estimating the Impact of the 1999 Pension Reform in Poland*, 2000-2050, CASE-CEU Working Papers Series, No. 27.

Gorzelak, Michal (1999): *Medium Term Fiscal Projection for Selected Countries in Transition: The Czech Republic, Hungary, Poland and Romania. The Government Side*, CASE – Center for Social and Economic Research, Warsaw, Reports, No. 19.

Halpern, Laszlo (1996), *Real exchange rate and exchange rate policy in Hungary*, Economics of Transition, Vol. 4 (1)

Halpern, Laszlo, and Judit Nemenyi (1999): *Fiscal Foundation of Convergence to European Union. Hungarian Economy Towards EU Accession*, paper prepared for the 5th Dubrovnik Conference on Transition Economies: *Ten Years of Transition: What Have We Learned and What Lies Ahead*, June 23-25, Dubrovnik, Croatia.

Halpern, Laszlo, and Charles Wyplosz (1995): *Equilibrium Real Exchange Rates in Transition*, Centre for Economic Policy Research, London, Discussion Paper, No. 1145.

Hanke, Steve H., and Kurt Schuler (1999): *A dollarization blueprint for Argentina*, Friedberg's Commodity & Currency Comments Experts' Report, Friedberg Commodity Management Inc., Special Report, February 1.

Havrylyshyn, Oleh, Ivailo Izvorski, and Ron van Rooden (1998): *Recovery and Growth in Transition Economies 1990-97: A Stylized Regression Analysis*, IMF Working Paper, WP/98/141, September.

IIF (1998): *Comparative Statistics for Emerging Market Economies*, Institute of International Finance, Inc., December.

IMF (1998a): *Growth Experience in Transition Economies*, International Monetary Fund, European II Department (in consultation with European I Department), September 4.

IMF (1998b): *Disinflation in Transition: 1993-1997*, International Monetary Fund, European I Department (in consultation with European II Department), September 4.

Jakubiak, Malgorzata (1999): *Saving, Investment, Financial Integration and FDI in Central Europe*, CASE – Center for Social and Economic Research, Warsaw, mimeo, March 31.

Kosterna, Urszula (1998): *On the road to the European Union. Some Remarks on the budget. The performance in transition economies*, CASE-CEU Working Papers Series, No. 1, January.

Levine, Ross and David Renelt (1992): *A Sensivity Analysis of Cross-Country Growth Regression*, American Economic Review, Vol. 82, pp. 942-63.

Liberda, Barbara, and Tomasz Tokarski (1999): *Determinants od Saving and Economic Growth in Poland in Comparison to the OECD Countries*, CASE-CEU Working Papers Series, No. 24.

Linn, Johannes F. (1999): *Ten Years of Transition in Central Europe and the Former Soviet Union. The Good News and the Not-so-good News*, paper prepared for the 5th Dubrovnik Conference on Transition Economies: *Ten Years of Transition: What Have We Learned and What Lies Ahead*, June 23-25, Dubrovnik, Croatia.

Maliszewska, Maryla (1998): *Modelling Real Exchange Rate in Transition: The Case of Poland and Romania*, in: *Real Exchange Rate, Foreign Trade and Economic Growth*, CASE - Center for Social and Economic Research, Warsaw, Studies and Analyses, No. 131.

Maliszewski, Wojciech (1998): *Medium-Term Fiscal Projection for Selected Countries in Transition*, CASE - Center for Social and Economic Research, Warsaw, Studies and Analyses, No. 151.

Markiewicz, Małgorzata (1998): *Fiscal policy and disinflation in transition economies*, CASE - Center for Social and Economic Research, Warsaw, Studies and Analyses, No. 127.

Mundell, Robert (1999): *The Priorities for Completing the Transition and the Model for the Future*, paper prepared for the 5th Dubrovnik Conference on Transition Economies: *Ten Years of Transition: What Have We Learned and What Lies Ahead*, June 23-25, Dubrovnik, Croatia.

Palacios, Robert and Roberto Rocha (1998): *The Hungarian Pension System in Transition*, Social Protection Working Paper Series; The World Bank, Washinton D.C.

Rutkowski, Michal (1999): *The Quest for Modern Solutions: Pension Reforms in Transition Economies*, paper for the Conference "Ten Years After: Transition and Growth in Post-Communist Countries", CASE – Center for Social and Economic Research, Warsaw, Poland, October 15-16.

Rybinski, Krzysztof, and Mateusz Szczurek (1998): *Current Account – Inflation Trade-Off. Lessons for Poland and Other Transition Economies*, CASE - Center for Social and Economic Research, Warsaw, Studies and Analyses, No. 147.

Sachs, Jeffrey D., and Andrew M. Warner (1996): *Achieving Rapid Growth in the Transition Economies of Central Europe*, CASE – Center for Social and Economic Research, Warsaw, Studies and Analyses, No. 73.

Schneider, Ondrej (1999): *Implicit Public Debt of the Czech Social-Security System*, CASE - Center for Social and Economic Research, Warsaw, Studies and Analyses, No. 167.

Siwinska, Joanna (1999a): *Public Debt Structure and Dynamics in the Czech Republic, Hungary, Poland and Romania*, CASE - Center for Social and Economic Research, Warsaw, Studies and Analyses, No. 162.

Siwinska, Joanna (1999b): *The External Public Debt of Baltic and Selected CIS Countries in Years 1992-1997: Estonia, Latvia, Lithuania, Kazakhstan, Kyrgyz Republic, Moldova, Russian Federation and Ukraine*, CASE - Center for Social and Economic Research, Warsaw, Studies and Analyses, No. 169.

Tomczynska, Magdalena (1999a): *Comparative Analyses of Direct Tax Systems in Selected Central European Countries: Poland, Czech Republic, Hungary and Romania*, CASE - Center for Social and Economic Research, Warsaw, Studies and Analyses, No. 161.

Tomczynska, Magdalena (1999b): *European Union Financial Transfers to Applicant Countries*, CASE - Center for Social and Economic Research, Warsaw, Studies and Analyses, No. 173.

Vajda, Zoltan (1999): *Macroeconomic Implication of the Pension Reform*, CASE – Center for Social and Economic Research, Warsaw, Reports, No. 20.

WEO (1998): World Economic Outlook, International Monetary Fund, May.

WEO (1999): World Economic Outlook, International Monetary Fund, April.

Winiecki, Jan (1990): *Post-Soviet-Type Economies in Transition: What Have We Learned from the Polish Transition Programme in Its First Year?*, Weltwirtschaftliches Archiv, Band 126, Heft 4.

World Bank (1997): *Poland – Reform and Growth on the Road to the EU*, Country Economic Memorandum, World Bank, November 26.

Chapter 2

THE APPROACH TO EU AND EMU MEMBERSHIP: THE IMPLICATION FOR MACROECONOMIC POLICY IN THE APPLICANT COUNTRIES

Jacek Rostowski

INTRODUCTION

Many commentators have noted the fact that the so-called "Eastern enlargement" of the EU is unique, in the sense that never before have countries which are so much poorer than the EU been admitted. Furthermore, they are being admitted to an EU which is far more internally liberalised (the single market) and integrated (EMU) than previously. Finally, the applicant countries are far more liberalised internally and open internationally than was the case with the previous enlargement to relatively poor countries (the so-called "Southern enlargement" of the 1980s). We believe that this unique combination of circumstances is likely to generate unanticipated problems for the applicant countries in their conduct of macroeconomic policy in the run-up to EU and later EMU accession. The problems we predict stem from the combination at one time of the following factors:

1. expected rapid growth in the applicant countries (far faster than the EU itself);
2. real appreciation resulting from the well known Harrod-Balassa-Samuelson effect;
3. free capital movements;

4. the need to satisfy the Maastricht criteria and join EMU within ten years.

These factors are likely to lead to high current account deficits, which it will be difficult for the authorities to limit to prudent levels. We describe the underlying pressures in Section 1, discuss suitable macroeconomic policy responses in Sections 2 and 3, and conclude in Section 4. At the core of our analysis lies an attempt to combine what we know about the macroeconomics of rapidly growing poorer countries with the standard prescriptions of the Mundell-Flemming model and the institutional requirements of the pre-EU and pre-EMU accession periods.

1. MEDIUM AND LONG-RUN TRENDS IN THE APPLICANT COUNTRIES.

There are three principal effects which are likely to exert a "demand" for current account deficits (and for the matching capital account surpluses to finance them):

1. Expected growth: people who expect to be richer in future than they are at present will behave rationally if they smooth their consumption path by borrowing today in order to consume more now, and repaying their debt later. At the level of a whole country this leads to foreign borrowing (capital inflow) and a current account deficit. If a number of countries expect their economies to grow, the faster growing ones should borrow from the slower. Applicant countries are expected to be fast growing for a number of reasons:
   - they have stopped pursuing the very bad economic policies which they had in the past under central planning (pervasive government control, extensive subsidies, massive foreign trade distortions, etc.);
   - considerable gains from learning by doing within the institutional infrastructure of the market economy which was initially non-existent (e.g. the bankruptcy courts, customs services, financial institutions), which can be expected to continue for some time to come;
   - new structural reforms which are coming on stream (e.g. pensions' reform, privatisation of utilities);
   - expected benefits of EU and EMU membership.
2. The well known Harrod-Balassa-Samuelson effect (H-B-S below) means that richer countries have higher price levels than poorer ones. Its corollary is that faster growing economies will experience real appreciation of their currencies relative to countries with slower growth (either as a result of higher inflation, or of nominal appreciation). The importance of this phenomenon in transition economies has been pointed out in the seminal paper by Halpern and Wyplosz (1995). The simplest

way to understand the H-B-S effect is to assume that economies produce two kinds of goods: tradeables (e.g. manufactures, primary products and agricultural products) where productivity differs between countries and can grow at different rates across countries, and non-tradeables (e.g. services and construction) where productivity is constant and uniform throughout the world.[1] Finally, one assumes that all goods, but in particular tradeables, are sold on perfectly competitive markets, and also that labour is homogeneous and labour markets are perfectly competitive. In such a world differences in income between any two countries are due exclusively to the productivity of their tradeable goods sectors. In the faster growing economy productivity in the traded goods sector rises faster than in the slower growing one, with the result that real wages must rise faster .[2] However, because of the homogeneity of labour and the competitiveness of labour markets, real wages must increase by the same amount in both the tradeable and non-tradeable sectors. Since productivity in non-tradeables is constant, this means that prices have to increase in this sector. The faster the growth rate of productivity in the traded goods sector the faster the rate of price increase in the non-traded goods sector. As a result, if the share of the two sectors is similar in the two countries, average prices will rise faster in the faster growing country even if the nominal exchange rate is constant, implying real appreciation. If the nominal exchange rate is not constant, then it is average prices adjusted for the change in the nominal exchange rate (i.e. in the currency of the foreign country) which will rise faster in the faster growing country, also implying real appreciation. Now, real appreciation means that national income measured in foreign currency rises faster than when it is measured in domestic currency. As a result the command of domestic residents over foreign resources increases faster than indicated by the growth of real GDP at domestic prices (in which the inflation in the non-tradeables sector is discounted). This higher than conventionally measured real growth justifies more smoothing of consumption, and a higher current account deficit than otherwise.

3. Equally important, if a large part of the government's debt is denominated in foreign currency (as is the case in many transition countries) then real appreciation leads to a decline in the ratio of public debt to GDP, and therefore of the ratio of public debt to the potential tax base. Even if Ricardian equivalence is only partial, residents can be supposed to expect a lower share of taxes in national income will be needed to service the existing public debt. This raises future disposable income and the desire to smooth consumption (and raise the current account deficit) along with it.

To illustrate the above points we start with an equation for the current account obtained from Obstfeld and Rogoff (1996):

$$CA_t = B_t - B_{t-1} = Y_t - C_t - G_t - I_t \quad (1)$$

Where B is the net foreign assets owned by the residents of the country (including their government), Y is national income, C is consumption, G government expenditure and I investment. It is assumed, for the moment, that G is fully financed by taxation. In the long run the current account should be in balance, the economy should have zero net foreign assets and therefore the net present value of consumption should equal the net present value of net income Z = Y - G - I. The representative consumer, faced with uncertainty, maximises the expected value of an inter-temporal utility function of the form:

$$U_t = E_t\{\sum_{s=t}^{\infty} \beta^{s-t} u(C_s)\} \quad (2)$$

where *t* is the present and *s* is the date of every future period, subject to the constraint[3]:

$$NPV(CA) = NPV(B) = NPV(Y - C - G - I) = 0 \quad (3)$$

which implies:

$$NPV(C) = NPV(Y - G - I) \quad (4)$$

The operator $E_t\ \{.\}$ is "a mathematical conditional expectation - a probability-weighted average of possible outcomes, in which probabilities are conditioned on all information available to the decision maker up to and including date *t*" (Obstfeld and Rogoff,1996 p. 79). C_t^* is what we call the level of consumption generated by the above procedure at time *t* . The current account is then given by:

$$CA_t = Z_t - C_t^* \quad (5)$$

So that the current account shows a surplus if $Z_t > C_t^*$ and a deficit if $Z_t < C_t^*$. Point (1) above (rapid expected growth of the applicant countries) implies that with consumption smoothing it will be usually the case that $Z_t < C_t^*$, and $CA_t < 0$. Second, the H-B-S effect means that growth of national income in real foreign currency terms will be faster than in real domestic currency terms, justifying a higher time path of C_t^* and larger current account deficits than would otherwise be the case. Third, real appreciation reduces the absolute value of B_t / Y_t and since $B_t < 0$ is normal in fast growing economies, this leaves scope for an increase in negative net foreign assets (net foreign liabilities or debt), which by eq.(1) leads to a larger CA deficit. Perhaps most useful of all, eq.(3) shows us that if the residents of an applicant country revise their expectations of the NPV (Y) upwards, as it has been argued happens at various times during he transition process[4], then they should also increase C_t^* for all t. If current Z_t does not increase by as much as C_t^*, and there is no reason why it should, then the current account deficit will also increase.

At the same time there are a number of "supply" factors, inducing capital inflows, which are likely to be present in the applicant countries:

1. Increased productivity in the tradeable goods sector and increased relative prices in non-tradeables lead to an increased return on capital in both sectors in the fast growing country. Observation of these trends will make foreign lenders willing to provide increased loans to the private sector within applicant countries.
2. The "Visegrad Three" all have full liberalisation of inward FDI flows (including repatriation of profits and principal). Furthermore, OECD membership means that they are already committed to freedom of outward capital flows and short term capital movements. Some countries believe that - in practice - the extent of these latter freedoms can still be limited at present.[5] Whether this is in fact so is unclear. In any event, upon EU entry truly fully free capital accounts will be unavoidable. Thus, much of the period preceding EMU entry will be one of fully free capital accounts.
3. Increased maturity of the institutional infrastructure will strengthen creditors' property rights and exit possibilities for shareholders.[6] The prospect of imminent EU membership can be expected to raise foreign investors' awareness of the progress which has been made in this regard.

From the perspective of foreign investors, high expected growth rates and real appreciation in applicant countries means increasing asset values. This may induce a further inflow of capital, causing further real appreciation together with a desire for higher current account deficits and higher private sector foreign debt on the part of applicant country residents, so that a "capital inflow - real appreciation" bubble may develop, with the real exchange rate rising ever more above its medium term equilibrium level[7] until, finally, the bubble bursts. Thus, setting a ceiling on the current account deficit at some prudent level may be a justified aim of public policy in the applicant countries. The dilemmas of conducting macroeconomic policy with such an aim and under the conditions which are likely to hold in the run-up to EU and EMU membership, is the subject of the next section.

2. FISCAL AND MONETARY POLICY IN THE APPROACH TO EU AND EMU MEMBERSHIP.

What policies will allow applicant countries keep their current account deficits at "prudent levels"? We first look at an adaptation of the consumption-smoothing model discussed in the previous section to help us analyse the policy implications in the medium-term, and then at short-term the Mundell-Flemming model.

We adapt the model by adding tax revenue as a determinant of the current account, and by specifying the medium-term determinants of the RHS of the CA equation. Including tax revenue is justified by the weakness of the empirical evidence for Ricardian equivalence (e.g. Wilcox, 1989). G and I can be spent on imports just like C and therefore subtract from any positive CA_t, while taxes subtract from disposable income which could be spent on imports. Since Y - C = S (savings) we rewrite eq.1 as follows (including the behavioural determinants of the variables on the right hand side):

$$CA_t = B_t - B_{t-1} = S_t(Y, \varepsilon) - (G_t - T_t) - I_t(r^*, \eta) \qquad (6)$$

We make the Keynesian assumption that savings depend on national income and the neo-classical assumption that investment depends on the world interest rate r*, and add the shift variables ε and η which represent the effects of (upward) changes in expectations regarding growth. Increases in the variable ε causes S to decline, while increases in η cause I to increase.[8] Changes in both variables are assumed to be random, but are restricted to being non-negative (i.e. if $\varepsilon_t < \varepsilon_{t-1}$ when random values of ε are drawn then we set $\varepsilon_t = \varepsilon_{t-1}$, and we do the same for η). Finally, consumers are assumed not to be able to anticipate future values of ε, or to calculate their expected value $E(\varepsilon_t) > 0$ (the same goes for η). We seek justification for these highly irrational expectations in the completely unprecedented nature of the transition from communism to capitalism.[9] Thus over time, but in a highly unpredictable way, the gap between I and S increases, increasing the current account deficit. The only way the authorities can offset this trend is to reduce the budget deficit G - T, possibly to the extent of turning it into a large surplus.

As in the earlier version of the consumption-smoothing model, an unanticipated reduction in the absolute value of B_t / Y_t (due to an increase in Y_t or to real appreciation) implies a reduction in net foreign liabilities/ GDP, since normally $B_t < 0$ in fast growing economies, and therefore brings about a desire by consumers to increase the NFL/GDP ratio. As before, this implies a reduction in B_t below B_{t-1}, and therefore a current account deficit.

However, we encounter an ambiguity regarding the policy implications of the model at this point: while the direct effects of a reduction in the budget deficit should reduce a current account deficit (the traditional two-gap model result), if a significant part of public debt is held abroad - as is the case in the applicant countries - an unexpected tightening in fiscal policy reduces government net foreign liabilities and therefore induces the private sector to increase its own net foreign liabilities. The result might be that total net foreign liabilities remain unchanged. In such a case (which we can call the "crowding in of private sector foreign debt") the current account deficit is unaffected by reductions in the fiscal deficit in the medium term.

This is the equivalent of so-called "Ricardian equivalence" but regarding the impact of fiscal policy on the current account rather than on aggregate demand. Although empirical evidence for standard Ricardian equivalence is weak, we believe it may be stronger in the present context because of constraints originating from the international suppliers of credit. We know that these often look at the total indebtedness of a country's residents, both public and private, when assessing an individual resident's credit risk. Of course, the extent to which this actually happens depends on the proportion of the reduction in the fiscal deficit which goes to reducing foreign public debt below its previously expected level. The lower this proportion, the stronger the standard effect of public sector deficit reduction on the current account deficit will be. We shall see below that similar doubts as to the efficacy of fiscal policy for current account deficit reduction resurface even in the context of the Mundell-Flemming model and its application to policy making in the short-term.

To analyse the implications of the effects we describe in the previous section for macroeconomic policy in the short term, we look at the Mundell-Flemming model with perfect capital mobility, risk neutral investors and fully flexible exchange rates. We assume that in the short term the exchange rate is not expected to change, i.e.

$$\rho_t + u_t = \rho^e_t = \rho_{t-1} \tag{7}$$

Where the last period's expectations of the current period's exchange rate (ρ^e_t), which are simply the last period's actual exchange rate (ρ_{t-1}) efficiently predict the current period's actual exchange rate (ρ_t , where u_t is a normally distributed error term). In such a case, if there were a difference between the rate of return on domestic and foreign assets, investors would put all of their money into the asset with the higher return. Since both kinds of assets are held it follows that their returns must be equal. Since exchange rate expectations are static, it follows that rates of return (i.e. interest rates) must be the same in the two countries:

$$i = i^* \tag{8}$$

where i is the domestic rate of interest, and i* is the world rate (given exogenously). This means that the LM curve (representing equilibria in the "money" market) becomes:

$$M/P = L(i^*, Y) \quad L_1 < 0, L_2 > 0 \tag{9}$$

while the "goods market equilibrium" IS curve becomes:

$$Y = C(Y - T) + I(i^* - \pi^e) + NX(Y, \rho P^*/P) + G$$

$$C_1 > 0,\; I_1 < 0, NX_1 < 0, NX_2 > 0 \tag{10}$$

where π^e is expected domestic inflation, P* is the foreign price level, P is the domestic price level and NX is net exports (remaining variables are as conventionally or previously defined).[10] The result in ρ,Y space is a vertical LM curve and an upward sloping IS curve:

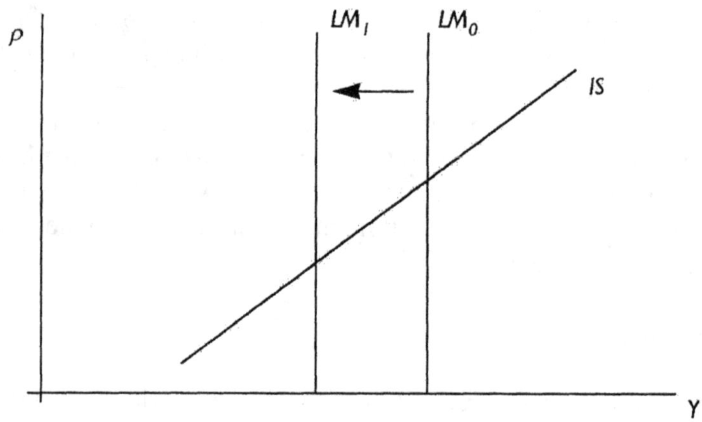

Figure 2.1.

Any tightening of monetary policy by the authorities is immediately offset "one for one" by capital inflows, because i cannot rise above i*. This capital inflow must be offset by a deterioration of the current account, so that the policy is in fact counterproductive.[11] Intuitively we can understand this if we remember that, given that the domestic interest rate is fixed at the level of the world rate, a reduction in M can only affect the exchange rate, which appreciates, reducing net exports.[12] If capital movements were not perfectly free in the very short term, so that the authorities could succeed in reducing M (in spite of their difficulty in raising i) this would have two offsetting effects. On the one hand it would reduce Y, increasing net exports (NX) and improving the current account balance. On the other hand, it would lead to a nominal appreciation of the domestic currency - a reduction in ρ - and if P (the domestic price level) is sticky downwards we would also have real appreciation, so that net exports would decline and the current account balance would deteriorate (see Figure 2.1, where ρ is defined as units of domestic currency/unit of foreign currency, so that a decline indicates an appreciation). Which of the two effects will be stronger depends on the various elasticities, but in neither case is the policy likely to be very powerful. Returning to the case of perfect capital mobility in the short term, expanding rather than contracting M will lead to capital outflow (to obtain the infinitesimally higher interest rate abroad) and therefore to nominal depreciation. In the short run there will also be real depreciation if prices are sticky, so that the current account deficit would be successfully reduced.[13] However, in the medium term increased M would lead to higher prices (not allowed for in the fixed price level Mundell-Flemming model), which would likely mean breaching the Maastricht criterion on inflation, and also to an erosion of the real depreciation and a reversal of the improvement in the current account. Thus, in the medium term, sustaining a "prudent" level of the current account through expansionary monetary policy would require accelerating inflation which would clearly be inconsistent with the Maastricht inflation criterion.

If the exchange rate is credibly fixed, then the domestic authorities have no influence over M. They have to respond to sales (purchases) of foreign (domestic) currency with a supply of central bank domestic (international) reserves, so that M becomes entirely endogenous and cannot affect the current account in any way. Monetary policy is thus unlikely to be effective in reducing a current account deficit whichever of the two exchange rate regimes, floating or fixed, is in force. This result is confirmed by empirical studies, which find that in the Mundell-Flemming model and its Dornbusch (1976) extension, changes in monetary policy are unable to predict either nominal or real exchange rate changes (Obstfeld and Rogoff, 1996 pp.622-6).

On the other hand, with fully free capital movements, the Mundell-Flemming model suggests that fiscal policy becomes highly effective in determining the current account balance, both under free and fixed exchange rate regimes. If the exchange rate floats and the fiscal deficit is reduced so that G - T in eq. (10) falls, then the IS curve in Figure 1.2 shifts to the left, leading to depreciation of the exchange rate without any effect on output:

aggregate demand falls as a result of the direct effect of the fall in G - T (together with any multiplier effects it may have) while the depreciation of the currency increases net exports (NX) by an exactly offsetting amount. National Income remains constant because it is determined by real money balances (M/P) in the money market equation (9), but the accompanying nominal depreciation leads to an improvement in the current account. The depreciation may have some inflationary effects over time, which may partially offset the current account improvement, however, with no increase in domestic M, such effects need not be very powerful:

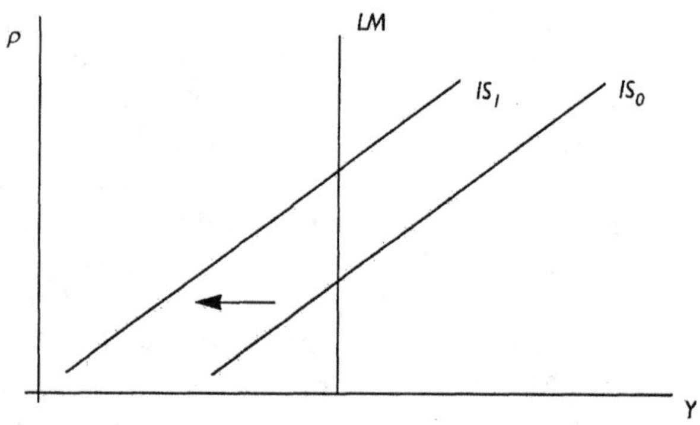

Figure 2.2.

With a fixed exchange rate the model consists in eq.(10) and:

$$\rho = \rho \qquad (11)$$

In Y, ρ space this gives the following equilibria:

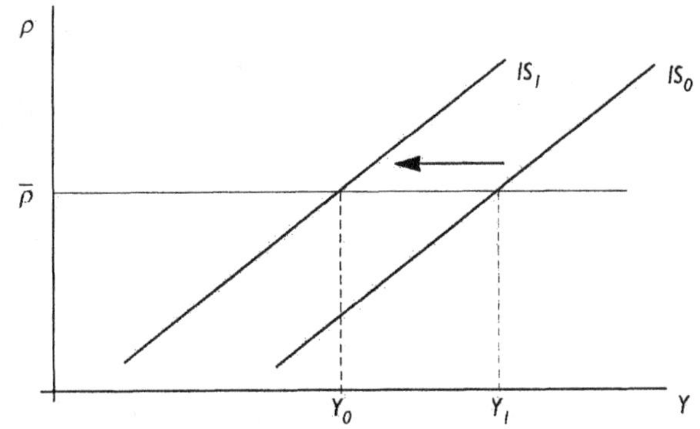

Figure 2.3.

A reduction in the budget deficit causes a fall in Y and thus an increase in (NX) helping to achieve the aim of a "prudent" level for the current account deficit. As previously stated, an attempt to reduce (increase) M merely leads to an increase (reduction) in the international reserves of the central bank, while M remains constant. The overall conclusion is that keeping the economy on course for EMU membership - in the face of the medium term effects (described in Section 2) which are pushing the applicant countries towards increasing current account deficits - implies ever tightening fiscal positions for these countries. Since the Czech Republic and Poland already have fiscal deficits well within the Maastricht fiscal policy criterion, achieving a prudent current account position may require them to run significant budget surpluses in their last pre-EMU entry years.

This conclusion, though, is brought into question by the medium term consumption-smoothing model we looked at earlier in this section. There we saw that the effect of fiscal policy on the current account might also be ambiguous. That result inspires one to ask whether there are other indirect effects of a tightening of fiscal policy which might cast doubt even in the short term on the conclusions we arrive at within the Mundell-Flemming framework. For instance, a tightening of fiscal policy could lead to a positive re-evaluation of the expected future worth of a country's currency. This could be due to the expected improvement in the country's current account and the greater solvency of its government (the issuer of the currency). The result could be appreciation rather than depreciation of the currency, and therefore an increase in the current account deficit rather than a reduction. That this might not be mere theorising is indicated by the view of some Hungarian economists that their currency's avoidance of rapid real appreciation over recent years has been due to the government's large fiscal deficit, something which cannot be explained in the Mundell-Flemming framework or even in the standard version of the medium term consumption-smoothing model. Furthermore, evidence from OECD countries shows that, while sharp reversals of fiscal policy may affect the current account deficit in the expected direction, the link between fiscal and current account deficits is usually insignificant (Obstfeld and Rogoff, 1996 pp.144-5). This is the kind of result which Knight and Scacciavillani (1998) have in mind when they draw the rather gloomy conclusion that exchange rate movements and current account changes may, in fact, be indeterminate.

3. INFLATION, INTEREST RATES AND EXCHANGE RATE REGIMES IN THE PRE-EMU ACCESSION PERIOD, AND THEIR IMPLICATIONS FOR CONFORMITY WITH THE MAASTRICHT CRITERIA.

Because of their expected rapid growth rate, the H-B-S effect may be very strong in the applicant transition countries. Thus, in the 1990s real appreciation has occurred at a rate of 2% per annum in Portugal and only 0.4% per annum in Spain[14], while in Poland it has averaged 7.5% during 1993-97. This difference seems to be related to the difference in growth rates, with the Portuguese and Spanish economies growing at under 2% per annum, while Poland grew at about 6%. As growth rates accelerate in the other applicant countries, we can expect rates of real appreciation to reach very high levels as well. The implications for the achievement of the Maastricht criteria for stage three of EMU by the applicant countries are profound.

First, it may be unwise for the applicant countries to achieve the inflation criterion, which at present requires that inflation not exceed the average of the three best performers within EMU +1.5%. If the H-B-S effect were to require a real appreciation of 7.5% per annum relative to the Euro zone (as Polish experience suggests it might), then this criterion would imply a nominal appreciation of at least 6% per annum.[15] Such a policy may entail two kinds of risks:

1. The current Maastricht inflation criterion is in fact unsuitable for countries in which a strong H-B-S effect operates, since it seeks to limit what is better thought of as a *relative price change* (between traded and non-traded goods) rather than as an increase in the overall price level. If, as we have assumed, prices are constant in the traded goods sector of the rapidly growing country while productivity increases rapidly, then the nominal exchange rate can also remain constant without affecting that country's trade or current accounts. Increases in the prices of non-traded

goods (resulting from the need to pay homogeneous labour higher wages in both sectors given the increase in its average productivity) need therefore have no effect on the current account or the equilibrium exchange rate. In fact, for prices to be constant in the rapidly growing country, its currency needs to appreciate nominally to such an extent that the ensuing fall in the domestic price of tradeables compensates for inflation in non-tradeables, so that:

$$- \alpha P_T (\partial\rho/\partial t)/\rho = (1 - \alpha)\pi_{NT} \qquad (12)$$

is required for $\pi = 0$ (where α is the share of tradeables in national income, P_T is the foreign currency denominated price of tradeables, ρ is the exchange rate defined as units of domestic currency per unit of foreign currency, π_{NT} is the rate of inflation on non-traded goods and π is the average inflation rate). But such a nominal appreciation implies a deterioration in the trade and current accounts of the rapidly growing country, which the growth in the productivity of labour in its tradeables sector by itself does not require, and which is therefore likely to be a move *away* from the equilibrium exchange rate.[16] It will also depress the output of tradeables, so that the Maastricht criterion can be thought of as "exporting depression" to the tradeables sector of the applicant countries.

2. If nominal appreciation is sufficient for eq.(12) to hold, then the interest parity condition:

$$- [(\partial\rho/\partial t)/\rho]^e + i = i^* \qquad (13)$$

may well imply negative short-term nominal interest rates in the applicant country.[17] For example, if we take the rate of nominal appreciation implicit in (1) meeting the Maastricht inflation criterion and (2) having the same real appreciation as Poland did during 1993-7 (i.e. a nominal appreciation of over 6% per annum relative to the euro zone), then with $i^* = 4\%$, i needs to be -2%! In the spirit of Dornbusch [1976], we suggest that this anomaly may be avoided through an initial upward jump in the value of the domestic currency, so that subsequent expected appreciation is low enough for $i > 0$. However, it is also possible that an "appreciation bubble" may develop, with the exchange rate overshooting its sustainable level (and ultimately collapsing).[18] Alternatively, the expectation of nominal appreciation could put such downward pressure on the domestic interest rate that an explosion of of domestic credit ensues.

Second, there are a number of difficulties in devising a suitable exchange rate regime for the the CEE applicants for the period immediately prior to

EMU entry. This matter has been discussed by G.Kopits (1999). However, we believe that Kopits has underestimated the difficulties which may arise. There are a number of possible exchange rate arrangements in the pre-EMU period:

1. Fixed rate (this is currently the mechanism obtaining in Estonia). Hungary has a variant of this, a pre-announced crawling devaluation of the currency with a very narrow band of permitted fluctuations around the central rate. As inflation decreases in Hungary, and the rate of crawl is consequently reduced to zero, the Hungarian system will converge on the Estonian one (unless the band for permitted fluctuations is considerably widened). As we have seen, such a system is very likely to be incompatible with the Maastricht inflation criterion, simply because of the operation of the H-B-S effect. Expected rapid growth will lead to high levels of capital inflows which may result in the need to choose between (a) dangerously high CA deficits, or (b) inflation well above that due solely to the H-B-S effect.[19]
2. Wide fluctuation bands (+/- 15%) around the central rate as in the current ERM2. This holds at present in the Czech Republic and Poland, and is likely to lead to nominal appreciation and high CA deficits, but may give the possibility of fulfilling the inflation criterion. As Kopits points out, appreciation even beyond the "fluctuation band" does not infringe the Maaastricht exchange rate criterion. One danger is an "appreciation bubble", which leads to a rate which is unsustainable. This could lead to a collapse of the exchange rate before accession to EMU (which *would* be against the Maastricht requirements), or to an overvalued exchange rate at the time of joining, which could mean a lengthy period of low growth within EMU.[20]

4. CONCLUSIONS

1. The H-B-S effect means that there will be powerful pressures for real appreciation in the applicant countries in the medium term (Halpern and Wyplosz, 1995).
2. Rapid expected growth, the H-B-S effect (*via* its effect on the ratio of foreign debt/GDP) and various factors increasing the supply of foreign capital, mean that applicant countries are likely to run large and growing current account deficits.
3. Monetary policy will be either counter-productive, likely to risk the return of high inflation, or ineffective.

4. Only fiscal policy *may* have the potential to effectively limit current account deficits to what the authorities are likely to consider prudent levels (and this is so under both fixed and flexible exchange rate regimes). As a result of their need to tighten fiscal policy in each successive year while they are EMU pre-ins, countries with relatively low fiscal deficits at present such as the Czech Republic or Poland, may therefore need to run substantial surpluses (possibly of the order of several percentage points of GDP) by the time they join EMU. We should consider the extent to which this is likely to be politically feasible.
5. Tight fiscal policy may, however, prove ineffective in limiting current account deficits, as a result of its effect on the private sector's willingness to increase its foreign indebtedness. In that case there is a serious danger that a real appreciation boom-bust cycle may blow applicant countries off their course to EMU membership.
6. The Maastricht Treaty inflation criterion for EMU membership should not be applied to the CEE applicant countries when the time comes for them to join the Euro zone, although the exchange rate criterion should, of course, be maintained.
7. A fixed exchange rate policy in the run-up to EMU membership will make the attainment of the Maastricht inflation criterion completely impossible (which will not matter if the latter has been dropped). However, a wide-band ERM2 type of arrangement carries its own risks of high exchange rate volatility.

ENDNOTES

[1] In fact, it is sufficient to assume that productivity growth is lower in the non-traded goods sector, that its growth is uniform accross countries and that returns to labour have a larger share in the non-traded goods sector. For a formal treatment of how differential productivity growth in the two sectors affects the real exchange rate between two countries see Obstfeld and Rogoff (1996, pp. 204-12).

[2] This need not lead to any increase in either the domestic or foreign prices of tradeables produced by the fast growing country, since unit labour costs denominated in foreign currency remain unchanged (the same number of domestic workers can produce more tradeable goods and get paid proportionally more). For this reason the nominal exchange rate need not be affected in any way either.

[3] Where $NPV(CA) = NPV(CA_t + CA_{t+1} + CA_{t+2} + \ldots + CA_{t+\infty})$. The same holds for NPV (B) and NPV(Y - C - G - I), etc..

[4] This point has been made forcefully to us by Stanislaw Gomulka in personal communications.

[5] This is the view of Kopits (1999). The present authors suspect that the current degree of capital account liberalisation is so great in the "Visegrad three" countries, that remaining

controls are not effectively binding (i.e. they do not allow macroeconomic results, different from those which would occur in the absence of the controls, to be achieved).

[6] In the presence of limited liability and asymmetric information in the provision of finance, there is increased risk to lenders as leverage increases, so that only part of the current account deficit can be financed through the accumulation of foreign debt by the private sector. The rest is financed by foreign direct investment (FDI).

[7] And the current account deficit rising ever more above its sustainable level. The IMF has a very crude procedure for estimating the level of a country's sustainable current account deficit (Knight and Scacciavillani, 1998).

[8] We are grateful to Stanislaw Gomulka for suggesting this approach to us.

[9] A more acceptable way of putting this might be that $E(\varepsilon_t) = 0$, and the effects we are discussing will occur if the actual values of ε_t exceed this (the same goes for η).

[10] A more general formulation is:

$$Y = E(i^* - \pi^e, G - T, \rho P^*/P, Y) \qquad E_1 < 0, E_2 > 0, E_3 > 0, \quad 0 < E_4 < 1$$

[11] If the international reserves of the central bank increase, then the the exchange rate is not, in fact, fully floating.

[12] This reduces Y. Hence in a small open economy with a floating exchange rate, contractionary monetary policy affects Y *via* ρ rather than *via* i.

[13] Alternatively we can think of the expansionary monetary policy as causing a one to one offsetting capital outflow which by definition improves the current account. For the extent to which the final outcome necessarily involves or not a depreciation of the domestic currency see Kouri (1978).

[14] 1990-1997 for both countries.

[15] If inflation in the three best performers is 1.5% below the EMU average. If it is at the EMU average, then nominal appreciation of 7.5% would be required.

[16] Much depends on the nature of what is produced by the non-traded goods sector. If it is exclusively non-storeable services, then the result we described above indeed follows. If non-tradeables include assets (e.g. land or buildings, the returns to which are expected to increase with increased productivity in the tradeables sector and real appreciation in the non-tradeables sector), then the anticipation of these processes can be expected to induce a capital inflow, which will cause an appreciation of the equilibrium nominal exchange rate and will in fact help to stifle average inflation.

[17] Because ρ is defined as units of domestic currency/unit of foreign currency, appreciation involves a reduction in it (i.e. a negative growth rate of ρ), which therefore has to be subtracted from the domestic interest rate (giving a positive effect to the LHS of eq. (13)) to arrive at the foreign interest rate.

[18] The 15% band of the current ERM2 mechanism could well be sufficient for such a bubble to develop. Once it had done so it would likely be allowed to break through the ceiling, since the alternative would be to acquiesce in higher inflation.

[19] Due to the effect of capital inflow on the domestic money base. The ensuing inflation will ultimately lead to a high CA deficit as well.

[20] This seems to be the current problem in Germany.

REFERENCES

Dornbusch,R. (1976), *Expectations and Exchange Rate Dynamics*, Journal of Political Economy 84 (December) 1161-76.

Halpern,L. and C.Wyplosz (1995), *Equilibrium Real Exchange Rates in Transition*, Discussion Paper No. 1145, Centre for Economic Policy Research, London.

Kopits, G. (1999), *Implications of EMU for Exchange Rate Policy in Central and Eastern Europe*, IMF Working Paper No. WP/99/9, International Monetary Fund, Washington D.C.

Kouri, P. (1978), *International investment and interest rate linkages under flexible exchange rates* in R.Aliber ed. The Polital Economy of Monetary Reform, London: MacMillan.

Knight, M. and F.Scacciavillani (1998), *Current Accounts: What is their Relevance for Policymaking* in O.Radzyner and A.Schubert eds. Current Account Imbalances in East and West: do they Matter?, Oesterreichische Nationalbank, Vienna.

Obstfeld,M. and K.Rogoff (1996), *Foundations of International Macroeconomics*, Cmbridge: MIT Press.

Wilcox, D. (1989), *Social security benefits, consumption expenditure, and the life-cycle hypothesis*, Journal of Political Economy 97 (April) 288-304.

Chapter 3

PUBLIC DEBT AND FISCAL ADJUSTMENT IN SELECTED TRANSITION ECONOMIES: STRUCTURE, DYNAMICS AND POSSIBLE DEVELOPMENT PATHS FOR THE CZECH REPUBLIC, HUNGARY, POLAND AND ROMANIA.

Michał Gorzelak,

Wojciech Maliszewski

and

Joanna Siwińska

INTRODUCTION

Over 10 years after introducing the market economy, the Central & Eastern European countries that plan to achieve membership of the European Union (EU) and the European Monetary Union (EMU) still have a way to go. Years of central planning have produced a significant economic gap between them and developed countries. At least a part of these differences must disappear before the CEE countries' accession.

The four countries we consider entered the 1990's with very different economic problems and imbalances inherited from the centrally planned economy. Poland and Hungary, along with other problems, were burdened by a huge external debt. The change of economic systems in the early 1990s brought a completely new era in public financing, and a major change in the development of their public debt. The shift to market-based deficit financing has raised awareness of the serious consequences of excess deficit and debt. In the most indebted countries - Poland and Hungary - the ratio of public debt to GDP has declined substantially since 1990. Both countries managed to regain creditworthiness on international financial markets and to attract a substantial amount of foreign capital. In the Czech Republic, Hungary and Poland, the financing of debt has been shifted to domestic markets. Domestic debt markets have also matured, allowing a switch from short-term instruments toward those of longer maturity. In Romania - the least advanced country of the four - the domestic debt market has still not developed and the public sector has been financed mainly by funds raised abroad.

There are several threats to budget balances of the CEE countries. The most important are the costs of reforms that may be necessary in the near future. Examples include health care reform, pension reform, and structural reforms (in heavy industry or agriculture). These are expected to lead to increases in budget expenditures, possibly combined with decreases in some revenues. Of course, some reforms - such as pension reforms or government orchestrated restructuring of loss-making industries - may bring some expenditure cuts in the future. However, other reforms (such as medical insurance reform) will probably not reduce future budget expenditures. The same is true of environmental expenditures. All reforms initially involve additional costs, so extra financing will be needed.

The aim of this analysis is to describe the recent development of public debt in the four CEE countries, and to assess the fiscal policy adjustments necessary for achieving the Maastricht criteria for accession to the European Monetary Union. The chapter consists of two main parts. The first deals with historical data of the 1990s. Second, comes a two-step fiscal policy simulation for each of the four countries. The first step assesses the minimum requirements needed to fulfil the Maastricht criteria for the debt to GDP ratio and the deficit to GDP ratio. We estimate the required primary surpluses consistent with these criteria. In the second step we forecast future primary surpluses from forecasted government expenditures and revenues. A comparison of the required and forecasted primary surpluses reveals the extent of fiscal adjustments necessary for meeting the Maastricht criteria.

1. THE HISTORY OF DEBT DYNAMICS AND STRUCTURE DURING THE 1990S

1.1 Development of public debt during the 1990s

Figure 3.1 summarises the developments of the total gross public debt of the governments of the four countries. At the end of 1997 the biggest ratio of gross consolidated government debt to GDP existed in Hungary, where it amounted to 68% of GDP. In 1997 the gross debt of Polish central government equalled 48% of GDP. In Romania the general government debt equalled 33.5% of GDP and in the Czech Republic, which exhibited the smallest indebtedness ratio, the gross debt of the central government was 10,6% of GDP.

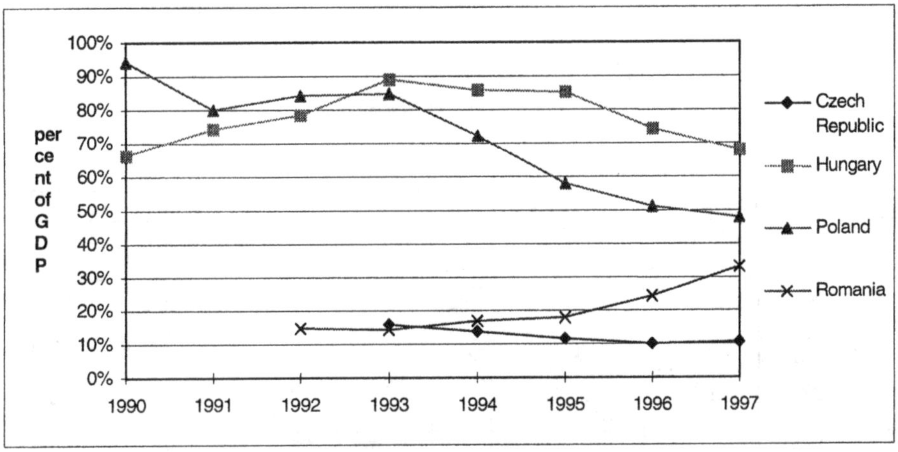

Figure 3.1. Gross debt of the central governments of the Czech Republic, Hungary, Romania and Poland, as a percent of GDP

Source: IMF, Czech - Statistical Appendix (1998), IMF, Hungary - Statistical Appendix (1997), Polish Ministry of Finance (1998) and IBCA, Sovereign Report - Republic of Romania (1997).

The developments of the gross public debt of the four countries during the 1990s are far from homogenous. Poland experienced the most dramatic debt ratio decline - of over 40 percentage points. The fall in total debt has been almost entirely attributable to the fall in the external debt ratio; the foreign indebtedness to GDP ratio decreased by 55 percentage points of GDP between 1990 and 1997, while in the same time the domestic debt ratio rose by only 10 percentage points of GDP. The lessening of foreign debt was mainly due to a negotiated reduction of debt towards the Paris and London Clubs. Sharp real appreciation of the national currency and quite rapid economic growth also helped to lower foreign debt relative to GDP.

Hungary experienced a sharp increase in the debt/GDP ratio from 1990 until 1993 - during that time debt rose by more than 20 percentage points, reaching almost 90% of GDP in 1993. In 1993-1994 the ratio of total debt to GDP stabilised and since 1995 there has been a sharp fall in this ratio. By the end of the century the authorities are intending to reduce the debt/GDP ratio below the 60 per cent Maastricht criterion.

Romania entered the 1990's with a very small public debt. During recent years, however, the debt to GDP ratio has risen noticeably. The chief reason was Romania's increased borrowing abroad. Nevertheless Romanian indebtedness is still is at a relatively low level.

In the Czech Republic the ratio of public debt to GDP is no cause for concern, but after a decline of 6 percentage point between 1993 and 1996, when both the external and domestic debt were decreasing, in 1997 this trend ceased and the ratio of total debt to GDP stabilised at the 1996 level. The ratio of public debt to GDP ratio is expected to rise rapidly in the next ten years when hidden dangers will come to the fore (Table 3.1).

Table 3.1. Public debt developments

	Czech Republic		Hungary		Poland		Romania	
	Domestic debt	External debt	Domestic debt	External debt	Domestic debt	External debt	Domestic debt	External debt
1990	n.a	n.a	40%	27%	12%	82%	n.a.	n.a
1991	n.a	n.a	38%	36%	16%	64%	n.a	n.a
1992	n.a	n.a	44%	35%	21%	63%	4%	11%
1993	9%	7%	50%	39%	23%	62%	2%	12%
1994	8%	6%	48%	38%	26%	46%	3%	14%
1995	8%	4%	43%	42%	23%	35%	4%	14%
1996	7%	3%	46%	28%	22%	29%	6%	18%
1997	8%	3%	n.a	n.a	21%	27%	8%	26%

Source: Czech Ministry of Finance, Hungary - Statistical Appendix, IMF (1997), Polish Ministry of Finance, IBCA, Sovereign Report, Republic of Romania (1997)

1.2 Determinants of public debt dynamics in the four countries after 1990.

The factors that have contributed to changes in the stock of the public debt in the four countries can be assessed by means of the following equation (see IMF, 1997):

$$\Delta B = I - P + O - S, \tag{1}$$

where Δ **B** is the change in public debt, **I** is interest payments, **P** is primary surplus, **O** is other items besides the budget deficit that affect indebtedness, such as devaluation losses, external debt reductions, issuance of bonds for bank recapitalization, or privatisation revenues, and **S** is monetary financing. This equation states, that debt will grow when the primary surplus together with monetary financing (seniorage) are smaller than interest payments on the debt together with non - budgetary items that affect indebtedness.

In order to compare debt dynamics across countries and analyse the sustainability of debt, it is useful to write equation (1) in terms of ratios to GDP (omitting monetary financing).[1] This results in:

$$\Delta b_t = -p_t + (i_t - g_t)b_{t-1}/(1+n_t) + o_t, \tag{2}$$

where **b** = B/GDP, **p** = P/GDP, **o** = O/GDP, **i** is the nominal interest rate and **n** is the nominal rate of growth of GDP.

Tables 3.2 to 3.5 below provide the decomposition of public debt dynamics, according to equation (2). The interest rate was calculated by adding the increases in foreign debt due to devaluation to the actual interest payments. Because we have not included seniorage, the non-deficit item **o** also includes a residual due to this inaccuracy.

Table 3.2. Decomposition of the change in gross debt of the Czech central government (in percent of GDP, unless otherwise indicated)

	1994	1995	1996	1997*
Change in debt (**Δb**)	-2.1%	-2.2%	-1.4%	0.4%
Primary surplus (**- p**)	-1.7%	-0.7%	-0.8%	-0.1%
$(\mathbf{i_t-n_t)b_{t-1}/(1+n_t)}$	-1.0%	-1.7%	-0.4%	1.1%
Non-deficit items (**o**)	0.6%	0.2%	-0.2%	-0.6%
Memorandum items:				
Change in domestic debt	-0.7%	-0.3%	-0.3%	0.2%
Change in external debt	-1.4%	-1.9%	-1.1%	0.1%
n (percent)	14	17.1	13.9	7.6
i (percent)	15.6	-0.1	9.9	19
Interest payments	1.2%	0.2%	0.9%	1.1%

Source: Czech Ministry of Finance, IMF, Czech Republic - Statistical Appendix (1997), own calculations; preliminary data

The main cause behind the increase in the Czech debt ratio in 1997 was a slowdown in GDP growth and a depreciation of the domestic currency as a consequence of the currency crisis. This has resulted in a positive difference between the interest rate on debt and the growth rate of GDP.

Table 3.3. Decomposition of the change in gross debt of the Hungarian consolidated central government (in percent of GDP, unless otherwise indicated)

	1992	1993	1994	1995	1996	1997
Change in debt (**Δb**)	4.3%	10.4%	-2.8%	-0.8%	-11%	-6%
Primary deficit (**- p**)	2.1%	3.4%	0.6%	-2.2%	-4.9%	-3.1%
$(\mathbf{i_t-n_t)b_{t-1}/(1+n_t)}$	-1.4%	1.3%	-1.9%	3.8%	-3.5%	0.1%
Non-deficit items (**o**)	3.9%	5.7%	-1.3%	-2.0%	-2.3%	-1.7%
Memorandum items						
Change in domestic debt	5.4%	6.1%	-2.2-%	-4.4%	3.2%	-6%
Change in external debt	-1.1%	4.3%	-0.6%	3.6%	-14.2%	0%
i (percent)	15.6	22.6	20.3	33	14.9	20.6
n (percent)	17.8	20.6	233	27	19.7	20.5
Interest payments	5.5%	4.5%	6.6%	9%	8.5%	9.1%

Source: IMF, Hungary - Selected Issues, (1997), p.23

In Hungary, in the early 90's the main aspects behind the debt ratio build up were the deteriorating fiscal deficit - a result of a sharp increase in government expenditures - and the issuance of a substantial amount of capitalisation bonds, mainly for the recapitalization and consolidation of banks, and in order to cover losses from earlier housing loans. All this resulted in an accumulation of domestic debt of over 10 percentage points of GDP. The fiscal adjustment process, that began in early 1995 and was achieved through sharp expenditure cuts, has resulted in a primary surplus that has been one of the key factors explaining the debt ratio decline over 1995-1997. Another element that has had a significant impact since 1994 are non - deficit related revenues, mainly from privatisation, which more that quintupled during 1994-1996. The fall in the total debt ratio was divided equally between internal and external debt: since 1995 both have fallen by over 10 percentage points of GDP. However the fall in external debt was concentrated in one year[2], while domestic debt fell first in 1995 and then again in 1997.

The ratio $(i_t-n_t)b_{t-1}/(1+n_t)$ has lowered the debt ratio in a number of years: the interest rate was much lower than GDP growth, mainly due to the fact that foreign exchange liabilities held by NBH did not bear any interest. Only in a few years was this term positive: in 1993 and 1995, reflecting the sharp depreciation of the forint, and in 1997, as a result of the swap of liabilities between the central bank and the government, which replaced the zero interest debt held by NBH with foreign exchange liabilities to the central bank. The full impact of this operation on interest payments is expected to be felt in 1998, but part of the domestic debt will continue to bear an interest rate below the market rate). It is noteworthy, that although fiscal consolidation started in 1995, the Hungarian debt ratio has been declining since 1994. The improvement in 1994 was due to large privatisation receipts, and the fact that the effective interest rate on debt has been smaller than nominal GDP growth, which in that year was caused to a large extent by real appreciation. In 1994 therefore, rather than fiscal policy, it was monetary policy that contributed to the decline of the debt ratio.

In Hungary interest payments on public debt are very high, the highest among the four countries. Payments have been growing rapidly, in 1997 constituting over 36% of total central budget expenditures and over 9% of GDP. This poses a very serious problem for fiscal policy as debt service payments are substantially larger than the primary surplus, which results in a large fiscal deficit and debt build-up, leading to a snowball effect of growing debt and interest payments. While real GDP growth is high, the economy can "outgrow" the debt and its burden, but when the pace of economic growth slows the authorities may find themselves on an unsustainable debt path of large fiscal deficits due to growing interest payments and an increasing debt to GDP ratio.

Table 3.4. Decomposition of the change in gross debt of the Hungarian consolidated central government (in percent of GDP, unless otherwise indicated)

	1992	1993	1994	1995	1996	1997
change in debt (**Δb**)	4%	1%	-16,3%	-14.4%	-6.8%	-3%
primary deficit (- **p**)	3%	-0.8%	-1.7%	-2.4%	-1.4%	-2.3%
$(\mathbf{i_t}-\mathbf{n_t})\mathbf{b_{t-1}}/(1+\mathbf{n_t})$	-0.2%	-2.6%	-9.4%	-10.4%	-2.8%	-0.4%
Non-deficit items (**o**)	1.1%	4.4%	-5.2%	-1.6	-2.6%	-0.3
Memorandum items						
Change in domestic debt	5%	2%	1%	-3.8%	-0.9%	-1%
Change in foreign debt	-1%	-1%	-17.3%	-11.6%	-5.9%	-2%
i (per cent)	38.1	30.8	15.7	10.2	18.1	21.1
n (per cent)	38.6	36.4	35.1	37.2	25.7	22.4
interest payments	3%	3.8%	4.4%	4.9%	4%	3.7%

Source: Polish Ministry of Finance, own calculations

The ratio of Polish debt to GDP has shrunk spectacularly and virtually all the decline in debt was due to a fall in external debt. There are two main factors that have influenced the decrease of external debt. Firstly, Poland was granted debt reduction by the Paris and London Clubs. In April 1991 an agreement was reached with the Paris Club, resulting in a reduction of the net present value of Polish debt by 50%. In September 1994 Poland negotiated a reduction of the debt held by the London Club by 49%, according to the Brady plan. The agreements were the main force behind the reduction of Polish external debt from 53 billion dollars in the end of 1991 to 42 billion at the end of 1994.

The second factor that has significantly contributed to the decline in the foreign debt ratio is the sharp real appreciation of the zloty. This has resulted in a negative difference between the nominal effective interest rate on public debt and the rate of growth of nominal GDP. This difference was also increased by the lower interest payments on external debt due to an 80% reduction in those payments granted by the official creditors as part of the 50% debt reduction of 1991. It is worth noting, that in comparison to the other three countries, the influence of the $(i_t-n_t)b_{t-1}/(1+n_t)$ factor in Poland has been the largest, the margin of the nominal growth rate over the interest rate reaching over 25 percentage points in 1995. The primary surplus, prevailing since 1992, has also contributed to the decline in the debt ratio, but not significantly. Only in 1997 when debt fell by 3% and the primary surplus reached 2.3% of GDP, could one say, that the fall in debt was due to fiscal developments.

The cost of debt service is high; in 1997 it accounted for 13% of total government expenditures and almost 4% of GDP. Debt service is growing relative to GDP and is now the chief reason behind the absolute growth of the public debt, as it has been much higher than the primary fiscal surplus. The decline in debt cost dynamics, noticeable in 1996 and 1997 is only temporary; it is due to a swap of t-bills for two and five year bonds, which will increase the costs in 1999 -2000. This together with debt service obligations on foreign debt that are expected to accumulate after the year 2000, will put a serious strain on government finances and requires a supply of savings, preferably to be made by government in the form of a primary surplus.

Just as in the case of Hungary, large debt service costs pose a serious threat of explosive debt growth. This problem has no easy solutions, as the cost of domestic debt service is proportional to the nominal interest rate which is close to the rate of inflation. The inflation rate is in turn quite strongly dependent on the level of the budget deficit, which is related to the cost of debt servicing.

Table 3.5. Decomposition of the change of gross public debt of the Romanian government (in percent of GDP, unless otherwise indicated)

	1993	1994	1995	1996	1997
change in debt (**Δb**)	-0.7%	2.8%	0.6%	6%	9.9%
primary deficit (**- p**)	-0.4%	0.5%	1.2%	2.1%	0.1%
$(i_t-n_t)b_{t-1}/(1+n_t)$	-0.9%	-2.2%	0.2%	-0.2%	-0.1%
Non-deficit items (**o**)	0.6%	1.7%	-0.8%	4.1%	9.9%
Memorandum items					
Change in domestic debt	-0.6%	0.5%	0.9%	2.3%	1.1%
Change in foreign debt	-0.1%	2.3%	0.3%	3.7%	8.5%
I	164.6	54.6	48.1	48.4	126.2
N	232.3	148.4	45.8	50.9	128.1
interest payments	0.8%	1.3%	1.4%	1.7%	4%

Source IBCA (1997), own calculations

The main reasons behind the sharp deterioration of Romania's debt ratio in 1996-1997 were off-budgetary and quasi-fiscal outlays. Official estimates indicate that in the 1996 quasi-fiscal subsidies amounted to 8.2% of GDP, bringing the total public sector deficit to 13.9% GDP (see IBCA, 1997). Until 1996 the government managed to keep the public debt from rising by monetizing the quasi-fiscal deficits. The acceleration of the growth of the debt after the election of 1996 is probably due to the halting of these practises by the new government.

The increase in the debt ratio mainly reflects borrowing abroad. Although in 1996 the IMF and World Bank suspended disbursements, which resulted in a fall in the share of total medium and long term debt owed to official creditors, the government took advantage of good conditions on international capital markets and raised funds by borrowing from private creditors (both from commercial banks and by issuing bonds). In 1997, the continued inflow of funds from private creditors was strengthened by increased borrowing from international financial institutions, made possible by the new stabilisation program supported by the IMF and World Bank.

Interest payments on government liabilities remained low until 1995 but the switch to private external creditors caused payments to increase sharply in 1997. This will put a large strain on a budget which is already suffering from falling output and deteriorating enterprise finances, which make it difficult to realise tax revenue targets.

1.3 The structure of public debt.

The structure of instruments used to finance public debt in the four countries has changed significantly during the 1990s: the share of securities has increased and their maturity has lengthened. This reflects the shift to a market-based system of deficit financing and a stabilisation of the securities market. The structures of public debt with respect to various debt instruments are presented in Tables 3.6 to 3.8.

Table 3.6. The structure of Czech public debt

Type of debt	1993	1994	1995	1996	1997
Total debt (I+II)	100%	100%	100%	100%	100%
I. Domestic debt	55%	57%	61%	69%	71%
I.1 Treasury bills and bonds	24%	34%	49%	66%	68%
Long-term bonds	13%	19%	25%	26%	31%
Short-term bonds & bills	11%	15%	24%	40%	37%
I.2 Long-term loans	31%	24%	11%	3%	0%
I.3 Short-term loans & advances	0%	0%	0%	0%	3%
II. Foreign debt	45%	43%	39%	31%	29%

Source: Czech Ministry of Finance

In the Czech Republic, as in the other countries, there is a strong tendency to substitute loan financing with securities. By 1996 and 1997 almost the whole of domestic debt was financed by bills and bonds.

Table 3.7. The structure of public debt in Hungary

Type of debt	1991	1992	1993	1994	1995	1996
Total public debt (I+II+III)	100%	100%	100%	100%	100%	100%
I. Domestic interest bearing debt	60%	52%	56%	56%	55%	50%
I.1 Deficit financing	34%	31%	35%	32%	32%	30%
I.1.1 Treasury bills & bonds	2%	4%	13%	17%	20%	21%
- treasury bills	1%	3%	7%	7%	8%	9%
- state bonds	1%	1%	6%	10%	12%	12%
I.1.2 NBH credits	32%	27%	21%	15%	12%	9%
I.2 Non-deficit financing	26%	20%	21%	24%	23%	21%
1.2.1 NBH other credits	24%	19%	14%	10%	8%	7%
1.2.2. Bonds	2%	2%	7%	14%	15%	13%
II. External debt of the central government	3%	6%	6%	6%	6%	7%
III. Non interest bearing debt held by NBH	37%	42%	39%	38%	38%	43%

Source: Hungary - Statistical Appendix, IMF (1997)

The structure of Hungarian government debt has been dominated by credit from the NBH and the non-interest bearing debt held by NBH. In 1996 treasury bills and bonds made up 34% of the debt, while 16% was credit from NBH and 43% was held by NBH. However during the 1990s the share of credit from the central bank has been falling rapidly in favour of financing through the issue of bills and bonds (since 1991 the NBH can finance the government only by purchasing marketable securities).

In 1992 a system of regular issues of t-bills was developed, and since then their role in deficit financing has been rising. Marketable bond issues for government financing started at the end of 1991, but their share has been increasing only since 1993: their part in total debt financing has risen since 1993 by 6 percentage points and in deficit financing from 7% in 1993 to 40% in 1996. Because budget deficits turned out to be a permanent phenomenon, the most important task faced by debt management was to increase the security of finance by increasing maturities. However, over a third of the deficit is still financed by short-term instruments.

Such a pattern of debt market development has also been observable in Poland, i.e.: at first the authorities introduced short term bills (3 and 6 months) and then, as the market matured and the reform program gained credibility, they began to issue longer-termed securities.

Non-deficit related financing constitutes over 20% of total public debt in Hungary. Here also financing by means of credit from the central bank has been decreasing in favour of bond financing. These bonds include, among others, securities issued to purchase the non-performing rubel debt owed to the NBH by Russia and the recapitalization bonds issued under the bank consolidation programs.

The structure of the government debt of Poland is provided in Table 3.8.

Table 3.8. The structure of the public debt in Poland

Type of debt	1992	1993	1994	1995	1996	1997
Total public debt (I+II+III)	100%	100%	100%	100%	100%	100%
I. Domestic debt	25%	29%	37%	40%	43%	45%
I .1. Deficit financing	11%	15%	21%	25%	28%	28%
I.1.1. Treasury bills	9%	14%	18%	17%	16%	15%
I.1.2 Bonds	2%	1%	3%	7%	12%	13%
I.2. Passive bonds (non-deficit financing)	6%	10%	13%	12%	12%	13%
II. Other	7%	3%	2%	3%	3%	4%
III. Foreign debt	75%	71%	63%	60%	57%	55%

Source: Polish Ministry of Finance

Since 1993 almost the entire Polish domestic debt has been financed by the issuance of bills and bonds, but until 1996 deficit financing was dominated by short term bills (with a maturity up to 52 weeks). As more long-term instruments were introduced - in 1994 fixed rate 2 and 5 years bonds and in the end of 1995 a 10 year floating rate bond, the share of medium and long term bonds grew rapidly. In 1997 they constituted 46% of deficit financing. This increases the safety of financing and also reflects the growing creditworthiness of the government and the credibility of the anti-inflation program.

Over 10% of the debt is non-deficit financing debt, which includes restructurization bonds, bonds for recapitalization of banks and bonds issued as part of the agreement with the London Club, which was in fact a method of swapping a part of foreign debt for domestic debt.

Exact data on the structure of Romania's domestic debt is not available. External borrowing has financed most government fiscal imbalances, therefore domestic debt is low, standing at 7% of GDP and 20% of total public debt in 1997. The market for the domestic debt is still underdeveloped. Existing domestic debt has been financed mostly by commercial banks. The majority of the paper has a maturity of 90 days. It was only in 1997 that legislation was put in place that provided for market-based T-bill auctions and secondary market trading, and for non-residents to buy domestic government securities.

1.4 The structure of public and publicly guaranteed external debt.

The maturity of public and publicly guaranteed external debt is provided in Table 3.9.

Table 3.9. Maturity of the Czech, Hungarian, Polish and Romanian public and publicly guaranteed external debt

	Czech Republic		Hungary		Poland		Romania	
	1990	1996	1990	1996	1990	1996	1990	1996
Total debt stock	100%	100%	100%	100%	100%	100%	100%	100%
Long-term debt	53%	65%	84%	89%	80%	100%	18%	76%
Short-term debt	47%	35%	16%	11%	20%	0%	82%	24%

Source: World Bank, World Debt Tables (1998)

The external public and publicly guaranteed debts of the four countries are dominated by long term debt, i.e. debt with an original maturity of more than one year. This is a favourable feature of the external debt as it smoothes the country's stream of obligations and increases the predictability of debt refinancing, safeguarding it from a sudden change in investor sentiment, although it limits the possibility of borrowing for a short period.

Most Czech and Hungarian public and publicly guaranteed external debt is owed to private creditors, which is the normal structure for a middle-income country. While in the Czech Republic loans from commercial banks dominate, in Hungary those loans are being swapped for bonds. In Poland and Romania most of the public and publicly guaranteed debt is owed to official creditors, a structure which is similar to that of low-income countries. However, in Romania during 1990-1996 the share of debt to private creditors rose by 35 percentage points. Romania's indebtedness toward private creditors increased substantially in 1996. The National Bank of Romania raised nearly 1 billion dollars through three bond issues; a three year Samurai bond (issued in March'96 at 340 basis points), a three year Eurobond (issued in June'96 at 305 basis points) and a five year Samurai bond (issued in September'96 at 315 basis points). In addition, the central bank borrowed 600 million dollars in the form of syndicated bank loans at a maturity of 1-3 years. These operations have increased the cost of debt servicing and shortened the average maturity, which has already lead to a sharp rise in debt payments in 1997.

2. THE BUDGET SURPLUS PROJECTIONS

The next sections describe two steps in our macroeconomic projection that has been prepared to show the possible future development of public debt and necessary fiscal adjustments. The first step tries to assess the fiscal adjustments required in the four transition countries to obtain the debt/GDP and the deficit/GDP ratios consistent with the Maastricht criteria. It shows the minimum primary surpluses of general government balances that are needed to keep debt/GDP at some assumed level. We assume a constant debt/GDP ratio for Hungary, Poland and Romania and an increasing ratio for the Czech Republic. These assumptions are stricter than the 60 per cent debt/GDP ratio specified in Maastricht treaty. However, in some scenarios the debt/GDP ratios required by Maastricht can be obtained even with relatively high fiscal deficits, well in excess of the 3 per cent deficit/GDP ratio. In cases when this second Maastricht criterion is not met one year before joining the EMU and after, we calculate the minimum primary surpluses required for keeping the deficit/GDP ratios at the 3 per cent level. In the second part of our projection we forecast the main elements of general government revenues and expenditures, providing an outlook to the future streams of general government primary balances. Comparison of primary surpluses required to satisfy the Maastricht criteria with the forecasted surpluses gives an assessment of fiscal adjustments necessary in the accession process. One must remember, however, that the second step uses a much larger set of assumptions, so its results may be less certain. Both steps use the debt/GDP ratios in 1999 as starting values.[3] Whenever it is possible, external forecasts of macroeconomic aggregates are used as inputs in projections.

2.1 The Government Budget Identity

The aim of the first analysis is an estimation of the future stream of primary surpluses consistent with given debt/GDP and deficit/GDP ratios and the assumed behaviour of other macroeconomic aggregates. The starting point is the government budget identity, which relates the primary deficit and nominal interest payments to possible sources of financing these expenditures (i.e. issues of domestic and foreign debt). The standard budget identity (with variables shown as a percentage of GDP) is as follows:

$$-p_t + b_{t-1}(1 + r_t)(1 + g_t)^{-1} + b^*_{t-1}(1 + r^*_t)(1 + a_t)(1 + g_t)^{-1} = b_t + b^*_t \quad (3)$$

Where p = the ratio of the primary surplus to GDP, b = stock of domestic debt to GDP ratio, b^* = stock of foreign debt to GDP ratio, r = real interest rate paid on domestic debt, r^* = real interest rate paid on foreign debt, g = real GDP growth, and a = domestic currency real depreciation rate.

In simulations we first set the required debt/GDP ratio. We assume that the total (foreign and domestic) debt/GDP ratios will remain constant for Hungary, Poland and Romania. For the Czech Republic we assume that the ratio will increase to achieve the 50 per cent level in 2010.[4] We assume for this country that the ratio of foreign debt to GDP will remain constant, and that the higher public debt/GDP ratio will be financed by borrowing on the domestic market.

To obtain values of future primary deficits/surpluses consistent with the required debt/GDP ratio, all variables in the budget equation, except the primary surplus, are assigned numerical values based on our prior assumptions and forecasts. The identity is then solved for the primary surpluses consistent with other projected variables. If the assumed debt/GDP ratio is consistent with a deficit higher than 3 per cent of GDP one year before the accession to the EMU or after, we calculate the primary surplus necessary for achieving the 3 per cent limit instead. In other words, we always use the more restrictive of the two Maastricht criteria. In all cases where the deficit/GDP criterion requires an adjustment in the debt/GDP ratio (i.e. when the former is binding and a reduction in the public debt/GDP ratio is required), we assume that only the foreign debt/GDP ratio will decrease. This assumption, and the assumptions above about changes in domestic and foreign debt/GDP ratios in the Czech Republic, are motivated by policymakers' concerns about the real exchange rate appreciation related to foreign capital inflows.

Our method is a simplification of the usual approach to the analysis of fiscal sustainability in developing countries, the main difference being that the budget identities of the Government (Treasury) and the Central Bank are not aggregated into a single budget identity of the consolidated Government. This is justified because the contribution of Central Bank profits to Government revenues is small and diminishing in the countries under investigation.

2.2 Behaviour of Real GDP Growth, Real Interest Rates and Real Exchange Rates

This accounting approach to policy consistency requires some assumptions about the behaviour of real GDP growth, real interest rates and real exchange rates. Usually, these variables are assumed to be exogenous to the fiscal balances in the identity. This assumption is certainly not realistic. All variables in the equation are endogenous and, ideally, a complete macro-econometric model would be required to determine their values. However, development of such a model is beyond the scope of this undertaking. The variables are determined by estimates available in the literature, or - for some numbers - by author's "best guesses".

The Foreign Interest Rate, the Risk Premium and EU accession issues

Since foreign currency denominated debt makes up a considerable part of total government debt in all four countries, a forecast of the foreign interest rate is needed to run the simulations. A large share of foreign debt is denominated in US dollars and the interest rates paid on this debt are obviously related to the rates on US Treasury obligations of the same maturity. In the simulations it is assumed that the real interest rate on US Treasury Bonds will be constant at the

3 per cent level, which is consistent with 5 per cent nominal interest rate and 2 per cent inflation, and thus with recent experience.

In addition, countries in transition must pay a considerable risk premium above the world interest rate. The behaviour of the risk premium depends on countries' default risk, which is in turn related to economic fundamentals as perceived by the market. Based on historical data and literature on this subject, it is assumed that for the Czech Republic, Hungary and Poland the risk premium will remain at its current level (1 per cent for the Czech Republic, 1.5 per cent for Hungary and 2 per cent for Poland). Also, it will fall only after accession to the European Union and ERMII, to 0,5% for all three countries, This assumption may seem unrealistic since the spread for the Czech Republic was already as low as 30 basis points (bps) before the 1997 Asian crises. However, as argued in Cline and Barnes (1997), this level was unsustainable. The spread for EU countries (e.g. Finland, Italy, Portugal, Sweden) increased to about 30 bps after the Asian crises and the slightly higher level for transition economies after accession seems to be a conservative but reasonable assumption. We also assume that full membership in the Monetary Union will bring full convergence of interest rates (and zero risk premium).

Two scenarios for joining the European institutions are considered. Early accession (ERMII in 2003 and EMU in 2005) means faster interest rate convergence, while postponed membership (ERMII in 2005 and EMU in 2007) generates a more persistent mark-up over foreign interest rates. In the case of Romania there are insufficient grounds for assuming any particular date of accession to the European Union, and we therefore extrapolate the current situation with a gradually declining risk premium. The last available (mid October 1998) level for the Romanian spread is 10 per cent but, since the risk premium has increased only recently, we assume a 7 per cent spread in 1998, 10 per cent in 1999 and then gradually declining (by one tenth annually) afterwards. The actual interest rate paid on Polish foreign currency denominated debt is significantly lower than in other countries due to the debt reduction agreement with the Paris Club. To account for the results of this agreement, the World Bank projection of principal and interest repayments is used for Poland until 2006. Thus, the share of low-interest debt declines over the projection horizon and new debt is assumed to pay the market interest rate.

Real GDP growth

Forecasting real GDP growth is far beyond the scope of this simulation, but several research institutes publish medium-term GDP projections for transition economies, which can be used here. For the 1998-1999 period we use the Consensus forecasts for Hungary and Poland, The Czech Ministry of Finance forecast for the Czech Republic and, for 1998-2000, our own forecasts for Romania. For the remaining years we consider two scenarios:

one with high (5 % per annum) and one with low (2% per annum) growth for all countries.

Real Domestic Interest Rates

To predict the future development of the real domestic interest rate we identify its domestic and foreign determinants. The domestic component is strictly related to GDP growth, and the second element is the real foreign interest rate. The weight given to the domestic determinant is assumed to decrease over time by one twentieth annually, to drop to 0.3 after EU accession, and further to zero after EMU accession. Again, there are two dates for joining the mechanism and in the case of postponed membership (EMU in 2007) the stronger influence of the domestic component is prolonged.

The initial weights given to the domestic component (0.3 for the Czech Republic, 0.5 for Hungary and Poland and 0.9 for Romania) reflect the present degree of integration of each country with international financial markets. The Czech Republic acceded to the IMF's Article VIII and OECD codes on capital liberalisation already in 1995, and its integration with international financial markets is higher than other transition economies. In Poland and Hungary capital account transactions, although liberalised, are still subject to significant restrictions. Romania has only recently introduced current account convertibility. These assumptions are modified for the Czech Republic in 1998-1999 and for Romania in 1998, according to the Czech Ministry of Finance forecast and our own forecast for Romania based on recent developments.

Real Exchange Rates

Productivity growth in the tradable sector and capital inflow exert significant pressure for real exchange rate appreciation through the Harrod-Balassa-Samuelson effect. Since the productivity gap is still wide between transition and developed economies, we expect that this tendency will continue in the future. Assumptions about productivity growth have to be consistent with the real GDP forecast. We assume unitary elasticity of the real exchange rate with respect to real GDP in the high (5 per cent) growth scenario and no real appreciation in the low (2 per cent) growth scenario. The unitary elasticity assumed in the first case is broadly consistent with data from the fast-growing transition countries.[5] In the two-year period preceding accession to the EMU, real exchange rate appreciation will be determined by accession criteria. At present these are the exclusion of exchange rate depreciation in excess of 15% from the central rate, and the requirement of very low inflation. However, since the period of strict adherence to these criteria will be short, and since it is not certain whether the current criteria will be obligatory for new member states, we do not embed these restrictions in our simulations. Once again, for the Czech

Republic for 1998-1999 and for Romania in 1999 we use different assumptions, based on the forecasts from the Czech Ministry of Finance and our own forecasts for Romania.

3. SIMULATION RESULTS: PRIMARY SURPLUSES NECESSARY FOR ACHIEVING THE DEBT/GDP RATIO CRITERIA

The series described above were used as inputs into eq.(3), and this produced the set of primary deficits (-) or surpluses (+). Figures 3.2 to 3.5 below present the simulation results and below we summarise the main findings.

The Czech Republic: Given our initial assumption about the evolution of the debt/GDP ratio (a gradual increase to 50 per cent in 2010), the Czech government is allowed to run high fiscal deficits, exceeding the 3 per cent ratio, in almost all scenarios. Consequently, starting from one year before EMU accession we calculate primary surpluses consistent with the deficit/GDP criterion. The deficit/GDP constraint is always binding in the post-accession period. Most of the time the allowed primary deficits are higher in the high growth scenario, because the higher growth and the related real appreciation of the currency reduce the debt/GDP ratio. Timing of the EU and EMU accessions does not have significant effects. The permitted primary deficits are always higher in the early accession scenario, but the cumulative differences (in terms of additional primary deficits) between late and early accession are negligible and amount to 0.8 per cent of GDP with the high growth assumption and 0.4 per cent with the low growth assumption. In all scenarios the permitted primary deficits diminish over time, since accumulating debt increases the cost of interest payments.

Hungary: Given the initial assumption about the constant debt/GDP ratio, some primary deficits are allowed in the high growth scenario but primary surpluses are always required in simulations with low growth. In the former case high growth and real currency appreciation reduce the debt/GDP ratio. The fiscal deficits slightly exceed 3 per cent of GDP and the deficit/GDP ratio criterion becomes binding starting from one year before accession to the EMU. In the low growth case the debt/GDP ratio is always binding. The cumulative difference between early and late accession amounts to 1.8 per cent of GDP in the high growth scenario (earlier accession allows for lower primary surpluses through lower costs of servicing the public debt) and 1 per cent under the low growth assumption.

Poland: The results for Poland are similar to the Hungarian case. Again, primary deficits are allowed in the high growth scenario but primary surpluses are required in the low growth scenario. The deficit/GDP ratio is binding in the former case, starting from one year before EMU accession. In the low growth case the debt/GDP ratio is always binding. The cumulative gains from early accession to the EMU are 1.2 and 0.6 per cent of GDP in the high and low growth scenarios respectively.

Romania: The initial indebtedness of Romania is one of the lowest among the countries investigated. However, poor macroeconomic performance and consequently very high risk premiums increase the costs of foreign debt service. Our assumption of slowly decreasing spreads makes the constant debt to GDP strategy feasible for the high growth assumption, when some primary deficits are allowed in the second half of the simulation period.[6] The strategy, however, seems to be difficult to implement in the low growth scenario.

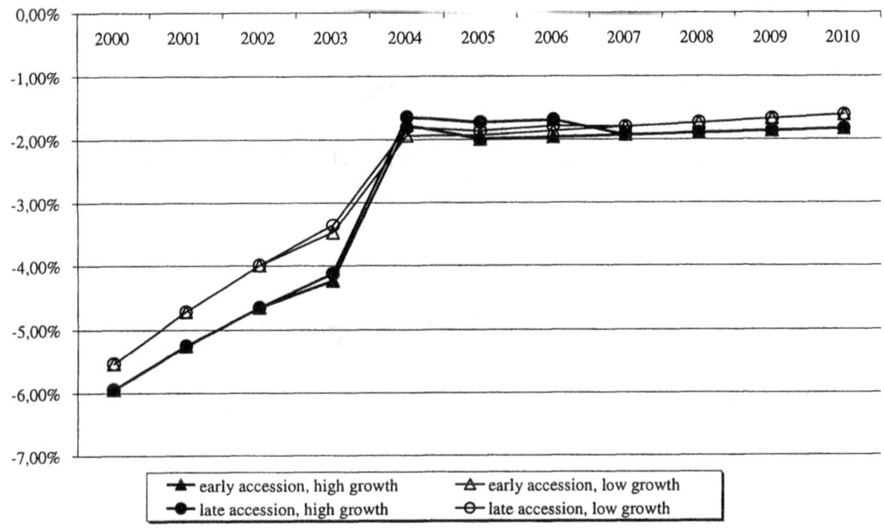

Figure 3.2. Czech Republic: required primary surplus (+) / deficit (-)

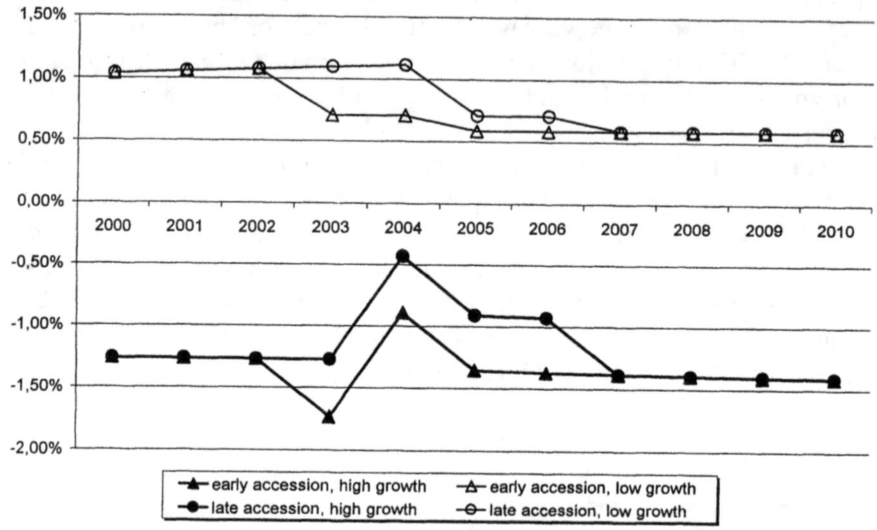

Figure 3.3. Hungary: required primary surplus (+) / deficit (-)

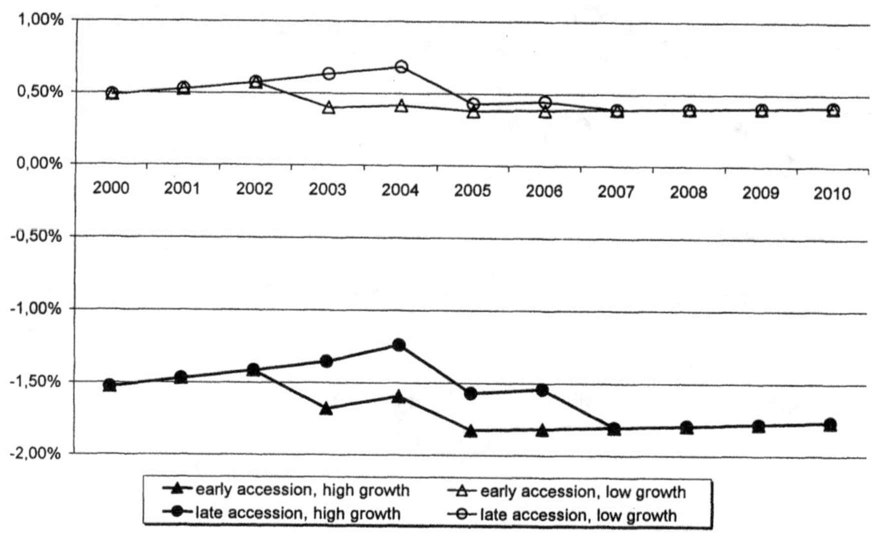

Figure 3.4. Poland: required primary surplus (+) / deficit (-)

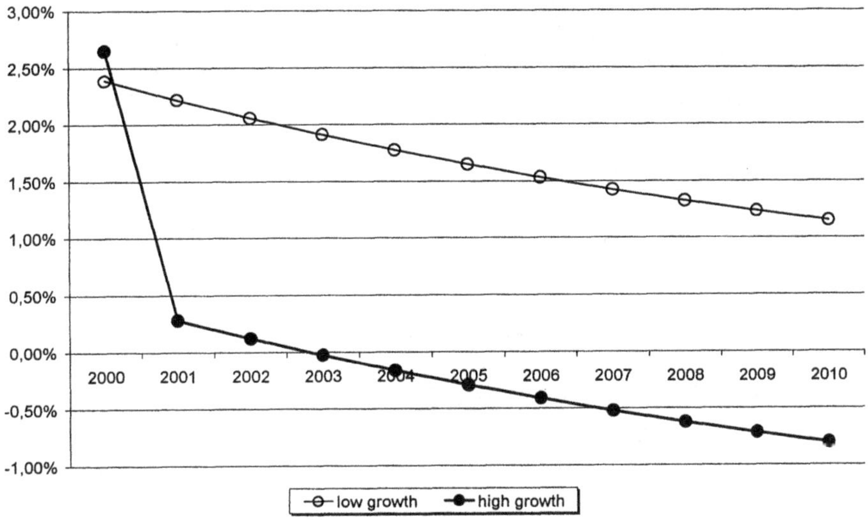

Figure 3.5. Romania: required primary surplus (+) / deficit (-)

4. FORECASTS OF GOVERNMENT REVENUES AND EXPENDITURES

In the second step of the projection we forecast the general government budget position assuming that no dramatic changes in the current proportions of the main elements of general government revenues and expenditures occur over the next 10 years. The revenues and expenditures of the national governments have been split into groups and some specific assumptions have been made for each of the elements, allowing us to calculate their behaviour based on the 1997 accounts (as published by the IMF). The primary deficits/surpluses of budgets are calculated for each year and the corresponding debt/GDP ratios are obtained from the budget identity (3) under identical assumptions as in the previous section.

One of our tasks was to develop a set of assumptions that could be used unmodified for all four countries. This would ensure full comparability of the simulation results. In order to avoid excessive complexity it was assumed that every element in the budget either stays constant in real terms, or grows at the same rate as GDP. For some items other assumptions have been made, related to the fact of expected EU accession. Although such an approach must include a degree of simplification, it is consistent and avoids unsubstantiated speculation.

It was generally agreed that in the short term budget revenues depend on the overall performance of the national economies (measured by the growth rate of GDP), while expenditures tend to stay at some constant real level. In other words, governments cannot push their costs below some minimum level, while revenues may fall rapidly when the economy gets into crisis. During years of growth, higher economic activity increases revenue, while expenditures may remain unchanged.

The table below presents the list of variables analysed, together with the assumptions that have been made regarding each of them.

Table 3.10. Decomposition of government revenues and expenditures

ANALYSED ELEMENTS	METHOD OF ESTIMATION	NOTES
REVENUES		
Tax revenue		
Direct taxes	Growth of GDP	
Indirect taxes	Growth of GDP	
International trade taxes	Constant real level	zero after EU accession
Other tax revenues	Growth of GDP	
Non-tax revenue	Constant real level	
EXPENDITURES		
Current expenditure:		
Wages & salaries	Constant real level	
Subsidies	Growth of GDP	
Transfers	Growth of GDP	
Interest payments	Calculated	formula described later
Other current expenditure	Constant real level	
Investment expenditure	Growth of GDP	

The following subsections provide further explanations of our assumptions.

4.1 Revenues

Taxes are assumed to grow at the same rate as GDP, with the exception of customs duties. The latter are equal to zero after EU accession. There will be no taxation on trade between EU members, while customs on external trade will no longer be the revenues of member states. Until accession, custom duties are assumed to maintain their real value, which is the effect of their gradual reduction in nominal terms in the pre-accession period combined with a growing volume of imports.

All "other" budget revenues are assumed to stay constant in real terms. These include all kinds of revenues that are not clearly specified or cannot be easily connected with GDP growth (for example, central bank transfers, capital revenues or dividends). This may be disputable as dividends may grow with GDP, as the profits of state owned or co-owned enterprises may grow with GDP. On the other hand, progress in privatisation may lead to a decrease in this kind of revenue.

The reason for treating all non-tax revenues in the same way is purely practical - the total number of categories has to be kept at a reasonable level. Increasing the number of categories requires more assumptions to be made, making the outcome more sensitive to random factors. The level of detail used in the simulation is therefore a compromise between the complexity of analysis performed, and the reliability of the final results.

4.2 Expenditures

On the expenditure side, wages and salaries are assumed to stay at a constant real level. This is another simplifying assumption, since economic growth and increases in productivity in some sectors may be expected to cause a rise in real wages in the whole economy. However, ongoing privatisation reduces the number of workers paid by the state. An attempt was made to include growth of real wages, depending on real GDP growth – 1 per cent annual growth of real wages in the low growth scenario, and 2 per cent with 5 per cent real GDP growth. However, the effects of this assumption turned out to be minimal.

The current ratios of subsidies and transfers to GDP are expected to remain stable. This reflects the redistributive function of the state as a tool for reducing income differences. The same is assumed for investment expenditures. All "other" expenditures are to stay at current real levels. As in the case of the revenue side, those expenditures that cannot clearly be identified or connected with GDP growth are treated in this way.

Interest payments, necessary for calculating the stream of debt/GDP ratios, are calculated from the formula:

$$ip_t = (b_{t-1} * r_t)(1 + g_t)^{-1} + (b^*_{t-1} * r^*_t)(1 + a_t)(1 + g_t)^{-1} \tag{4}$$

which is the relevant part of the government budget identity (3), and where ip equals the ratio of interest payments to GDP. The assumptions about real interest rates, real GDP growth and real exchange rate appreciation are the same as in the previous section.

4.3 Extra revenues and costs – EU transfers and the costs of reforms

As was mentioned, the CEE countries face several reforms related to the expenditure side of their budgets. Some countries have already started reforms, in others there are no plans for introducing such reforms as yet. In this projection we will try to assess the fiscal impact of the reforms. Health care reform, public pension reform and environmental expenditures are included.

It is worth noting that not all of the above mentioned expenditures are "true" costs of reforms, which would never occur if the reform were not performed. Some outlays have to be made just because they were not made in the past, as in the case of pension system reform. If pensions are to be financed from savings accumulated by the pensioners themselves (through pension funds) and not from taxes on the earnings of their children, a part of already existing pension liabilities must be paid out of the state budget during a transitory period. Such extra financing is not a new kind of expenditure, but just a payoff of existing implicit debt. The implicit debt of the pension system is merely converted into an explicit one. Extra financing from the state is needed in this case, just as much as for the "real" cost-drivers such as environmental expenditures.

The Czech Republic and Hungary have already implemented health care reform. A similar process has just started in Poland. Both countries noted an increase in health care expenditures, by about 2 per cent of GDP annually. One may believe that a similar outcome will occur in Poland. We assume that in Poland in the first 4 years of the reform there will be an annual increase of expenditures related to health care of 0.5 per cent of GDP, and that subsequently a constant burden of 2 per cent of GDP will be added to expenditures. No figures are assumed for Romania.

Pension system reform is being introduced in Poland, Hungary and Romania. According to external projections (Gomułka, 1998), the reform will cost the Polish government some 1.7 per cent of GDP yearly (on average). A simplified estimation is used for Romania: numbers for Poland were adopted, adjusted proportionally to current ratios of pension expenditures to GDP in this country. For Hungary another external estimate has been used (Vajda, 1999).

All three countries will have to increase their environmental expenditures, in order to fulfil EU directives after accession. We assume that after EU accession current environmental expenditures (value of new assets and technologies acquired for environmental projects) will have to be doubled in all of the countries.

The numerical values corresponding to these assumptions are collected in the table below (expenditures as a share of GDP). For convenience, it is assumed that environmental expenditures will maintain constant shares of GDP.

Table 3.11. Costs of reforms

Expenditures	'99	'00	'01	'02	'03	'04	'05	'06	'07	'08	'09	'10
Czech Republic:												
Environment					3,80	3,80	3,80	3,80	3,80	3,80	3,80	3,80
Hungary:												
Pension system		0,35	0,70	1,05	0,92	0,79	0,66	0,53	0,39	0,26	0,13	0,00
Environment					1,50	1,50	1,50	1,50	1,50	1,50	1,50	1,50
Total		0,35	0,70	1,05	2,42	2,29	2,16	2,03	1,89	1,76	1,63	1,50
Poland:												
Pension system	1,11	1,19	1,26	1,34	1,41	1,49	1,57	1,64	1,72	1,8	1,87	1,95
Health care	0,5	1,00	1,50	2,00	2,00	2,00	2,00	2,00	2,00	2,00	2,00	2,00
Environment					1,60	1,60	1,60	1,60	1,60	1,60	1,60	1,60
Total	1,61	2,19	2,76	3,34	5,01	5,09	5,17	5,24	5,32	5,4	5,47	5,55
Romania:												
Pension system	0,51	0,55	0,58	0,62	0,65	0,69	0,72	0,76	0,79	0,83	0,86	0,90

Source: Statistical Yearbooks, own computations.

The totals have been added to the general government expenditure of the countries.

Some additional government revenues are expected as a result of the EU accession. Transfers, grants or other targeted inflows may be expected from the EU to help new members to overcome the difficulties of the transition and accession periods. An external estimate (Tomczyńska, 1999) was used here, modified for the particular needs of this projection. The table below presents expected final net transfers of EU funds, as a percentage of applicants' GDP:

Table 3.12. Accession revenues

% of GDP	2001	2002	2003	2004	2005	2006	2007	2008	2009	2010
High growth scenario										
Czech R.	0,19	0,18	0,32	0,40	0,46	0,52	0,56	0,53	0,51	0,49
Hungary	0,19	0,18	0,31	0,39	0,45	0,51	0,55	0,52	0,50	0,47
Poland	0,56	0,54	0,93	1,16	1,36	1,52	1,64	1,56	1,49	1,42
Low growth scenario										
Czech R.	0,20	0,20	0,36	0,47	0,57	0,67	0,76	0,74	0,73	0,71
Hungary	0,20	0,20	0,35	0,46	0,56	0,66	0,74	0,73	0,71	0,70
Poland	0,60	0,58	1,06	1,38	1,67	1,96	2,21	2,17	2,12	2,08

Source: Tomczyńska (1999), own computations

As with the costs of reforms, these numbers have been added to the general government revenues of the three countries.

4.4 Simulation Results

Figures 3.6 to 3.13 present the simulation results for the four countries and two growth scenarios. Since the exact dates of accession to the EU only have small effect on the simulation results (as compared to real GDP growth), only one accession date is analysed here. The "optimistic" scenario was chosen, assuming full membership in the EU for the Czech Republic, Hungary and Poland in 2003, and membership in EMU in 2005. No accession dates are forecasted for Romania (at least in the period up to 2010). The series in the graphs are calculated as follows:

The "required" primary surpluses are calculated from the debt/GDP and deficit/GDP constraints as explained above and correspond to the series in Figures 3.2 to 3.5. The constraints on the debt/GDP ratio are based on our assumptions (the constant or increasing ratio strategy) and are stricter than the relevant Maastricht criteria. Nevertheless, even these strict assumptions on the evolution of public debt are sometimes not sufficient to guarantee a fiscal deficit/GDP ratio below the 3 per cent limit. In cases where the latter constraint is binding, we adjust the debt/GDP ratio accordingly

The "forecasted" primary surplus is calculated from our forecasts of government expenditures and revenues.

The primary surplus series "forecasted/required when constraints binding" is calculated from the forecasted primary surpluses when the constraints specified by the Maastricht criteria do not apply (i.e. more than one year before the date of the EMU accession) or are not binding. Whenever the constraints are binding, we calculate the primary surpluses necessary to adjust the deficit/GDP ratio or debt/GDP ratio to the relevant criterion. Since, despite the stringency of our assumptions, the "required" primary surpluses in some cases allow for very lax fiscal policy and a fast accumulation of debt in the initial (pre-accession) period, high primary surpluses are often required to adjust fiscal indicators shortly before and after accession to the EMU. In these cases a comparison between the "forecasted" and the "required" primary surpluses in the post accession period is not informative since the "required" surpluses show the necessary adjustments from much higher debt/GDP ratios. In the "forecasted/required when constraints binding" simulation, the accumulation of the debt is slower at the beginning of the period. This simulation shows adjustments necessary for meeting the EMU accession criteria under the most plausible forecasts for pre-accession fiscal policy.

The series on public debt ("required", "forecasted" and "forecasted/required when constraints binding") correspond to relevant primary surplus series. In calculating these series we assumed in the case of the Hungary and Poland that primary surpluses are used to reduce the foreign debt/GDP ratio, whereas primary deficits are covered by new domestic borrowing. For the Czech Republic we assumed that the foreign debt/GDP ratio remains constant. For Romania we assumed that primary surpluses and deficits reduce and increase domestic and foreign debt equally.

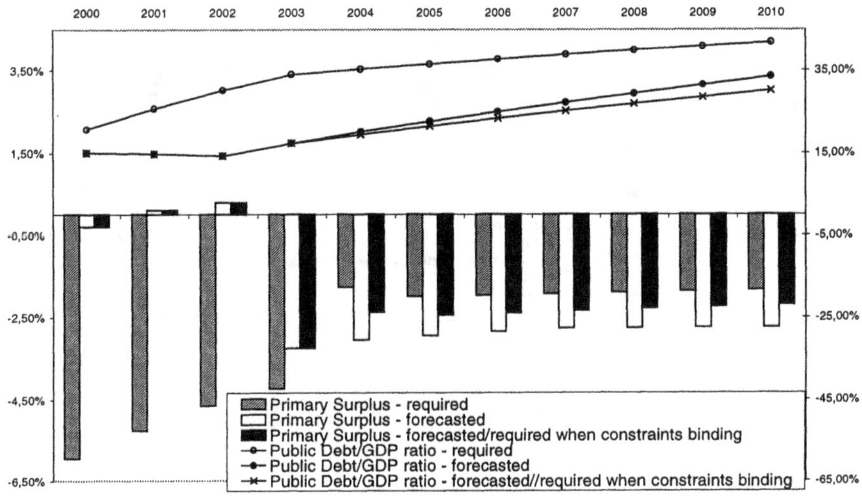

Figure 3.6. Czech Republic, high growth

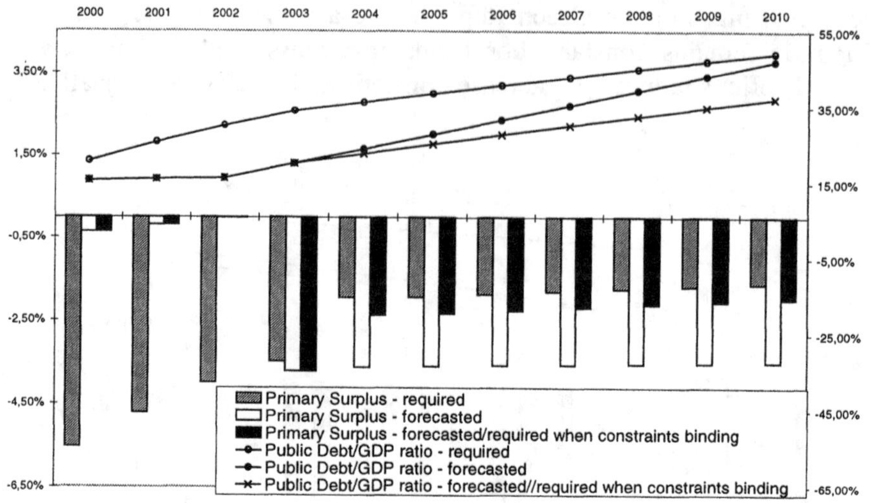

Figure 3.7. Czech Republic, low growth

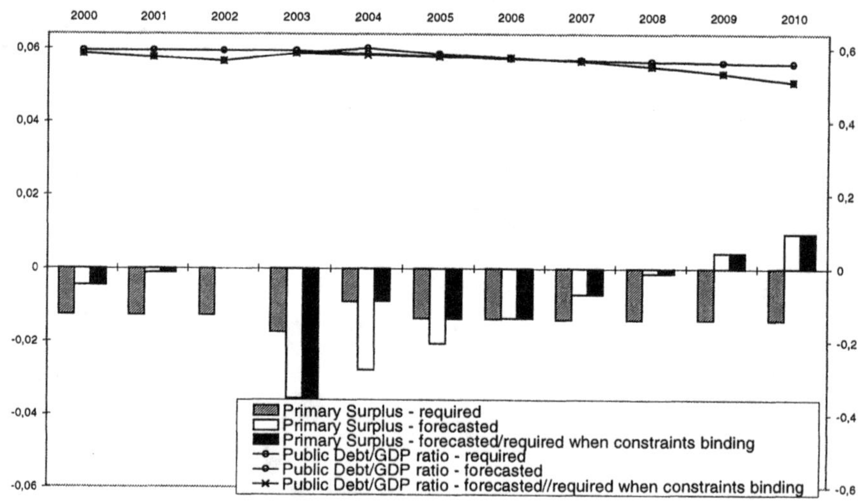

Figure 3.8. Hungary, high growth

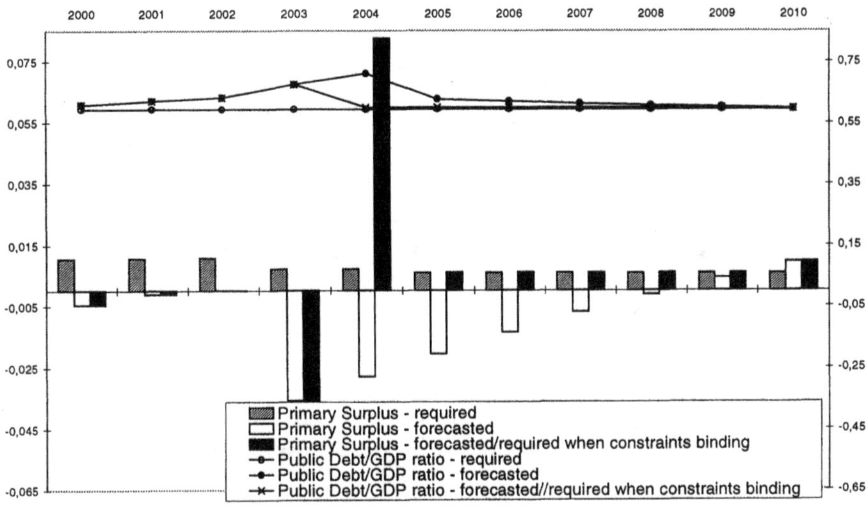

Figure 3.9. Hungary - low growth

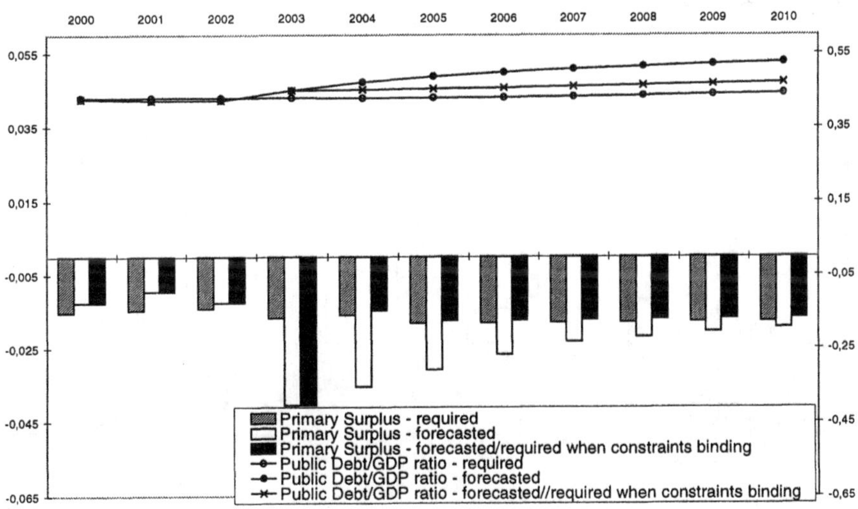

Figure 3.10. Poland, high growth

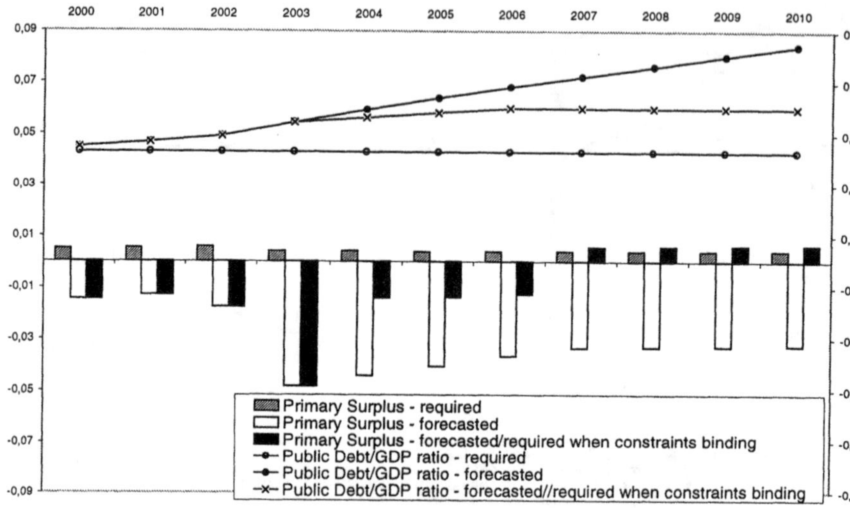

Figure 3.11. Poland, low growth

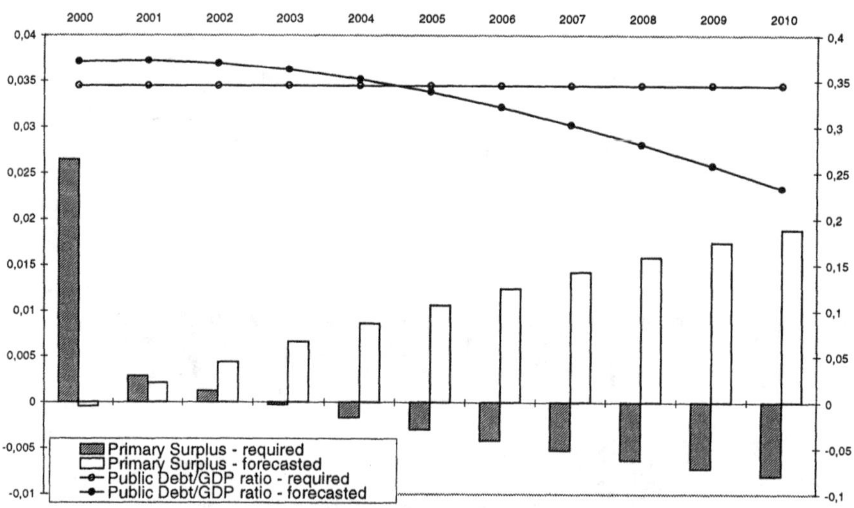

Figure 3.12. Romania, high growth

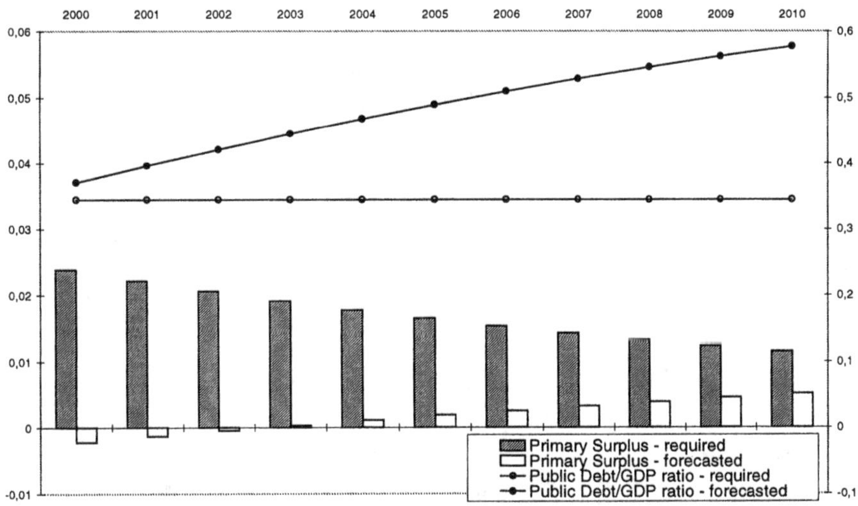

Figure 3.13. Romania, low growth

A comparison of the "required" and "forecasted" primary surpluses reveals that our constraints on the debt/GDP strategy (constant ratios for Hungary and Poland and an increasing ratio for the Czech Republic) are not binding before EMU accession in the high growth scenarios. Under the low growth assumption the constraint is still non-binding for the Czech Republic. In all countries joining the EU, fiscal expenditures related to accession are high and lead to substantial primary deficits in the years following accession. High growth mitigates the problem of fiscal adjustment when it is assumed. In the Czech Republic the difference between the "forecasted/required when constraints binding" and the forecasted primary deficit is lower than 1 per cent of GDP under the high growth assumption. In Hungary the "forecasted/required when constraints binding" primary deficit is lower than "forecasted" only in two years (2004-2005) after the accession and a small surplus is achieved at the end of the period. In Poland the differences are more persistent but they diminish over time and exceed 1 per cent of GDP only in three post-accession years (2004-2006). In the low growth scenario the "forecasted/required when constraints binding" primary deficits after the accession are always lower than the "forecasted". In Hungary and Poland the Maastricht criteria require primary surpluses at some point of the simulation period, while our forecasts indicate some substantial primary deficits in the post-accession years. Fiscal adjustments will be required to overcome this inconsistency if the new members decide to join the monetary union soon after the EU accession. In our forecasts the bulk of EU-related expenditures fall on expenditures related to environmental protection. For political and macro-economic policy reasons (Rostowski, Chapter 2) it is likely that the imposition of the Maastricht criteria will be given priority and that environmental expenditures will be lowered or postponed.

The difference between the high and low growth scenarios is even more pronounced in the case of Romania. The high growth scenario allows for small primary deficits, even under the stringent assumption of a constant debt to GDP ratio. In the low growth scenario the Romanian government is required to run large primary surpluses to keep the ratio constant.

5. SUMMARY AND CONCLUSIONS

During the 1990s the stock and structure of the public debt of the four countries has undergone major changes. Hungary and Poland, the two countries that entered the transition period with the largest debt burden, managed to lower their debt to GDP ratios substantially. The improvement in the Hungarian debt ratio can be attributed first, to the conduct of fiscal policy that resulted in primary surpluses, second, to an inflow of non-deficit revenues, mainly privatisation receipts, and third, to a high nominal growth rate of GDP in terms of foreign currency that was greater than interest payments, resulting in the economy "outgrowing" the debt.

In the case of Poland the debt ratio improvement can be attributed mainly to external debt reduction, which was the result of the agreements with the Paris and London Clubs. Other important factors were the fast rate of real GDP growth and the real appreciation of zloty that resulted in the nominal rate of GDP growth in terms of foreign currency being bigger than debt service payments.

The remaining two countries, which at the beginning of the decade had relatively low public debts - the Czech Republic and Romania - did not experience such a spectacular debt ratio decline. Romania experienced a debt ratio increase, although its indebtedness is still under the 60% of GDP ratio specified by the Maastricht Criteria, and is lower than the public liabilities' ratio of both Hungary and Poland. The debt build-up has occurred in Romania since 1994, and was especially dynamic in 1996 and 1997. The chief reasons have been non-deficit and quasi-fiscal imbalances. In 1997 the Czech Republic also noted a debt ratio increase, although so far very small in magnitude. The increase was mainly due the currency crisis and the floods, both of which hit the country in 1997, and resulted in a reduction in GDP growth.

The structure of the debt of the four countries has also undergone major changes. In the Czech Republic, Hungary and Poland the share of foreign debt has fallen in favour of domestic debt. In Romania, on the other hand, the share of foreign debt has substantially increased. The shift to market financing of the debt has resulted in a growing share of securities in domestic debt financing. The progress in the development of government debt markets and the growing credibility of the governments concerned, has allowed an increase in the maturities of bonds.

Government sectors of transition economies, in addition to explicit public debt, are also burdened with high implicit public debt in the social security system. The estimate for Poland (Gomulka and Jaworski, 1998) illustrates the magnitude of the problem - Poland's implicit debt is 200% to 270% of GDP. As the necessary change to a capital-funded system is implemented, this debt will gradually become explicit.

For further economic development and stability, sustainable financial policies are crucial. Although the debt ratios of Hungary and Poland are falling and both countries display primary surpluses, and the debt ratios of the Czech Republic and Romania are relatively low, each of the countries faces hazards that threaten further fiscal sustainability. In the second part of the paper we analysed the sustainability of fiscal policy in the four transition countries. For the applicants to the European Union and to the European Monetary Union, the natural benchmark for such an analysis is consistency with the relevant Maastrich criteria: ratios of public debt and deficit to GDP. For Romania we consider a constant public debt to GDP ratio to be a condition for fiscal sustainability.

The Czech Republic seems to be in the best situation, but it is not certain whether the country will manage to keep its fiscal deficit under control. The Czech Republic has still not resolved the problem of hidden public debt arising from bad debts in the banking sector. According to OECD estimates (OECD 1998), its true indebtedness is underestimated by as much as 7% of GDP. Because of its low initial indebtedness and hidden liabilities, we assume a gradually increasing debt/GDP ratio in our simulations. These assumptions allow for a very lax fiscal policy in the simulation period. Under these very mild conditions, the forecasted primary deficits are higher than the permitted ones after EU accession. Debt build-up before accession diverts the economy onto an unsustainable path, making the fulfilment of the Maastricht criteria unfeasible, especially under the low growth scenario. Although the forecasted primary deficits before the accession are much lower in absolute terms than the allowed limits, reducing the threat of rapid debt build-up, the forecasts presented here differ from the analysis by

Schneider and Štepanek (Chapter 7). The evolution of public debt in their forecasts closely resembles our limit case of lax fiscal policy with the debt/GDP ratio gradually increasing to 50 per cent in 2010. Our results indicate that the Maastricht criteria may not be attainable under such a scenario.

Hungary and Poland are even more vulnerable to negative shocks. Both countries face large interest payments - in Poland they reached almost 4% of GDP in 1997 and in Hungary a huge 9% of GDP. These payments are larger than the primary surpluses run by the governments of both countries and therefore add to their debt build-up. Any change in the economic environment that results in a contraction of GDP growth may cause interest payments to outweigh the nominal GDP increase, which may lead to a snowball effect of growing debt ratios and interest payments. Poland, although its interest payments are smaller at present, will face a debt service build-up after 2001. Any problems with the roll-over of its debt, caused for example by a deterioration in the country's investment rating, might cause serious problems in servicing the debt. Our simulation results confirm the fragility of both countries' fiscal positions. In the high growth scenario for Hungary the permitted primary deficits are larger in absolute terms than the forecasted ones, with the exception of the two post-accession years. In the low growth scenario small primary surpluses are required to meet the Maastricht criteria, but we forecast substantial primary deficits instead. The simulation results for Poland are very similar to the Hungarian case. In the high growth scenario forecasted primary deficits are broadly matched by the allowed limits. In the low growth scenario we forecast high primary deficits, while some primary surpluses are required for compliance with the Maastricht criteria.

Summing up, it is necessary that policymakers in the three candidate countries make an effort to implement further fiscal adjustment, especially by curbing government spending and improving its quality (IMF 1998). All the advanced transition countries appear to spend more than their long-run revenue generating capacities can sustain, and more than efficiency calls for. In order to comply with the Maastricht criteria all countries will probably be forced to make additional fiscal adjustments in the period covered by our projections. These adjustments will mainly affect the expenditure side, as the ratio of total revenue to GDP is already quite high.

The situation of Romania is the most fragile. Although its debt to GDP ratio remains low, in 1996-1997 it increased by nearly 16 percentage points of GDP. The underlying cause was a huge fiscal imbalance, arising from a large quasi-fiscal deficit and off-budgetary transfers. Although the authorities committed themselves to a stabilisation program, backed by the IMF and World Bank, most criteria agreed upon with the IMF were not met, including the fiscal deficit target. These budgetary imbalances were exacerbated by large off-budgetary losses resulting from the failure to close or privatise loss-making state enterprises (IIF 1998). The country is heavily dependent on foreign loans, but a lack of political stability and slow reforms significantly increase the costs of borrowing. Fiscal policy will not enter onto a sustainable path without deep structural reform of the economy. In our simulations the high growth scenario reflects the successful implementation of such reforms. Under this assumption the constant debt to GDP ratio strategy seems to be very easy to implement. In the low growth - slow reforms - scenario the required primary surpluses are much higher than the forecasted ones, making the achievement of a constant debt to GDP ratio unfeasible. Moreover, the low growth scenario is far more plausible for Romania than for the more advanced transition countries. The warning signal coming from the simulation is thus that much clearer.

ENDNOTES

[1] The estimates of seniorage until 1994 can be found in Buiter (1997).

[2] In 1995 NBH repaid around 4 billion dollars of its external debt, using its currency reserves.

[3] We use the 1997 data for forecasting primary surpluses since those were the latest available at the time of preparing the forecast. The source for most of the data is the IMF. The 1999 debt/GDP ratios are obtained from the Czech Ministry of Finance, National Bank of Hungary, IMF and National Bank of Romania.

[4] The annual growth of this ratio is consistent with a debt/GDP ratio asymptotically approaching the 60 percent level.

[5] The Harrod-Balassa-Samuelson effect in transition economies is investigated in Wyplosz and Halpern (1995), Halpern (1996) and Maliszewska (1998).

[6] The high primary surplus required in the high growth scenario for the year 2000 comes from our GDP growth forecast for that year (1 per cent).

REFERENCES

Anand, R. and van Wijnbergen, S. (1989), *Inflation and the Financing of Government Expenditure: an Introductory Analysis with an Application to Turkey*, World Bank Economic Review 3

Barr, D. and Campbell, J. (1996), *Inflation, Real Interest Rates, and the Bond Market: A Study of UK Nominal and Indexed-Linked Government Bond Prices*, NBER Working Paper 5821

Bernheim Douglas, *A Noeclassical Perspective on Budget Deficits*, Journal of Economic Perspectives, Vol. 3, 1989

Barro Robert, *Are Government Bonds Net Wealth?,* Journal of Political Economy, No.82, 1974

Buiter, W.H. (1993), *Consistency Checks for Fiscal, Financial and Monetary Policy Evaluation and Design, mimeo*, World Bank

Buiter, W.H. (1997), *Aspects of Fiscal Performance in some Transition Economies Under Fund-Supported Programs*, IMF Working Paper, April, WP/97/31

de Castello Branco Martha, *Pension Reform in the Baltics, Russia and other Countries of the Former Soviet Union (BRO).* IMF Working Paper, WP/98/11, February 1998

Citrin Daniel, Lahiri Ashok, *Policy Experiences and Issues in the Baltics, Russia, and Other Countries of the Former Soviet Union.* Occasional Paper 133, IMF, December 1995

Cline, W. and Barnes, K. (1997), *Spreads and Risk in Emerging Markets Lending*, Institute of International Finance Research Paper No. 91-1, November 1997

Czyżewski, A. and W. Orłowski (1996), *Scenariusze makroekonomiczne rozwoju gospodarki polskiej w latach 2000-2005*, CASE Studies And Analyses No. 101, Warsaw.

de Fontenay Patric, Miesi-Ferreti Gian, *The role of Foreign Currency Debt in Public Debt Management,* IMF Working Paper, WP/95/21, February 1995

Gomułka, S. and J. Jaworski (1998), *Implicit Public Debt Of the Polish Social Security System,* CASE - CEU Working Paper Series No. 14, Warsaw.

IBCA (1997), *Sovereign Report, Republic of Romania*, IBCA.

IMF, *International Capital Markets*, November 1997,

IMF, *World Economic Outlook*, May 1998

IMF (1997), *Hungary: Statistical Appendix*, IMF Staff Country Report No. 97/104, IMF, Washington D.C.

IMF (1998), *Czech Republic: Statistical Appendix*, IMF Staff Country Report No. 98/37, IMF, Washington D.C.

IMF (1998), *Republic of Poland: Selected Issues and Statistical Appendix*, IMF Staff Country Report No. 98/51, IMF, Washington D.C.

Maliszewska, M. (1998), *Modelling Real Exchange Rate in Transition: The Case of Poland and Romania*, CASE Studies & Analysis

OECD, *OECD Economic Outlook*, June 1998, OECD.

Sachs J. and F. Larrain (1993), *Macroeconomics In The Global Economy*, Prentice Hall, New Jersey.

Schneider, O. (1999), *Implicit Public Debt of the Czech Social Security System*, CASE Studies And Analyses No. 167, Warsaw.

Styczeń, M. (1999), *Socio-demographic Forecast of* Poland, 1997-2050, for Modelling Incomes and Social Security Retirement Pensions, CASE Studies And Analyses No. 168, Warsaw.

Tomczyńska, M. (1999), *Europen Union Financial Transfers to Applicant Countries*, CASE Studies And Analyses No. 173, Warsaw.

Vajda, Z. and B. Nestor (1999*), Does a "Pensions Overhang" Threaten the Macroeconomic Stability of the Developed Countries?*

World Bank (1999), *World Development Indicators*, World Bank, Washington D.C.

Halpern, L. (1996), *Real exchange rate and exchange rate policy in Hungary, Economics of Transition*, Vol. 4 (1)

Halpern, L. and Wyplosz, C. (1995), *Equilibrium Exchange Rate in Transition*, CEPR Discussion Paper, No. 1145.

Chapter 4

EVALUATINGE GOVERNMENT POLICY IN TRANSITION COUNTRIES

Max Gillman

INTRODUCTION

A view of a government's macroeconomics policy versus what is known as „microeconomic reform" is that the former shifts around the burden of the problem while the latter solves the problem. In economic terms, if there is a distortion in incentives, the first-best solution is to eliminate the distortion. Such macroeconomic problems with microeconomic solutions may be a disincentive to work that raises long-term unemployment because of moral hazards problems arising out of an unemployment insurance system that subsidizes not working. Or it may be incomplete insurance across states of nature because of a „free" national health care system that induces substitution towards low-quality health care. Or it may be incomplete consumption smoothing intergenerationally because of a government pension/social security scheme that inefficiently creates moral hazard by inducing early retirement. Or it may be incomplete smoothing of consumption intertemporally because of a lack of integration into international capital markets, because of unenforceable property rights, high and varying inflation rates, or high and accelerating government debt.

Evaluating the government reform policies of the Central European nations, as they seek integration in international markets, requires fresh examinations of what role governments actually play in democratically inclined societies: something beyond the mix of monetary and fiscal policy within an IS-LM multiplier framework. Intertemporal analysis over the horizon of optimal agents means 1) that with Ricardian equivalence between debt and taxes, there is no multiplier from deficit spending. 2) It means that with the Fisherian equation that sets the nominal interest rate equal to the expected inflation rate plus the marginal product of capital, there is no multiplier from printing money at a faster rate. Rather than postulating multipliers from current period government spending, optimization over time leaves us to examine how the government raises capital intertemporally and how it invests its capital. And this is one way to think of microeconomic reforms: how the government raises and spends capital and controls freedom of economic, social and political exchange through regulations. How do we examine the broad effect of policy through the sequences of incremental reforms? Can we discern directions in which governments and the private sectors are headed?

1. NEOCLASSICAL MEASURES

Different ways to evaluate government policy have been used with neoclassical methods that generally focus on the economy's performance and only indirectly reflect government action. Three categories of such measures are the 1) marginal factor products, 2) tax and growth rates, and 3) debt ratios.

1.1 Marginal factor products

From an arbitrage-type perspective, with the integrated-market law of one price, the real interest rate is itself a summary measure of how a developing country is viewed. Computation of a real rate follows by assuming that the deterministic Fisher equation of interest rates holds, and that the actual inflation rate equals the expected inflation rate. This means that for countries in which the inflation rate has been accelerating or decelerating unexpectedly, the ex post actual rate will not equal the ex ante expected inflation rate and the ex post real rate cannot be computed this way. And this problem is evident when the computed ex post real rate is a negative quantity. In the Central European transition countries, such a computed negative real rate is commonplace in countries with highly variable inflation rates.

One way to compute the real rate that minimizes this problem is to choose a nominal interest rate that builds in a risk premium for inflation rate variance. This is consistent with the generalized Fisher equation under uncertainty, which in certain cases gives the nominal interest rate as the expected inflation rate plus the deterministic real rate plus what has been called an inflation risk premium. (Bogacheva, 1999; see Lucas and Stokey, 1987; Bansil and Coleman, 1996). The government's treasury debt interest rate generally may include some of this risk premium. But these rates are more commonly thought of as the risk-free rate for the particular country, and using this to compute a real interest rate aggravates the problem of finding negative real rates, since the treasury debt rate is relatively low. In the on-line International Financial Statistics, which supplies a degree of homogeneity across national accounts, there is a „lending rate" which generally is the highest nominal interest rate reported and one that would be more likely to include an inflation risk premium. There are two consistently available inflation rate indicators, the consumer price index and the producer price index. The producer price index (PPI) gives a generally lower rate of inflation. Computing the real rate as the lending rate minus the PPI gives an upper bound on the real rate that can be reasonably well compared across countries.

Table 4.1 shows the real interest rate for the 1990's for several Central European countries plus Germany and the United States for comparison.

Table 4.1. The real interest rate in 1990's

Real Interest Rate	Czech	Germany	Hungary	Poland	Slovenia	US
Lending Rt - %ch Ppi mort.bond						
1990		0.072				0.100
1991		0.066	0.009	0.043		0.085
1992		0.069	0.102	0.113		0.063
1993	0.031	0.063	0.030	0.031		0.060
1994	0.037	0.062	0.085	0.027	0.212	0.071
1995	0.037	0.048	0.043	0.080	0.106	0.088
1996	0.048	0.060	0.038	0.129	0.158	0.083
1997		0.040	0.035		0.139	0.084
mean	0.038	0.060	0.049	0.070	0.154	0.079
standard deviation	0.007	0.011	0.033	0.044	0.044	0.014
Correlation with US	0.67	-0.14	-0.52	0.20	-0.98	1.00

The Czech Republic has had a low and steady real rate; Hungary has had a higher and more variable rate; Poland has had a still higher and more variable rate; and Slovenia has had an even higher rate as variable as Poland's. This suggests that the higher average rates are partly to compensate for greater variability. In Slovenia, there are numerous capital controls that may cause the rate to be higher than say Poland's, with equal variability. The high rate in Germany and even higher rate in the US, both with equally low variability, suggest a higher marginal product of capital than in the transition countries.

Why would the marginal product of capital be higher in Western countries than in transition countries? Convergence theory in the exogenous growth framework predicts that countries with higher marginal products and the same technology will grow faster as all countries converge to the same rate of growth of output, as capital flows to the higher marginal product areas. However, even with a scarcity of capital in developing countries, capital will not flow into these countries if the human capital stock is low and as a result the return on physical capital is actually lower than in the West. This is the argument of Lucas (1989). This logic and Table 4.1 suggest that the stock of human capital may be lower relative to the stock of physical capital in the above transition countries, and so the return on physical capital is lower.

Alternatively, the degree to which the Hungarian, Polish, and Slovenian rates are above the German rate may be for other reasons than a premium due to variability. For example, a) a lack of full integration in capital markets can result because of insufficient domestic property right enforcement such as bankruptcy laws that lead to a low collateral value on loaned capital. This conceivably can make the return to owners of capital low because of leakage of capital to non-owners, perhaps, as has been the Czech experience. b) With solid property rights, market segmentation can constrain investment to be financed out of domestic savings, raising marginal products in transition countries such as Hungary and Poland. c) Similarly, government restrictions on capital flows can cause segmentation that raises the marginal product of capital, perhaps, as in Slovenia. d) And incentive-compatibility problems with debt repayments can decrease international capital finance and increase marginal products, perhaps, as in Romania, Ukraine, and Russia.

A related gauge of a country's progress and relative ranking amongst nations is its real wage, and how fast it rises. The rate of increase in the real wage is a rough measure of the return to the average level of human capital, comparable to the real rate of interest on physical capital. In equilibrium on the „balanced-growth" path, the net rates return to human and physical capital should be equal. Taxes reduce the net returns to both types of capital, and leisure can act as a tax on human capital that decreases its net return.

Table 4.2 shows the percent change in the real wage in the 1990's for several Central European countries plus Germany and the US.

Table 4.2. Percentage Change in Real Wage.

% change in	Czech	Germany	Hungary	Poland	Slovenia	US
RealWage (Wage Index/Ppi)						
1991		4.50	-6.50	11.20		3.10
1992		5.30	8.10	7.00		1.80
1993		5.50	7.00	5.90	24.50	1.00
1994		1.00		1.20	8.90	1.40
1995	10.10			12.60	5.20	-1.00
1996	13.20			11.60	7.50	1.00
1997	12.80				5.00	3.00
mean	12.03	4.08	2.87	8.25	10.22	1.47
standard deviation	1.38	2.10	8.13	4.37	8.15	1.39

The computation takes the wage series in the International Financial Statistics and deflates it with the PPI, before calculating the percentage change. It shows high rates of „return" to human capital in Czech and Poland in recent years, of over 10%, compared to a US rate near 1%. Compared to the real rate of interest on physical capital, the Czech human capital rate is higher, the Polish rates were about the same in 1996, while the US growth rate in wages was much below its return on physical capital.[1]

The high rates for Czech and Poland support the notion of a scarcity of human capital relative to physical capital there. Although it is well known that Central European nations have high literacy and attenuation rates, this general human capital is only a part of the composition of human capital. The other is specific human capital from on-the-job training and learning-by-doing, that comes most readily in industries building comparative advantage in international markets. This is what presumably is at lower lèvels in Central European human capital. The low wage rate growth in the US may be a reflection more of a stratified labor market than of the human capital return. The unskilled wage growth rate should reflect productivity gains. But the Central European productivity gains likely also result from more jumps in human capital to higher skill levels.

A step further than examining the marginal factor products that is not investigated here is to examine how transition country business cycle facts compare to international evidence. The literature on international real business cycles details how various aggregates co-move with output (Backus, Kehoe, and Kydland, 1995; Cooley and Hansen, 1995). Table 4.3 shows real output and the correlation amongst countries. There is a high positive correlation amongst the US, Germany, Poland, Czech, and Slovenia, while Hungary and Romania move opposite of the US.

Table 4.3. Real GDP and its Correlation

Real GDP							
	US	Slovenia	Romania	Poland	Hungary	Germany	Czech
1989	5697.4					2297.3	
1990	5743.8		857.9		2089.3	2429.4	
1991	5687.9		747.2	457.74	1840.7	2750.6	
1992	5842.7		646	447.6	1784.4	2811.1	
1993	5973.1	174.3	655.1	443.19	1774.1	2778.5	498.7
1994	6183.6	183.6	681.1	449.2	1826.4	2858	514.7
1995	6308.4	191.1		486.11	1853.6	2913.7	547.4
1996	6544.8	197		508.5		2952.4	568.9
1997	6802.1	204.4				3012	574.4
Correlation of Real GDP							
	US	Slovenia	Romania	Poland	Hungary	Germany	Czech
US	1.00	0.99	-0.56	0.79	-0.32	0.77	0.95
Slovenia	0.99	1.00	1.00	0.95	0.99	1.00	0.98
Romania	-0.56	1.00	1.00	0.93	0.96	-0.92	1.00
Poland	0.79	0.95	0.93	1.00	0.79	0.99	0.99
Hungary	-0.32	0.99	0.96	0.79	1.00	-0.86	0.93
Germany	0.77	1.00	-0.92	0.99	-0.86	1.00	0.97
Czech	0.95	0.98	1.00	0.99	0.93	0.97	1.00
Corr. of Real Interest Rate with US GDP	0.09	-0.37		0.43	-0.09	-0.86	0.97

Germany moves most closely with Poland and Czech, and opposite of Hungary. Opposite movements within an integrated market are explained in the business cycle literature by shocks to technology specific to the particular country or industry. For example, this suggests that Hungary may be specializing in industry that is not as pronounced in Germany.

Business cycle evidence generally includes a procyclical real interest rate and a possibly procyclical real wage. The degree to which transition countries are found to fall within the range of evidence would suggest a degree of integration in world markets, and would reflect some degree of market stability. Table 4.3, using the real interest data from Table 4.1, shows a slight positive correlation of the US real interest rate with US GDP. There is a higher correlation of the Polish real interest rate and US GDP; a slight negative correlation of the Hungarian real interest rate and US GDP; and a strong negative correlation of the German real interest rate and US GDP.

1.2 Endogenous growth and taxes

The marginal factor prices and the business cycle evidence can suggest some degree of market integration. They are indicators of the health of private markets which governments support and constrain, and only indirectly reflect government policy. The other such key indicator is the growth rate of real GDP. Endogenous growth theory tells us that the balanced-growth rate of output equals the amount that the marginal product of capital (physical or human) exceeds the Fisherian rate of time preference, normalized by a coefficient for the preference for intertemporal substitution, generally taken to be between 1 and 2. Thus with the same preference parameters, nations have output growth rate differentials determined by differences in their marginal product of capital.

Table 4.4 shows the growth rates amongst several Central European nations and Germany and the US, and the correlation between the growth rate and real interest rate of each country. Germany, Hungary, Poland, and Slovenia show such a positive correlation between real interest rates and output growth rates, although Czech and the US show a negative correlation.

Table 4.4.. Growth Rate of GDP

Growth Rate of Real Gdp	Czech	Germany	Hungary	Poland	Romania	Slovenia	US
1990		0.058					0.008
1991		0.132	-0.119	-0.183			-0.010
1992		0.022	-0.031	-0.022	-0.135		0.027
1993		-0.012	-0.006	-0.010	0.014		0.022
1994	0.032	0.029	0.029	0.014	0.040	0.053	0.035
1995	0.064	0.019	0.015	0.082		0.041	0.020
1996	0.039	0.013	0.013*	0.046		0.031	0.037
1997	0.010	0.020	0.044	0.069	-0.066	0.038	0.039
1998	-0.027		0.051	0.048	-0.073	0.042	
mean	0.024	0.035	-0.002	0.006	-0.044	0.041	0.022
standard deviation	0.034	0.044	0.059	0.084	0.071	0.008	0.017
Correlation of own real Int rt, grth rt.	-0.29	0.32	0.36	0.37		0.57	-0.33

* Hungarian Central Statistical Office 1997-98: Central European Economic Review, Vol VII No.4

Endogenous growth theory also emphasizes that it is the net marginal product of capital, net of marginal taxes on capital that determines the growth rate. Thus the tax burdens of nations should negatively affect the growth rates. Recent extensions of this growth theory to a monetary setting find the same kind of negative growth effect from the inflation tax. The inflation rate acts on exchange and induces greater substitution on leisure. And greater leisure use induces a lower return on human capital. These taxes are a more direct gauge of government action.

Table 4.5 shows the total revenue as a share of GDP. This captures not only the average tax rate but also includes other items such as asset sales from privatization efforts. Hungary, Poland, and Slovenia show similar levels and gradual declines in the levels. Czech and Germany are at similar levels but Czech shows a declining trend and Germany a rising trend. The US share has been low and relatively stable, while Romania's share has dropped to a level below that of Czech. Hungary and Romania show the most variability.

Table 4.5. Revenue as a share of GDP

Revenue/GDP	Czech	Germany	Hungary	Poland	Romania	Slovenia	US
1989		0.296					0.183
1990		0.289	0.529		0.347		0.183
1991		0.285	0.509		0.373		0.179
1992		0.317	0.480		0.365		0.176
1993	0.348	0.318	0.484		0.319	0.426	0.179
1994	0.332	0.326	0.478	0.419	0.299	0.415	0.184
1995	0.327	0.323	0.430	0.409	0.296	0.417	0.188
1996	0.311	0.316	0.425	0.398	0.279	0.408	0.192
1997	0.304	0.320		0.388		0.400	0.200
mean	0.324	0.310	0.476	0.404	0.325	0.413	0.185
standard deviation	0.017	0.016	0.038	0.013	0.037	0.010	0.007

Table 4.6 shows the share of the increase in base money in total GDP, where base money is defined as reserves plus currency. The mean and standard deviation consistently move together across the sample. Both are highest in Hungary and Romania, and about half those numbers in Poland. Czech, Germany, Slovenia, and the US have means near 1% with low variability.

Table 4.6. Change in Base Money Relative to GDP.

Change in Base Money/GDP	Czech	Germany	Hungary	Poland	Romania	Slovenia	US
1990		0.016					0.009
1991		0.010	0.130	0.051	0.077		0.006
1992		0.022	0.051	0.053	0.121		0.008
1993		0.002	0.051	0.021	0.088		0.010
1994	0.021	0.003	0.043	0.028	0.059	0.024	0.010
1995	0.015	0.005	0.069	0.056	0.051	0.015	0.005
1996	0.010	0.007		0.027	0.043	0.009	0.006
1997	0.000	-0.001		0.035	0.065	0.013	0.009
mean	0.012	0.008	0.069	0.039	0.072	0.015	0.008
standard deviation	0.009	0.008	0.036	0.014	0.026	0.006	0.002

Table 4.7 shows the inflation rates, defined as the percentage change in the Consumer Price Index, across a larger sample of Central European nations and Germany and the US, ranked according to mean across disparate years as data allows.

Again is the striking relation between the level of the mean and the level of the variance; they rise together uniformly, except for the US and Czech, across the sample countries. Generally the countries in Table 4.7a are subject to analysis because they have relatively stable inflation. But after Slovenia, the countries in Table 4.7b historically have such high and variable inflation rates, that the real interest rate is often negative, a reflection of de facto debt repudiation, and the investment climate consequently is poor in terms of integration in the capital markets. Recently the inflation rates have come way down to low steady levels in Croatia and Latvia, and to somewhat higher levels in Ukraine and Russia.

Table 4.7a. Inflation Rate.

	Germany	US	Slovakia	Czech Rep.	Moldova	Hungary	Poland
Inflation Rates							
1991	3.64	4.23				34.23	76.71
1992	5.06	3.03				22.95	45.33
1993	4.46	2.95				22.45	36.87
1994	2.73	2.61	13.41	10.06		18.87	33.25
1995	1.84	2.81	9.89	9.10	12.07	28.30	26.80
1996	1.49	2.93	5.81	8.82	22.12	23.49	20.15
1997	1.75	2.34	6.11	8.45	10.96	18.28	15.91
1998	0.29	1.61	6.80	10.80		14.30	11.80
mean	2.66	2.81	8.40	9.45	15.05	22.86	33.35
standard deviation	1.62	0.74	3.23	0.96	6.15	6.21	20.78

Table 4.7b. Inflation Rate.

	Slovenia	Latvia	Romania	Bulgaria	Russia	Croatia	Ukraine
Inflation Rates							
1991			230.62			122.22	
1992	156.62	243.27	211.21	91.30		632.50	
1993	31.90	108.77	255.17	72.88	874.62	1483.62	4734.91
1994	19.77	35.93	136.76	96.06	307.38	107.33	891.19
1995	12.63	24.98	32.24	62.05	197.41	3.95	376.75
1996	9.68	17.61	38.83	123.01	47.57	4.34	80.33
1997	9.09	8.45	154.76	1082.26	14.62	4.13	15.94
1998	8.00	4.70	64.00	46.20	27.60	5.70	10.50
mean	35.38	63.39	140.45	224.82	244.87	295.47	1018.27
standard deviation	54.12	86.80	88.15	378.92	329.21	524.99	1851.55

A consequence of high inflation rates can be lower growth rates of GDP. This is supported in endogenous growth theory and in empirical studies (Gillman et al, 1999, de Gregoria, 1996). Table 4.8 shows the correlation of inflation rates and GDP growth rates for the sample of countries found in Table 4.4. The evidence shows a strong negative correlation for Poland, Hungary, the US, and Czech, a slight negative effect for Romania, a slight positive effect for Germany, and a strong positive correlation for Slovenia. The literature on the growth-inflation effect has identified a negative non-linear effect, whereby the negative correlation is stronger at low inflation levels than at high ones. The lower level of the negative effect for Romania compared to the higher levels of the negative effect for Poland, Hungary, and the US is consistent with these results.

Table 4.8. Growth-Inflation Effects

Correlation of Annual Growth Rate of GDP and Inflation Rate for 1990-1998						
Czech	Germany	Hungary	Poland	Romania	Slovenia	US
-0.557	0.080	-0.858	-0.946	-0.113	0.799	-0.764

From data in Tables 4 and 7, plus the inflation rates in 1990 for Germany and the US of 0.027 and 0.054 respectively.

1.3 Debt

Considering inflation rates as summary evidence of the monetary policy, the summary measure for fiscal policy often is taken to be government debt levels relative to GDP. Some literature views debt as a something of a free ride, in the sense that we do not have to worry about debt at all, as in traditional IS-LM models. More neoclassically, we can build overlapping generations economies in which debt increases net wealth because the burden of repayment is put more heavily on unborn generations that have no weight in the utility function that is maximized (Obstfeld and Rogoff, 1996). As a counter to such thinking, the Barro-Ricardo logic makes debt merely a set of future tax payments that dynastic-family utility functions fully include. Indeed it is the unfunded entitlement programs that cause such onerous marginal wage tax rates in Eastern European countries that have inherited a legacy of massive communist era social welfare programs.

When debt is focused upon it is usually in the context of its magnitude relative to national output, making the debt/GDP measure a combination of government and private sector activity. [2] Table 4.9 shows the debt/GDP for Central European nations plus Germany and the US from 1989-1997, as IMF data is available.

Table 4.9. Debt to GDP ratios.

Debt/GDP	Czech	Germany	Hungary	Poland	Romania*	Slovenia	US
1989		0.224					0.413
1990		0.247					0.444
1991		0.239	0.741				0.481
1992		0.261	0.785		0.150		0.503
1993	0.159	0.286	0.897		0.140		0.517
1994	0.141	0.302	0.871	0.723	0.170	0.154	0.510
1995	0.114	0.373	0.860	0.579	0.180	0.168	0.507
1996	0.101	0.388	0.724	0.511	0.230	0.222	0.499
1997	0.101	0.390		0.480	0.330	0.241	0.474
mean	0.123	0.301	0.813	0.573	0.200	0.196	0.483
standard deviation	0.026	0.066	0.073	0.108	0.071	0.042	0.035

*Data for Romania from Siwinska (1999).

The small and shrinking Czech debt is notable, as is the rising Romanian debt. Germany and Slovenia also show rising levels while Hungary and the US exhibit a rising and falling trend. It is difficult to make much more out of such numbers by themselves. But one important consideration suggested by the evidence, in light of other evidence on growth rates and marginal products, is that different governments may in effect be choosing different positions on a risk-yield frontier, in the sense of the capital asset pricing tradeoff. Certainly, Hungary with the highest debt ratio seems not exceedingly more likely to default than Czech with the lowest debt ratio. But at the same time, the yield to governments, if measured by the increase in taxes from economic expansion, is higher in Hungary with its high growth rate than in Czech with its low growth rate.

Table 4.10 compares, for low inflation countries, their mean debt/GDP for 1994-1997 and their GDP growth rates for 1994-1998.

Table 4.10. Debt/GDP and Growth Rate of GDP: Risk-Yield Tradeoff?

Mean	Czech	Slovenia	Germany	US	Poland	Hungary
Debt/GDP, 1994-97	0.114	0.196	0.363	0.498	0.573	0.818
Gr Rt GDP, 1994-98	0.024	0.041	0.020	0.033	0.052	0.035

There is some sense in which the higher debt counties of US, Poland, and Hungary have had higher growth rates that Germany and Czech, suggesting a lower risk, lower yield preference for Germany and Czech. However from this perspective, Slovenia is an outlier. This may be because of its capital restrictions, or because the debt/GDP is a mixed measure of private and government activity, rather than a measure of only government activity as would be desired for applying a risk-yield framework.

2. A MEASURE OF A GOVERNMENT'S DEBT-EQUITY RATIO

Private firms choose how risky they want their finance structure to be. Highly leveraged, with a high debt-equity ratio and seeking a high growth rate of return, or less highly leveraged, with possibly a more stable but lower yield. The market uses the debt-equity ratio in part in evaluating the risk of default by firms, since when the company is highly leveraged, the contractual interest payments on debt are large relative to the non-contractual dividend payments on equity ownership. A downturn in revenue creates a greater likelihood of default in a more highly leveraged firm.

For evaluation of the risk of government finance, the debt/GDP measure is related to the concept of a debt-equity ratio, but requires some additional assumptions to view it in this way. A benefit of the extension of the debt/GDP measure to a perspective of the debt-equity ratio is a broader way to evaluate directly the government policy of transition countries, in which default is possible.

A federal government like a private firm has two basic means of external finance: borrowing through debt and selling equity. When IBM sells debt, it is limited by wanting to avoid having high contractual interest payments that risk default. When IBM sells equity stock to raise capital, it is limited by wanting to avoid „diluting" the unit share value of the stock. This share circulates in a secondary market but has no other value than the financial yield to investors. When the government sells debt, it faces the same limit of wanting to avoid high contractual interest payments that are too high relative to a downturn in tax payments plus seigniorage, since this also risks default. The difference between private and public finance relates mainly to its equity shares. The government „sells" its equity when it buys goods and services with freshly printed money. The stock of fiat money has no par value, similar to the unit equity share of a firm, in that it cannot be converted into anything else like gold, as with commodity money. Fiat money has no debt features. And its value is diluted when the government issues more of it, like private equity. As long as IBM issues equity at a rate below the rate of demand for its equity, the unit share price will keep rising. Likewise the government's fiat will depreciate in value only if its issuance exceeds in rate of growth the demand. However, unlike IBM's stock, the government's fiat serves also as a means of exchange. If Panama became a „dollarized" with IBM stock instead of U.S. currency, then IBM would enjoy an additional demand for its equity beyond its rate of return, and IBM would reap seigniorage: it could issue more without dilution of its equity value. So this is the main difference in the equity finance. The government's fiat enjoys the additional transaction demand. In addition, the government can induce differential default on its debt, without a court system of bankruptcy restructuring of debt as with private firms, through unexpectedly high money printing and inflation (equity dilution) that breaks the implicit contract of paying a certain real interest rate on its debt.

Government revenues are mainly its tax receipts, from all sources plus asset sales for example through privatization. Its issuance of money also adds to its capital. And from here we can define a notion of the equity value, or net worth, of the government, not an obviously well defined concept. First, to define the asset value of the government, we could try to determine the present discounted value of the government's profit stream, as for a private firm. But then what are the profits for a government? In a sense they are the new taxes generated (or lost) plus seigniorage by having set and enforced the property rights covering markets such that the markets could expand (or contract). With an economy growing, markets expand, taxes increase, and the government reaps this tribute in return for supplying the flow of services in the form of defining property rights.

Assuming that the government reinvests all profits, then all past incremental increases in the economy's output and taxes, carried forward without interest, are captured by the current tax revenues expected at the end of the year. And the future increase in taxes is captured by the future increase in output, factored by the average tax rate. This suggests that the current and future discounted tax revenues plus seigniorage can be defined as the asset value of the government. The real discount rate, denoted r, for such future tax revenues from the expansion of the economy should be the risk-free real interest rate, denoted r_f, plus a premium, denoted p, for the degree of inefficiency with which the government uses the new taxes to maintain or improve its services; or $r \equiv r_f + p$. This interest rate will simply be measured by the real interest rate in the economy, where the particular market rate will be chosen as a retail rather than wholesale rate so as to be more likely to include the full premium. The revenue at time t can be expressed as the average federal tax rate τ factored by the real output, y_t, plus the rate of growth of the money stock σ factored by the real money supply, denoted here by $m_t \equiv M_t / P_t$, where M is the nominal money stock and P the aggregate price level. Assuming constant average tax, money supply growth, and real interest rates, then the infinite discounted stream is

(1)

$$\frac{\tau y_t + \sigma m_t}{1+r} + \frac{\tau y_{t+1} + \sigma m_{t+1}}{(1+r)^2} + \frac{\tau y_{t+2} + \sigma m_{t+2}}{(1+r)^3} + \ldots$$

Assuming real output and real money demand grow at constant rate g, this asset value equals

(2)

$$\frac{(\tau y_t + \sigma m_t)}{1+r} + \frac{(\tau y_t + \sigma m_t)(1+g)}{(1+r)^2} + \frac{(\tau y_t + \sigma m_t)(1+g)^2}{(1+r)^3} + \ldots = \frac{(\tau y_t + \sigma m_t)}{r-g}$$

The equity value at time t, denoted e_t, of the federal government can then be defined as the asset value minus the real debt at time t, denoted, d_t:

(3)

$$e_t \equiv \frac{(\tau y_t + \sigma m_t)}{r-g} - d_t$$

And the debt-equity ratio is given by

(4)

$$\frac{d_t}{e_t} = \frac{d_t}{\dfrac{(\tau y_t + \sigma m_t)}{(r-g)} - d_t}$$

Defining velocity v as the ratio of real output to real money, or $v_t \equiv y_t / m_t$, the inverse equity-debt ratio can be written as a function of the debt-output ratio, velocity and the other parameters:

(5)

$$\frac{e_t}{d_t} = \frac{(\tau + [\sigma / v_t])}{(r-g)(d_t / y_t)} - 1$$

The equity-debt ratio depends negatively on the debt-output ratio, the money velocity, and the real interest rate, and positively on the average tax, money supply growth and output growth rates. Given computation of real interest rate, data exists so that this can be readily computed for any country. Note that $\sigma / v = \sigma M / Y = (\Delta M / M) M / Y = \Delta M / Y$, where M and Y are the nominal base money stock and nominal income, so that this can be measured by the increase in the nominal base money relative to nominal GDP, as in Table 4.6.

3. EMPIRICAL ESTIMATION OF THE DEBT-EQUITY RATIOS

Calculation of the Debt/Equity ratios in Table 4.11 below uses the IMF data of the Tables 4.1, 4.4, 4.5, 4.6, and 4.10, for the real interest rate, the growth rate of GDP, the share of taxes (revenue) in GDP, the change in the money base relative to GDP, and the debt/GDP ratio. As with debt/GDP ratios, the evidence here shows a sense in which the low growth rate countries of Czech and Germany have the low debt/equity ratios compared to the high growth rate countries with higher debt/equity ratios. But now Slovenia, which has a low debt/GDP ratio but a high growth rate, fits in the high debt/equity, high growth group of countries rather than being an outlier as in the debt/GDP comparison of risk/yield. We also find that the variability of the debt/equity ratio rises with the mean across countries in an unbroken pattern, thereby exhibiting greater monotonicity in this than the inflation rate data.

Can anything be said about the levels of the debt/equity ratio? Consider some private corporation examples for comparison. From 1991 to 1998 the high growth Intel Corporation had long term debt equity ratios as in Table 4.12. These are of a low level comparable to the governments of countries in Table 4.11.

Table 4.11. Debt to Equity Ratios

Debt/Equity	Czech	Germany	Poland	Slovenia	Hungary	US
1990		0.012				0.268
1991		-0.050			0.174	0.325
1992		0.043			0.243	0.106
1993		0.067			0.063	0.115
1994	0.019	0.033		0.125	0.103	0.105
1995	-0.004	0.034		0.053	0.051	0.216
1996	0.013	0.058		0.157		0.128
1997	0.025	0.025	0.111	0.134		0.114
mean	0.013	0.043	0.111	0.117	0.146	0.172
standard deviation	0.013	0.036	0.000	0.045	0.081	0.086
Gr Rt GDP, 1994-98	0.024	0.020	0.052	0.041	0.035	0.033

Table 4.12. Intel Corporation

INTEL CORPORATION: Debt-equity ratios, 1991-98							
1991	1992	1993	1994	1995	1996	1997	1998
0.079	0.111	0.133	0.111	0.083	0.059	0.130	0.039
mean: 0.093, standard deviation: 0.034							

Another corporation, IBM, had a debt-equity ratio of 1.5 in 1998, considerably higher, and private corporations often have such ratios above 1. Using revenues as the profit stream in the government debt-equity ratio arguably makes the levels low compared to private corporations. But with a consistent methodology, countries still can be compared on this basis to each other, and the evidence suggests the possibility of using a framework of risk-yield tradeoffs.

4. EVALUATION OF CHANGES IN THE DEBT-EQUITY RATIO

Applying the concept of yield-risk to gauge government policy does not imply that high debt is necessarily good because it guarantees high yield, although if along the efficiency frontier, it may lead to higher, albeit possibly more variable, GDP growth. The government may not be close to the efficiency frontier at which the yield-risk tradeoff is optimally chosen as a result of tangency between preferences and the production possibility curve that uncertainly transforms current social capital into future social capital at some risk. The process of getting to the efficient frontier is a major dilemma for transition countries. This is done by more efficiently transforming government revenues into a flow of property rights services, in particular with respect to the communist-era social welfare entitlements for health, pensions, education, disability, and the ill-defined and enforced tax base.

On a gradual approach to a reasonable policy that can be roughly considered along the efficiency frontier, policy tensions can arise when attempting to decrease the debt/equity ratio. Increasing hear-horizon revenues through higher marginal tax rates may sacrifice future tax revenues because of lower economic growth. Similarly increasing the tax base without lowering the marginal rates would raise the effective marginal rates and also sacrifice growth. Relying on high seigniorage requires high inflation rates and recent research indicates that this is an inefficient form of taxation relative to factor and consumption taxes (Lucas, 1993; Aiyagari et al, 1998).

Raising tax and inflation rates increases the liquidity perhaps in the short run, but increases avoidance, decreases the tax base, lowers economic growth, and decreases the future stream of taxes. The ability of the government to pay interest payments on debt through tax revenues is the way in which the concept of Ricardian equivalence is manifest (see Barro, 1990). However the subtext of the practice of such equivalence is that such liquidity of the debt comes at the cost of a marginally increasing dynamic cost in terms of decreased economic growth. This hidden feature of Ricardian equivalence creates perhaps the central problem of a high debt-equity ratio: liquidating the future growth of the economy through higher marginal tax rates helps avoid insolvency at the cost of lower net worth, and a higher expected future debt-equity ratio. Thus as the debt-equity ratio is analyzed, a look at the pace of changes in the quality of government spending and in the marginal tax rates, including inflation rates, gives an indication of the likely future debt-equity ratio.

5. QUALIFICATIONS AND CONCLUSIONS

The data set used is for illustrative purposes. Using the International Financial Statistics has the advantage of a well-screened data set that is comparable across countries, but has disadvantage of missing data points. As no econometric analysis has been performed on the data set, and as the missing data points are clearly identified in the tables, it is clear that the results are discussed given these limitations. Filling in missing points with less internationally accepted data may be possible, but does introduce less confidence in the consistency of the data set taken as a whole.

The chapter finds a certain risk-yield tradeoff in the cross-country comparison of the calibrated debt-equity ratios and the growth rates of GDP. This is robust to some changes in the data years used, and the countries were selected in a non-biased way based on whether a debt-equity ratio could be computed. For example, while almost having enough data for Romania, some key data, necessary for computation of the debt-equity ratio, were missing and could not be filled in from national accounts data. As this is a first postulation of the theoretical concept of a debt-equity ratio as applied above to governments, the data succeeded in illustrating how the concept can be used to interpret a broad measure of government performance in Central European countries. And the data shows how these countries can be compared to Western economies in this measure. Further work to extend the database across years, countries, and regions would be interesting.

The concept of the debt-equity ratio brings together how the central dilemmas of governments are resolved in terms of the need for to raise capital, the efficacy of how it is raised, and the effectiveness with which it is invested. It offers an alternative summary measure related to older discussions of macroeconomic tradeoffs and of the industrial policy of the government. It is in place of the 1960s type discussions of taking a position of a certain inflation-unemployment equilibrium along a supposedly stable Phillips curve, which turned out not to be stable. And it is alternative to the 1980s idea of governments actively participating in supporting industries in some type of industrial policy, which turned out to be an international set of weak private bank loans.

The concept here merges these under the 1990s type emphasis on microeconomic reform that leads to more efficient markets and more effective government policy. In this the capital of the government is viewed, as is the capital of the finance theory of private firms. This views efficient governments as taking a position along the central finance tradeoff of risk and yield, as dependent on their national cultures or preferences. It views inefficient governments in terms of whether they are moving towards such an efficiency frontier. And it views the investment of international capital markets as diversifying across idiosyncratic risks that are systemic to a country or a region in part because of the particular risk-yield tradeoff taken by the government of that country or region.

ENDNOTES

[1] See de Gregoria (1996), Fischer (1993), Bruno and Easterly (1998), Gomme (1993), Ireland (1994), Chari, Jones, and Manuelli (1996), Jones and Rossi (1993), Gillman et al (1999), and Stokey and Rebelo (1995).

[2] A country's level of international reserves is sometimes cited as evidence about the strength of government finances. Certainly with fixed exchange rates, international reserves are necessary to support an overvalued currency.

REFERENCES

Aiyagari, S. Rao, R. Anton Braun, and Zvi Eckstein (1998*), Transaction Services, Inflation, and Welfare, Journal of Political Economy*, vol. 106, no. 6, 1274-1301.

Bansil, Ravi, and Wilbur John Coleman (1996), *A Monetary Explanation of the Equity Premium, Term Premium, and Risk-Free Rate Puzzles*, Journal of Political Economy, 104:1135-1171.

Backus, David K., Patrick J. Kehoe, and Finn E. Kydland (1995), International Business Cycles: Theory and Evidence, in Cooley (ed.): Frontiers in Business Cycle Research, Princeton University Press, Princeton, pp. 331-356.

Barro, Robert J. (1990), *Macroeconomic Policy*, Harvard University Press, 1990.

Bogacheva, Elena (1999), *Demand for Money and Interest Rates in a Representative Agent Economy with Costly Credit*, manuscript, CERGE-EI.

Bruno, Michael and William Easterly (1998), *Inflation Crises and Long Run Growth*, Journal of Monetary Economics, 41, 3-26.

Chari, V.V., Larry E. Jones, and Rodolfo E. Manuelli (1996), *Inflation, Growth, and Financial Intermediation,* Federal Reserve Bank of St. Louis, Review, May/June.

Cooley, Thomas F., and Gary Hansen (1995), Money and Business Cycles, in Cooley T. (ed.): Frontiers in Business Cycle Research, Princeton University Press, Princeton, pp. 175-216.

De Gregorio, Jose (1996), *Inflation, Growth, and Central Banks*, Policy Research Working Paper, No. 1575, World Bank, February.

Fischer, Stanley (1993), *The Role of Macroeconomic Factors in Growth*, Journal of Monetary Economics, 32, 485-512.

Frenkel, Michael, and Gil Mehrez (1997), *Inflation and the Misallocation of Resources*, manuscript presented at the 1997 European Economic Association Meetings, Toulouse.

Gillman, Max, Michal Kejak, and Akos Valentinyi (1999), *Microfoundations of Inflation and Growth: Non-linearities and Financial Development*, forthcoming Institute of Advanced Economics working paper, Vienna.

Gomme P. (1993), *Money and growth revisited, Journal of Monetary Economics*, 32, 51-77.

Ireland, Peter N. (1994), *Money and Growth: An Alternative Approach*, American Economic Review, 84(1), March, pages 47-65.

Jones, Larry E., and Peter E. Rossi (1993), *Optimal Taxation in Models of Endogenous Growth*, Journal of Political Economy, June, 485-517.

Lucas, Robert E., Jr. (1989), *Why Does Not Capital Flow from Rich to Poor Countries*, Proceedings, American Economic Review, March, pp. 242-251.

Lucas, Robert E., Jr. (1993), *On the Welfare Cost of Inflation*, manuscript, University of Chicago.

Lucas, Robert E., Jr., and Nancy L. Stokey (1987), *Money and Interest in a Cash-in-Advance Economy*, Econometrica, 55: 491-513.

Obstfeld, Maurice, and Kenneth Rogoff (1996), *Foundations of International Macroeconomics*, MIT Press, Cambridge.

Siwinska, Joanna (1999), *Public Debt Structure and Dynamics in the Czech Republic, Hungary, Poland, and Romania*, CASE - Center for Social and Economic Research, Warsaw, Studies and Analyses, No. 162.

Stokey, Nancy L., and Sergio Rebelo (1995), *Growth Effects of Flat-Rate Taxes*, Journal of Political Economy, vol. 103, no.3 (June), 519-550.

Chapter 5

A GREAT LEAP FORWARD? PENSION DEVELOPMENTS AND REFORMS IN THE CZECH REPUBLIC, HUNGARY, POLAND AND ROMANIA.

Stanisław Gomułka

INTRODUCTION

All transition countries inherited pension systems based on the principles of pay-as-you-go and defined-benefit (PAYG-DB). In the early years of operation, such systems had advantages over a fully funded, defined-contribution (FF-DC) system. For, under a PAYG-DB arrangement, those who retire receive pension benefits immediately and contributions initially tend to exceed the payments. These advantages, however, disappear later on, when population (and employment) growth rates decline and when people live longer after retirement. Under such circumstances, a FF-DC program has the advantages of greater flexibility and transparency, hence greater financial viability. The changeover from PAYG-DB systems to FF-DC systems is therefore a worldwide trend. In transition economies, this trend was reinforced by a crisis of pension finances due to three additional factors (1) large transformational recession, (2) extension of pension insurance to farmers and (3) rapid expansion of the informal economy. Factor 1 increased expenditures as early retirements became a popular way of containing the unemployment problem; it also reduced revenues as employment declined. Factor 2 increased net expenditures since farmers' contributions have been insignificant. Factor 3 reduced revenues. These factors have therefore made this changeover more urgent and, in some countries, more rapid.

This chapter focuses on pension problems, developments and reforms in four transition countries: the Czech Republic, Hungary, Poland and Romania, during the 1990s.* Its main purpose is threefold, to explain the large differences in these developments among the FOUR, to relate them to corresponding developments in some of the key European Union (EU) and OECD countries, and to explain the main aims and principles of the reforms.

1. PENSION DEVELOPMENTS DURING TRANSITION

A comparative survey of pension systems in transition countries (see Cangiano, Cottarelli and Cubeddu, 1998) identified a number of common features, or 'stylized facts', with respect to pension developments. These are as follows:

(i) Early retirement reached significant proportions in most countries, as the pension system was used to cushion the effect of transition on open unemployment.

(ii) The system dependency ratio (the ratio between pensioners and contributors) has been rising rapidly, reflecting both a sharp decline in the number of contributors and a rapid growth of the number of pensioners.

(iii) The fall in the number of contributors reflected both a large drop in total output and a sharp increase in the share of the informal economy in that output.

I propose to augment this list by three additional stylized facts:

(iv) The cushioning use of the pension system – fact (i) - was more common in Central and Eastern Europe (CEE) than in the countries of the FSU. It was also more common in countries where restructuring was deeper and faster.

(v) In several countries, the rise in the ratio between pensioners and contributors reflected the extension of pension protection to farmers. And,

(vi) The relaxation of health criteria for entitlement to invalidity pensions reflected poorer work prospects, possibly also increased incidences of corruption among the medical profession.

Despite these common features, developments in pension finances have been remarkably diverse. As can be seen from Table 5.1, this diversity also applies to the four countries, which concern us here. The diversity is driven mainly by two factors: an exceptionally high number of non-retirement pensioners in Poland and an exceptionally low replacement rate in Romania. The first factor is making Poland an outlier not only in Central and Eastern

Europe, but also worldwide. The second factor is making Romania similar to the countries both of the FSU and most of the OECD (Chand and Jaeger, 1996, Table 6), but different from the main EU countries: Germany, France and Italy, where replacement rates are close to those of Hungary and Poland.

Given the weight of non-retirement pensions in Poland, it is instructive to look in greater detail at the composition of these pensions. This is done in Table 5.2 for all categories of pensioners in several years and in Table 5.3 for several types of pensioners outside agriculture in a single year, 1996

Table 5.1. Major trends in pension finances of the FOUR, 1990-1998

Category	Czech Republic	Hungary
Size of pension expenditures, % of GDP	Broadly constant at about 8% net of tax and about 10% if taxable	Broadly constant at about10.5%
Number of pensioners: (a) % of population of of pensionable age (b) % of contributors	Increasing: (a) from[4] 116% in 1990 to 117% in 1998	Increasing: (a) from[4] 105% in 1990 to 130 in 1995
Average pension% of wages	Declining from 62% in 1990 to 44% in 1995, then broadly stable	Declining from 64.4% in1991 to 55-58% in 1996-98
Contribution rate in 1996, % of wages	26	30.5
Retirement age	62 for men since 1996 and 57-61 for women (depending on number of children) in 2007	Progressively raised and unified to 62 for men (2001) and women (2009)
Dependency ratios: (a) old age[5] (b) system[6]	About 33, stable About 60, stable	About 36, stable Increasing sharply from 53 in 1990 to 84 in 1996
Size of contribution revenues, % of GDP	Broadly constant at about 8-9%	Declining from 11% in1991 to 8-9% in 1995-98
National PAYG financial balance, % of GDP	Small surplus	Deteriorating from balance to a deficit of 1-2%

Category	Poland	Romania
Size of pension expenditures, % of GDP	Increased from 6.5% in 1989 to nearly 15% in 1995, then about stable	Declined in 1990-1, then broadly stable
Number of pensioners: (a) % of population of of pensionable age (b) % of contributors	Increasing: (a) from[4] 128% in 1989 to 148% in 1995	Increasing: (a) from[4] 73% in 1989 to 80% in 1995
Average pension% of wages	Increasing from 43% in 1989 to 65% in 1995, then declining somewhat	Declined from about 47% in 1990 to 36% in 1998
Contribution rate in 1996, % of wages	45.5	25.5 (32.5 as of 1999)
Retirement age	To be raised progressively to65 for men and 60 for women until 2010 from effective ages of 59 and 55 respectively	62 for men and 57 for women, to be raised to 65 and 62 respectively
Dependency ratios: (a) old age[5] (b) system[6]	About 33, stable About 60, stable	n.a. n.a.
Size of contribution revenues, % of GDP	Increasing from 7.8% in 1989 to 11.8% in 1995, then stable	Declining from 6-7% in 1990-93 to below 5% in 1996
National PAYG financial balance, % of GDP	Deteriorating from a surplus of 1.4% in 1989 to a deficit of 3.2% in 1995, then broadly stable	Deteriorating from a surplus close to 1% to a deficit close to 1% during the 1990's

Notes: 1) Assumes 2% rate of growth of real pensions and 3% discount rate. 2) Current beneficiaries only 3) Outside agriculture 4) Pension age population refers to: in the Czech Republic and Hungary, women over the age of 55 and men over the age of 60; in Poland and Romania, all over 60; 5) 60+ years old as a percentage of 20-59 years old, 6) Pensioners as a percentage of contributors or employees.

Sources: For the Czech Republic, official data as reported by Schneider (1999) and IMF (1998). For Hungary, Cangiano et.al. (1998), Augustinovics (1997), Palacios and Rocha (1997), and Nestor and Vajda (1999). For Poland. Polish Government (1999), Gomulka and Jaworski (1998) and Gomulka and Styczen (1999). For Romania, Cangiano et.al. 1998) and De Menil et.al. (1999).

Table 5.2. Poland: non-retirement pensions and pensioners, 1989-99

Category	1989	1995	1998
A. Pensioners			
I. Non-retirement, as % of retirement			
1. Outside agriculture	139	117	114
2. In agriculture	30	63	73
3. Total	98	100	104
II. Non-retirement, as % of population			
1. Outside agriculture	10.4	12.2	12.8
2. In agriculture	5.3	10.3	10.6
3. Total	9.4	11.8	12.4
B. Pensions expenditures			
I. Non-retirement, as ratio of retirement			
1. Outside agriculture	1.2	0.8	0.9
2. In agriculture	0.4	0.6	0.7
3. Total	1.0	0.8	0.8
II. Non-retirement, as % of GDP			
1. Outside agriculture	2.9	5.7	5.5
2. In agriculture	0.3	0.9	0.9

Note: With respect to agriculture, the population is taken to be 20% of the total and GDP to be 5% of the total.
Source: Government (1999), Table 1.

Table 5.3. Poland: non-retirement pensions, pensioners and public implicit debt in 1996, outside agriculture

Type of benefit	Percent, 100 = retirement pension		
	Number of pensioners	Average pension	Implicit debt
1. Men, invalidity of category			
I	12	85	12
II	43	70	41
III	51	62	47
2. Women, invalidity of category			
I	9	89	8
II	28	74	26
III	30	62	26
3. Survivors, all	84	70	58

Source: Gomulka and Jaworski (1998).

Data in Tables 5.2 and 5.3 imply that the problem of large non-retirement pension expenditures has in terms of the number of pensioners been inherited from pre-transition period, but its weight, in terms of expenditures in relation to GDP, has increased during transition. Moreover, the model of pension payments established outside agriculture has during the 1990s been extended to the agriculture population, aggravating further the pressure on public finances.

These data also show that non-retirement pensions outside agriculture were already unusually numerous in 1989, probably reflecting the exceptionally strong bargaining power of Polish workers for many years before the start of transition. The observed rapid convergence of the incidence of non-retirement pensions in agriculture to that outside agriculture after 1989 also reflects the implementation of pension privileges granted to farmers before 1989. However, Poland is the only country of the Four among all transition countries (except Slovenia), where the replacement ratio increased sharply during transition since 1989. This increase took place at the start of transition, mainly in the year 1991. The sharp rise of the replacement rate was unintended by the authorities, since the indexation rule used was based on wages. The simultaneous increases of this rate and of the ratio of pensioners to contributors at the start of transition undermined public finances during the entire transition period. As early as 1993 an attempt was made to reverse this upward trend of pension expenditures as a proportion of GDP, by the introduction of the "0.91" rule, which reduced pensions by 9%. However, by 1993 pensioners in Poland constituted one third of the entire electorate. Under their pressure, after 1994 the 0.91 rule was gradually phased out. The threat of a fiscal crisis in the pension system persuaded the authorities, in 1996, to replace the wage indexation rule by a price indexation rule. This change proved effective in halting the upward trend of the ratio of pension expenditures to GDP. Indeed, since 1996, this ratio started to decline somewhat.

The number of pensioners as a proportion of the population of pensionable age is an indicator of the extent of early retirement privileges and the treatment of farmers. This proportion increased in all the four countries, but especially sharply in Poland and Hungary. Again, Poland and Romania are clear outliers.

Also we now have comparable estimates of the size of the implicit pension debt in the four countries (Table 5.1). This debt for the category of the already retired turns out to be close to 100% of GDP in the Czech Republic, Hungary and Romania, but close to 200% of GDP in Poland. Again the key reason for this difference is the unusually large number and size of non-retirement (invalidity and family) pensions in Poland. These pensions cost about 6.5% of GDP in Poland, which is about twice the cost in Hungary, about 3 times the cost in the Czech Republic and about 5 times the cost in Romania.

2. THE FOUR COMPARED WITH 2ND WAIVE OF EU ENTRANTS

Comparisons of the four analyzed countries with the four countries, which represented the 2nd waive of EU entrants may also be of interest. These data are given in Table 5.4. In addition, the key data on pension expenditures and pension liabilities for major industrial countries are given in Table 5.5. Both the magnitude and the inter-country variation of these data are similar just as in our four transition countries

Table 5.4. Social pension expenditures by type of benefit (1994, in percent of GDP)

Country	Retirement	Invalidity	Survivors & family	TOTAL
Greece	8.5	1.4	1.7	11.6
Ircland	4.3	1.4	3.4	9.1
Portugal	6.1	2.1	3.2	11.4
Spain	7.4	1.8	2.5	11.7

Source: Eurostat, Social Protection Entrepreneurs and Receipts, 1980-1994, after Rostaguo and Util (1998, Table 1).

Data presented in Table 5.4 are similar to those for the Czech Republic and Hungary. Poland's spending on survivors' and family pensions (1.9% of GDP in 1998) is also in line with the four EU countries. The aspect, which makes Poland an outlier, is mainly the size of invalidity pensions (4.5% of GDP in 1998). Compared to the unweighted average for the four EU countries (6.6% of GDP in 1994), Poland spends more on retirement pensions (8.0% in 1995 and 7.7% in 1998), but the difference is relatively small and declining. Romania, on the other hand, is a clear case of under-protection. In 1998, only 46% of the active population were covered by the social insurance system (De Menil et.al., 1999). Moreover, the replacement rate has become unusually low during transition (Table 5.1). Consequently, Romania's pension expenditure, at about 5.5% of GDP, is a major factor in keeping the country's public finances under control.

Table 5.5. Public pension schemes: expenditures and liabilities (in percent of GDP)

Country	Expenditure in 1990	Implicit pension debt 2	
		Present retirees	Present workforce
Germany1	12.3	106	115
France1	13.3	128	136
Italy	14.2	171	187
Japan	5.7	68	98
USA	6.9	32	77

Notes: 1) 1992, 2) Assumes a sudden transition to a fully funded system, making the estimates comparable to those for our four countries.
Source: Chand and Jaeger (1996).

A large variation in public pension expenditures can be found also among the most developed countries (Table 5.5). It is noteworthy that these expenditures in the Czech Republic, Hungary and especially, Poland are comparable to the highest among these countries.

3. KEY PROBLEMS OF THE PRE-REFORM SYSTEM

The radical market-oriented reforms, which the Four and other transition countries adopted at the end of the 1980s and the beginning of the 1990s, did not extend to the pension system. Not only in the Czech Republic and Romania but also in Hungary (until 1998) and Poland (until 1998) the system remained fully state-managed, highly redistributive, and financed on a pay-as-you-go (PAYG) basis. Social security contributions continued to be strictly proportional to wages and paid fully by the employer. These contributions did not go into individual accounts, but into the single account of the State Pension Authority. Thus, they were effectively a form of tax collected for the specific purpose of financing current pensions. Employees remained largely unaware both of the size of their cumulative contributions and of any link between these contributions and future pensions. The pensions themselves were calculated not on the basis of the cumulative contributions of individuals, but by a formula which in addition to contributions was taking into account several other factors as well. For most of the 1990s this formula in Poland was,

$$\pi i = 0.24w^* + 0.013niwi + 0.007miwi + \pi i^* \qquad (1)$$

where πi is the pension paid to an individual "i" at the point of retirement, w^* is the national average wage, wi is the average wage of the person "i" during the last several years (from 2 to 10) of work, ni is the number of years of work and mi is the number of non-contributory years.[1] Finally, π^*i stands for the pension right on account of privileges for which the individual might be eligible because of the type of work he or she had performed. We may note in formula 5.1 the large size of the redistributive component, $0.24w^*$, which is augmented by the impact of privileges for some categories of workers. [2] Both redistributive components weaken the link between current earnings and future pensions, thus reducing the incentive to work.

Any individual "i" would judge the size of his or her pension in terms of the replacement ratio, $\pi i / wi$. The presence of large redistributive terms in (1) implies that this ratio would be high for people for whom the ratio of their own wage to the average wage, wi/w*, is low. Let ρ be the replacement ratio such that the wage wi buys the same standard of living as the pension ρwi. The value of ρ is person-specific, but is usually taken to be in the range between 2 and 0.8. Suppose ρ = 0.7. The actual average replacement ratio for old-age pensioners rose, in the 90s, to a level between 0.7 and 0.8 in Poland and a level between 0.6 and 0.7 in Hungary. Thus for a large proportion of current employees in these two countries, their expected pension would have been close to or larger than 0.7 times their own earnings. Such employees would have no incentive to make private savings out of their current earnings.

The fairly radical reform policies and the rather fast economic restructuring of the 1990s rapidly aggravated the problem of financing the state pension system, from both the revenue side and the expenditure side. The number of contributors to the social security system has declined due to increased unemployment and growing evasion. On the other hand, to alleviate the social cost of transformation, early retirement was allowed and the criteria for granting disability pensions were liberalized. These measures meant a rapid rise in the number of pensioners. To meet the escalating pension bill, higher payroll taxes were imposed on the firms. The result was a higher labor cost, which became a factor discouraging employment and encouraging evasion (Golinowska 1997a,b, Golinowska and Hausner 1998, Palacios and Rocha 1997).

During the 1990s, demographic changes did not make a significant contribution to the financial difficulties of the pension system in the 1990s. However, demographic projections indicate that such changes could become a major additional source of tension within the next 10 to 20 years (Styczen, 1999). In the Czech Republic and Hungary, the demographic factor has already become a source of financial tension.

4. IMPLICIT PUBLIC DEBT OF THE PRE-REFORM PENSION SYSTEM

The PAYG-DB pension system may be viewed as a social pact involving three overlapping generations: those who work currently finance pensions of those who have already retired in exchange for a promise that their own pensions will in future be paid by the next generation of workers.

The reform adopted by Hungary and Poland and planned by Romania changes this arrangement in a fundamental way, as social security contributions of current workers go in part to personal accounts (pillar I) and in part to private pension funds (pillar II). The capital accumulated in pillar II can no longer be used automatically by the state to pay the pensions of people other than those who effectively own it. Moreover, capital accumulated in pillar I has also individual owners. Both capitals can be used to pay current pensions, but the payments would represent a debt of the state.

Two questions may be asked. Firstly, what would be the capital needed at the beginning of the reform to settle all the future pension obligations of the state with respect of those who are already who beneficiaries? Thus suppose that the transition to the new system is instantaneous, so that current contributions cannot be used at all to finance any current pensions. As this capital is not available to the pension system, it would have to be borrowed to meet future obligations to current pensioners. Therefore, the capital is a form of public debt. Because of the terms of the social pact, this debt is not a part of the official public debt before the reform. However, this debt is implicit in pension obligations and will become gradually explicit after the reform, in the course of gradual switching to the new system. The second question concerns the current value of the pension entitlements of those who, because of their past social security contributions or poor health or family circumstances, have already acquired some pension rights by the start of the reform. The capital represented by those rights is another form of the implicit public debt of the present pension system. In Tables 5.1 and 5.3 estimates of this implicit debt are reported. For the FOUR they are based on a common estimation method.

For the people who are already pensioners, the following approach is used. Suppose a specific benefit in the initial year is Y0, and assume that its rate of growth will be constant. The benefit is assumed to be defined fully by the type of pension, the age of person, and the sex of person. It is also assumed that the rate of growth of benefits is common, a constant g. The question is what should be the initial fund K0 that is just high enough to pay the benefits Y1, Y2,….,YT during an expected lifetime T, assuming that the capital still unspent at any time during this period produces a rate of return r? Thus K0 is a solution to the following problem:

$$Kt=(1+r)Kt-1-Yt \qquad (2)$$

$$KT=0 \qquad (3)$$

$$Yt=(1+g)Yt-1 \qquad (4)$$

Where t=1,2…,T. The terminal value of the capital, KT, is zero as the fund is to be spent fully by year T. The solution to this problem is:

$$K_0 = Y_0 \sum_{i=1}^{T} \left(\frac{1+g}{1+r} \right)^i \tag{5}$$

The required initial capital is thus the present value of all future payments: Y1, Y2,....,YT with the rate of return r being the discount rate. In (5), both Y0 and T are specific for particular group of pensioners in the initial year, taken to be the first year under the new system. For example, for old-age pensioners outside agriculture in Poland there were 102 groups considered: 51 age classes – from 40 years old and younger to 90 years and older - for each of the two sex categories. The capital K0 was compared separately for each group characterized by an age class, a type of pension, and a sex category. The numbers Y0 and T vary as between groups, but both were assumed to be common for all members of any specific group (Gomulka and Jaworski, 1998).

The method used to estimate the implicit pension debt with respect to those who acquired some pension rights by the beginning of the new system requires no new data. It is assumed, however, that the age composition of all new pensioners will be the same over time as that observed initially. This stationarity assumption also applies to the expected lifetime and the size of benefits of all members of each age group.

To explain the method, let us consider all the people who were in the initial year, say 1996, of age 21, 22, 40, and who become pensioners at the age 40. Let

V (40,20-k, 1996+k)

be the present value of all the expenditures on pensions for these 40-year olds at the point of retirement. These people become pensioners in the year 1996+k, after working and acquiring pension rights during (20-k) years of work. It is assumed that pension rights are proportional to the duration of work and subject to growth in real terms at a rate g. Hence

(6)

$$V(40,20-k,1996+k) = \left(\frac{1+g}{1+r} \right)^k \left(\frac{20-k}{20} \right) V(20,20-k,1996)$$

where k=1,...,20, and r is the discount rate. Therefore the total present value of pension rights for those people will be

$$TV = V(40,20-k,1996)\sum_{k=1}^{20}\left(\frac{20-k}{20}\right)\left(\frac{1+g}{1+r}\right)^{k} \qquad (7)$$

As the value V(40,20-k, 1996) is known, we can compute (7) for any magnitude of g, selected to be 0, 2 and 4 per cent, and for any value of r, chosen to be equal to 3 per cent.

The method presented above was used to estimate implicit public (pension) debt in all four countries. The estimates have been done separately for already retired and for those still working. The results are as follows (Table 5.6).

Table 5.6. Implicit pension debt, in percent of GDP

Country	g in %	Already retire: Men, Old	Already retire: Men, other age	Already retire: Women, Old	Already retire: Women, other age	Working: Men, All kinds	Working: Women, All kinds	Total, All kinds
Czech Republic	0	22	14	30	14	59	59	199
	2	25	18	36	18	76	77	251
	4	29	23	43	26	99	105	324
Hungary[2]	0	Not available		Not available		Not available	Not available	293
	2							407
	4							600
Poland[3]	0	42	40	47	38	34	50	251
	2	50	48	55	44	42	62	302
	4	61	58	66	52	54	78	370
Romania[4]	0	25	9	43	23	48	63	211

Sources: Schneider (1999), Vajda (1999), Gomulka and Jaworski (1998), De Menil et al. (1999).

5. AIMS AND PRINCIPLES OF THE REFORMS IN HUNGARY (1998) AND POLAND (1999)

In both Hungary and Poland the pension reform was intended to address the key problems: large expenditures and disincentives to work and savings. These problems are in turn related to low effective retirement ages, liberal disability criteria, high replacement ratios, large redistribution through the pension formula, and privileges for some categories of workers. There was also a need to diversify the institutional architecture in two ways: by complementing compulsory contributions with voluntary ones and by complementing the state social security system with private pension funds. The motivation of the reforms was thus both microeconomic and macroeconomic. There were two main microeconomic concerns. One was to create a far tighter link than under the old system between pension benefits and pension contributions, thereby strengthening the incentive to work and the disincentive to evade. Addressing this concern required a drastic lowering of the redistributive component and the establishment of individual accounts to make the system more transparent. The other central microeconomic concern was to lower the obligatory social security contributions paid by the employer, in order to reduce labor costs and increase employment. The key macroeconomic aims of the reform were also two. One was to bring down, in both countries, the aggregate levels of public expenditures on pensions, as proportions of GDP, from the very high levels they had reached during the first phase of economic transformation. Such reductions were needed to make public finances less of an obstacle to growth, by reducing the total taxation burden and the budget deficit, and to make it rather an instrument of growth, by increasing public resources for education and infrastructure investment. The other aim was by to induce the working population to save more on a voluntary basis. These micro and macro objectives were mutually compatible, and their achievement required a radical reform of the pension system. The reform was becoming urgent also for demographic reasons. These were the same as those found in many developed countries: longer post-retirement life and lower birth rate.

The reform is limited to retirement (old age) pensions outside agriculture. It involves the creation of a new institutional architecture and the introduction of new rules concerning contributions and benefits. Five principles can be identified as having guided these changes. Namely:

a) The diversification principle: Security and efficiency of the pension system must be enhanced, and to do this is by diversifying the system between state and private funds and between obligatory and voluntary contributions. Moreover, the savings measures introduced in the obligatory part of the system must be sufficiently strong to pay for much of the cost of the reform.
b) The distribution principle: The public part of the new system should continue to be of the PAYG type, while being made less redistributive and more transparent.
c) The capital-funding principle: The private part of the system should be capital funded and well regulated.
d) The savings principle: The expenditure-savings measures introduced in the obligatory part of the system must be sufficiently strong to pay for any cost of reform, and
e) The gradual phasing-in principle: The phasing-in of the new system must be spread over a prolonged period of time, and should not involve people near retirement.

We shall briefly discuss these principles in turn.

Principle a. The system of retirement pensions for workers consists of three pillars: (I) state, (II) open pension funds and (III) other pension funds. Only pillars II and III are private, and only pillars I and II will receive obligatory contributions.

Principle b. Obligatory contributions are to remain proportional to earnings, a form of payroll tax, but will now be subject to a cut-off point equal to 2.5 times the average wage. To make the tax more transparent, half of the contribution paid before the reform by employers is added to wages and paid by employees. The key innovation, however, has been the establishment of personal accounts to which all the obligatory contributions of those in the new system would be assigned. These personal contributions, if not used as pensions, can be inherited by survivors.

Principle c. The private pension funds, which constitute pillar II, receive a specified part of all the obligatory contributions. However, a key question which reformers had to address was: How does one protect future pensioners from inefficient pension funds? In Poland, a two fold solution was adopted. Firstly, contributors are free to move their savings between funds. Secondly, it is laid down that any recognized fund must, as a condition of remaining in business, guarantee to all its contributors a rate of return not less than 2 percentage points below the pension industry's average rate. This solution is likely to force less efficient funds out of business. To prevent a collapse of the industry into a monopoly, it will be necessary to issue from time to time new licenses to new funds.

Principle d. The part of the obligatory contributions, which is diverted to pillar II represents a loss of revenue to pillar I. Thus, the reform implies a deterioration of public finances in the initial phase of its implementation. To contain this deterioration, supplementary reforms are needed in pillar I. The most important of these are tighter criteria for entitlement to invalidity pensions, increasing the effective retirement age in (Poland, from 56 in 1997 to 60 for women and 65 for men; Hungary progressively raised and unified to 62 by 2001 (men) and 2009 (women)), by reducing the scope for early retirement, and reducing the rate of growth of real pensions, in Poland to a minimum of 0.15 in the years 1999-2000 and 0.20 from 2001 of the growth rate of real wages. In Hungary the indexation rule was changed from net wages to a weighted average of gross nominal wages and prices; starting in 2001, the weights are to be 0.5 and 0.5, the so-called Swiss formula. Further expenditure-saving reforms are needed to replace the subsidy component, in Poland about 95% of total spending, of the pension system for farmers.

Principle e. A gradual phasing-in of the reform is intended, to protect the rights of older workers. Hence is the provision of the Polish reform that all people aged 50 and above remain in the old system, while those between 30 and 50 years old will have the right of choice, and only those aged 30 and below are all compelled to join the new system. This arrangement has two advantages: it reduces sharply the political resistance to reform and it helps to contain the financial costs of its implementation. The Hungarian arrangement is even more flexible, as the new system is mandatory only for new entrants to the labor force, while all the existing workers have the right either to opt in or remain in the old system.

6. REFORM DEVELOPMENTS AND PENSION PROJECTIONS

In this section I shall first briefly review and then compare the pension reforms, which have been implemented or approved for implementation. The purpose of this comparative review is to seck the reasons for any differences in the reform programs.

In general, three approaches to the reform of a PAYG-DP pension system are possible: (i) reformers within the system, (ii) complete shift to a fully funded system and (iii) an intermediate arrangement in the form of a multi-pillar (typically three pillars) system. The Czech Republic adopted strategy (i), Hungary and Poland strategy (iii), and Romania is about to adopt also strategy (iii).

6.1 The Czech Republic

The Czech authorities have prepared long-term scenarios of the financial position of the public pension system for 1997-2020, taking into account demographic developments. The key finding was that "if the current replacement rate is maintained and the retirement age increases in accordance with the pension law, the premium tariff would need to increase from the current 26 percent to 36 percent in 2020", (IMF, 1998, p.43).

Pensions are not subject to any tax in the Czech Republic, and this distorts comparisons with other countries. If taxes were applied, pension expenditures would be some 1.5% of GDP higher than officially reported. Compared to Poland, the Czech Republic has two disadvantages. One is that the unemployment rate, which was very low during most of the 1990s, started to increase sharply under the weight of the 1997-1999 recession and is likely to continue increasing in response to subsequent restructuring. The other disadvantage is the absence of any significant pool of labor in agriculture that would swell the number of contributors to the pension system in the future.

Nevertheless, the Czech authorities decided against a wholesale pension reform, even of the intermediate and gradual three-pillar type proposed by the World Bank and adopted by Hungary and Poland. Such a wholesale reform would make explicit a substantial part of the implicit pension debt accumulated under the present system. According to Schneider (1999), "This debt is often cited as the insurmountable barrier for any (substantial) reform proposal". The Czech response to the threat of a substantial increase of the premium tariff has been to adopt changes to the present PAYG-DB system and to implement them gradually. These changes involve above all a gradual increase in the retirement age, linking benefits more directly to contributions, and adopting a price indexation formula for pensions, which is intended to lower the ratio of pensions to wages.

6.2 Hungary and Poland

In the post-WWII period, demographic trends in Hungary were similar to those in the Czech Republic. However, during the 1990s, restructuring went far deeper in Hungary, leading to a much sharper increase in the ratio of pensioners to contributors (Table 5.1). The replacement rate declined in both countries, but the decline was sharp in the Czech Republic and quite moderate in Hungary. In Poland this rate increased sharply during the 1990s.

It would thus appear that the countries, which undertook more significant restructuring, such as Hungary and Poland, were also under greater social pressure, to which they succumbed, to keep the replacement ratio high. In these countries the pension system became an extension of the social protection safety net to ease opposition to restructuring reforms. The macroeconomic implications of this combination of deeper restructuring and larger pension transfers were larger budget deficits and higher payroll taxes in Hungary and Poland than in the Czech Republic. The further implication was that the financial pressure to reform the pension system was also greater in Hungary and Poland.

The threat of a major macroeconomic instability forced Hungary to adopt a tough stabilization program in 1995. In 1996, a government initiated reforms of the pension system. The relevant legislation was adopted in July 1997 and, in January 1998, Hungary became the first transition country to begin implementing a 3-pillar pension system. The motivations, aims and specific principles of the Hungarian reform (Palacios and Rocha, 1997) are the same as, or similar to, those which Poland adopted one year later (Gomulka and Styczen, 1999). A broad description of these principles was given in section 6 above.

In both countries, the reform applies only to retirement pensions. However, in Hungary these pensions accounted, in late 1990s, for some 80% of all pension expenditures, as against 55% in Poland. The latter proportion indicates that much of the pension problem in Poland still remains to be solved. As indicated earlier, Poland remains the world leader in pensions other than old age (mainly invalidity and family pensions), which are internationally exceptionally high in terms both of their number in relation to the labor force and levels in relation to wages. Moreover, there remains the problem of what to do with the financing of pensions for the agricultural community.

6.3 Romania

As noted earlier, so far, pension expenditures in Romania have been kept low in relation to GDP. However, simulations indicate that the contribution rate must increase from 25.5% in 1996 (and 32.5% in 1999) to 41.5% in 2040 in order to maintain the 1998 ratio of pensions to wages (De Menil et.al, 1999). In 1998, this ratio, at 36.2%, was much lower than in Hungary and Poland (Table 5.1). Therefore, Romania is expected to experience social pressure to increase that ratio in the future. This pressure and the expected increase of the coverage of the population by pension insurance are two major factors, which prompted Romanian government, in 1999, to propose a reform of the state pension system along the Hungarian-Polish model (De Menil et.al., 1999).

7. CONCLUSIONS

Demographic trends during the years 2000-2050 (for which projections are typically made), are expected to be similar in the FOUR to the major EU countries. Populations will be either stable (Poland, Romania, France, UK) or declining (Hungary, the Czech Republic, Germany, Italy). Dependency ratios (65+ to 15-64 years olds) are projected to increase in most countries, including our FOUR, at a historically unusual pace. These ratios in the four EU countries listed above are expected to increase from about 24% in 2000 to about 40-45% in France and UK and 50-60% in Germany and Italy (Chand and Jaeger, 1996). In Poland this ratio is projected to increase from 17.7% in 2000 to 40.9% in 2050 (Styczen, 1999), and in Hungary from about 25% in 2000 to about 40% in 2050 (Palacios and Rocha, 1997). The elderly population itself is projected to age considerably in most countries. This is indicated by the 'very elderly' ratio (75+ to 65+), which is expected to increase, in the four EU countries, from about 40-45% in 2000 to about

60% in 2050. This ratio in Poland is projected to increase from about 40% in 2000 to about 51% in 2035 and then to decline to 42% in 2050 (Styczen, 1999).

Pension systems and pension expenditures show large variations among countries worldwide. This variation appears to reflect mainly demographic factors and differences in the level of insurance protection, the latter tending to increase with the level of development. What concerns the four transition countries analyzed in this chapter the greater pension expenditures in Hungary and Poland are in part inherited (especially in Poland) and in part caused by the more radical restructuring reforms. These greater expenditures have in turn prompted these two countries to start replacing gradually their PAYG-DB system with a three-pillar mixed system, with private pension funds constituting a large component of the reformed system.

ENDNOTES

* London School of Economics, Department of Economics, and CASE. The author wishes to acknowledge the helpful suggestions of the co-editors of this book, Marek Dabrowski and Jacek Rostowski. This chapter draws on my joint work with Piotr Jaworski and Marek Styczen. This work was reported in discussion papers circulated by CASE and the Central European University, and is listed in the references section.

[1] These include years spent in higher education, an unpaid leave for mothers of 3 years per child up to a maximum of 6 years, and the period when a disability pension was received.

[2] The most significant privileges were granted to miners, soldiers and police, but some privileges were also given to teachers, rail workers, steelworkers, sailors and others.

REFERENCES

Augustinovics, Maria (1997), *Introduction*, in: *Pension Systems and Reforms: Britain, Hungary, Italy, Poland, Sweden*, EC's Phare ACE Programme 1995, Final report, Budapest.

Cangiano, Marco, Carlo Cottarelli, and Luis Cubeddu (1998), *Pension Developments and Reforms in Transition Economies*, IMF Working Paper, WP/98/151.

Chand, Shetta K., and Albert Jaeger (1996), *Aging Populations and Public Pension Schemes*, IMF Occasional Paper, No.147.

Chlon, Agnieszka, Marek Gora, and Michal Rutkowski (1999), *Shaping Pension Reform in Poland: Security through Diversity*, mimeo.

De Menil, Georges, Stephane Hamayon, and Mihai Seitan (1999), *Romania's Pension System: The Weight of the Past*, CASE - Center for Social and Economic Research, Warsaw, Studies and Analyses, No. 177.

Golinowska, Stanislawa, Zofia Czepulis-Rutkowska, and Maria Szczur (1997), *The Case of Poland*, in: *Pension Systems and Reforms: Britain, Hungary, Italy, Poland and Sweden.* ACE Phare Programme 1995, Final report, Budapest.

Golinowska, Stanislawa, and Jerzy Hausner, (1998), *Political Economy of the Pensions Reform*, CASE Reports, No. 15, Warsaw (in Polish).

Gomulka, Stanislaw, and Piotr Jaworski (1998), *Implicit Public Debt of the Polish Social Security System*, CASE-CEU Working Papers Series, No. 14.

Gomulka, Stanislaw and Marek Styczeń (1999), *Estimating the Impact of the 1999 Pension Reform in Poland*, 2000-2050, CASE-CEU Working Papers Series, No. 27.

Hausner, Jerzy (1998), *Security Through Diversity: Conditions for Successful Reform of the Pension System in Poland*, Collegium Budapest, DP, No.49, Budapest.

IMF (1998), *Czech Republic: Selected Issues*, IMF Staff Country Report, No. 98/36

Koch, Manfred, and Christian Thinaman (1997), *From Generosity to Sustainability: The Austrian Pension System and Options for its Reform*, IMF Working Paper, WP/97/10.

Nestor, Barbara, and Zoltan Vajda (1999), *Does a Pensions Overhang Threaten Macroeconomic Stability? The Case for Hungary*, Central European University, mimeo, May, Budapest.

Palacios, Robert and Roberto Rocha (1998), *The Hungarian Pension System in Transition*, Social Protection Working Paper Series, The World Bank, Washington D.C.

Polish Government (1999), *Strategy of Public Finances and Economic Development: Poland 2000-2010*, June, Ministry of Finance, Warsaw.

Rostaguo, Massimo V., and Francesca Utili (1997), *The Italian Social Protection System: The Poverty of Welfare*, IMF Working Paper, WP/98/74.

Sadka, Efraim, and Vito Tanzi (1998), *Increasing Dependency Ratios, Pensions and Tax Smoothing*, IMF Working Paper, WP/98/129.

Schneider, Ondrej (1999), *Implicit Public Debt of the Czech Social-Security System*, CASE - Center for Social and Economic Research, Warsaw, Studies and Analyses, No. 167.

Styczen, Marek (1999), *Socio-demographic Forecast of Poland, 1997-2050, for Modelling Incomes and Social Security Retirement Pensions*, CASE - Center for Social and Economic Research, Warsaw, Studies and Analyses, No. 168.

Vajda, Zoltan (1999), *Macroeconomic Implication of the Pension Reform*, CASE – Center for Social and Economic Research, Warsaw, Reports, No. 20.

World Bank (1995), *Hungary: Structural Reforms for Sustainable Growth*, Washington D.C.

World Bank (1997), *Poland: Country Assistance Review*, The World Bank, Operations Evaluations Department, Washington D.C.

Chapter 6

SEARCHING FOR THE LAFFER CURVE IN TRANSITION ECONOMIES

Mateusz Walewski

INTRODUCTION

The Laffer Curve has been very controversial from the very beginning. This simple idea has had both powerful supporters, such as former U.S. president Ronald Reagan, who was convinced by its transparent logic, but also very renowned opponents such as James Tobin, who called it "as ancient as it is trivial". Tobin argued that the idea was purely political, and that neither economic theory nor empirical research had been able prove that any such relationship really existed.

This modest paper does not try to resolve this discussion. It is merely a simple empirical analysis based on a poor data set that tries to answer a very simple question: Does any evidence exist for the Laffer Curve, or at least some kind of a Laffer-like relationship in three countries of Central Europe: the Czech Republic, Hungary and Poland.

The Chapter is constructed in the following way. The next section very briefly reviews discussion of the subject over the last 20 years. It also presents a selection of earlier empirical results. The Section 2 develops an index of income tax rates (Tax Burden Index – TBI) that has been constructed by the author especially for this paper. The same section also presents the main sources of data used in the chapter. Section 3 presents the results of statistical, graphical and econometric analysis of the data. Tables, empirical results and graphs are presented in Section 4.

1. THE LAFFER CURVE

As the popular story goes; at the end of seventies, during a meeting with Ronald Reagan Arthur Laffer drew on the napkin a curve describing the theoretical relationship between tax revenues and tax rates. The curve presented by Laffer was bell shaped (see Figure 6.1). It meant that after some critical point increasing taxes not only does not lead to further increases in revenues, but revenues actually start to decrease. Laffer tried in this way to convince the president that lowering tax rates can lead to an increase in revenues.

The idea underpinning this relationship seems to be quite simple. It is obvious that with taxes equal to zero there are no revenues. Therefore the left hand side end of the curve seems to be perfectly defined. Pure logic indicates that in the case of a 100% tax rate, no one would like to work and pay taxes, and therefore budget income would also be zero, or very close to zero. Therefore, under the assumption of continuity, a function describing the relationship between tax rates and budget revenues has to have some maximum (point "MAX" on the Figure 6.1). Laffer called the negative sloped part of the curve "the prohibitive range".

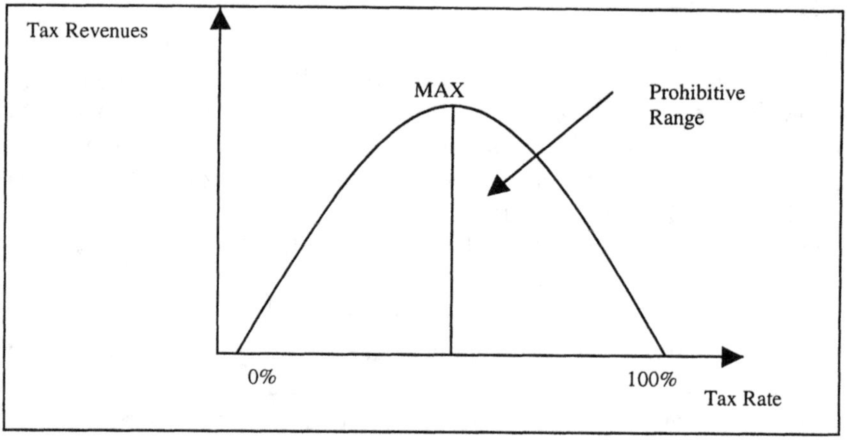

Figure 6.1. The Laffer Curve

The are two possible theoretical explanations for the existence of the relationship described by Laffer. The first refers to the theory of labor supply and demand, and is illustrated in Figure 6.2 [1]

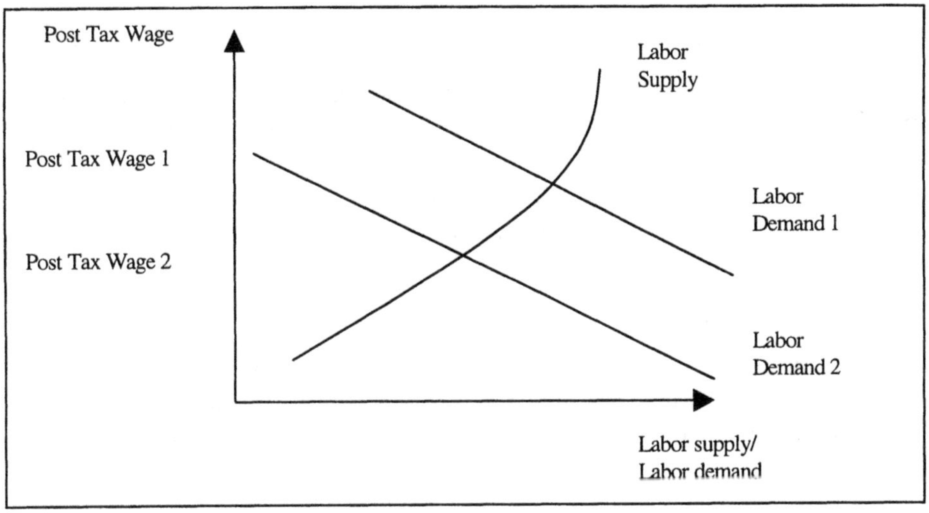

Figure 6.1-MW The Labor market derivation of the Laffer Curve

Let us assume that the labor supply is a positive function of the post-tax wage, i.e. the wage received by the employee, and the labor demand is a function of the pre-tax wage, i.e. the cost of the worker to the employer. In this situation a change in the tax rate leads to a shift in the labor demand function, which shifts inwards (from Labor Demand 1 to Labor Demand 2 on the Figure 6.2-MW) when taxes increase. This shift leads to a decrease in the number of hours worked, lowering aggregate output, and therefore the tax-base. It leads also to a decrease in the post tax wage. When this effect dominates over the positive effect of increased taxes we find ourselves on the negatively sloped part of the Laffer Curve, i.e. in its "prohibitive range".

Although the logic of the Laffer Curve presented above seems to be very attractive, there are a number of doubts, some of them concerning the basic assumptions of the derivation. One of the main problems with the Laffer Curve is that it assumes a monotonic relationship between tax rates and hours worked. However, looking at this relationship in more detail, one should take into account all changes in wages and prices resulting from the change in tax rates. For example, adapting a quite simple general equilibrium model, it is possible to show that the Laffer Curve does not need to be continuous and may not have any interior maximum (Malcolmson 1986). Everything depends the on prevailing technology and the elasticity of labor supply. For certain perfectly plausible shapes of production functions a more negative elasticity of labor supply implies a more positive slope for the Laffer Curve, (so that tax revenues never decline as tax rates increase. The magnitude of the labor supply elasticity as such is also important - for example for adult males in the U.S.A it has been shown to be close to zero (Mirowski 1982). Therefore, Malcolmson (1986) suggests that it is impossible to determine the shape, or even existence of the Laffer Curve on a purely theoretical basis. Only empirical work can show us whether such a relationship exists or not. On the other hand, if one wanted to determine the shape of the Laffer Curve empirically in a really convincing manner, one would have to build a model allowing for all possible general equilibrium effects of tax increases.

However, even if one assumes that the supply of labor does not cause a Laffer-type relationship between tax rates and revenues, one can argue that although economic agents do not work less as taxes increase, they do put more of their effort into the underground economy, and that this causes budget losses. One can describe the mechanics of this process using the following formula (Sultan 1999):

$$B^{te}+B^{cc} <=> C^{e}+C^{h}+p*i*C^{r}+C^{pd}+C^{pp} \quad (1)$$

Where:
B^{te} The amount of tax that is evaded
B^{cc} Compliance costs saved
C^{e} Direct costs of evading
C^{h} Costs of hiding evasion
p Probability/risk of being caught
i Certainty of the punishment if caught
C^{r} Value of the risk
C^{pd} Personal Discomfort
C^{pp} Peer pressure or tax morality

One can roughly assume that we find ourselves on the positively sloped part of the Laffer Curve as long as the left-hand side of equation 1 is smaller then the right-hand side. As soon as the total costs of tax evasion become lower then the sum of tax evaded plus the costs of "paying" taxes, we reach the prohibitive range of the curve. The higher a tax rate and the more complicated a tax system, the bigger the probability that the left-hand side of equation 6.1 will be bigger then the right-hand side. High tax rates mean high B^{te}. Complexity and lack of transparency of a tax law means both: high B^{cc} and low C^{e},C^{h} and "p", since there are more opportunities to evade taxes and it is much easier to hide tax evasion. When the tax system is complicated it is also much easier to avoid taxes without breaking the low, therefore some cost elements simply disappear.

However, this leads to a need to estimate the shadow economy if one is to evaluate the magnitude of the Laffer effect. However doubtful they may be, there exist numerous estimations of the shadow economy both for developed and for developing countries. (Kloc, 1998). For example according to Kaufmann & Kaliberda (1995 - cited in Kuzmin, 1999), levying a 20% Value Added Tax on only a quarter of the Ukrainian shadow economy would increase budget revenues more then enough to eliminate the entire budget deficit. I think that these numbers bring home to us magnitude of the shadow economy in developing countries. Hence, although there are no reasons to believe that this problem is as overwhelming in Central European Countries as it is in the former USSR, this does not mean that it is negligible.

Empirical analysis of the Laffer hypothesis has been carried out both for the USA and for Europe. In 1979 Canto, Joines and Webb tried to use simple ARIMA models using US data to estimate the effects of tax rates on economic activity. The results indicated a positive effect for the Kennedy tax cut of 1964. Mariger (1995) estimated the effect of the 1988 tax cut on labor supply using a panel of married man and women for the years 1985-1988. He found that the reform increased hours worked by no more then 2 percent. Hsing (1996) using US time series data for the years 1959-91, estimated that the revenue maximizing tax rate oscillates between 32.67% and 35.21%. As far as European analyses are concerned, Van Ravenstein and Vijlbrief (1988) estimated the revenue maximizing marginal tax rate in Holland to be 70.1%.

2. THE TAX BURDEN INDEX AND DATA SOURCES

Thus, neither the presence nor the shape of the Laffer Curve are as obvious as pure logic would suggest. This paper is not sophisticated enough to either prove anything or to try to estimate the functional form of the Laffer Curve. Nevertheless, it tries to examine whether there are any signs of the presence of such a relationship in three countries of Central Europe.

However, there is one more problem one has to cope with when trying to analyze any relationship, variables have to be well defined and measurable. In this case that is not easy. What is needed is a measure of average taxation. If one used a measure of tax rates only, one would measure only one, and not the most important, factor determining the impact of the tax system in a country. One can imagine two countries with exactly the same tax rates, but with completely different "taxes burdens". Different tax thresholds could result in major differences in tax burdens, even setting aside different tax reliefs, allowances and other details of tax law. This is why the measure of average taxation used in this paper tries to take into account both tax rates and tax thresholds.

A Tax Burden Index (TBI) has been constructed in the following way:

TBI = First Tax Rate * First Ceiling + Second Tax Rate*(Second Ceiling-First Ceiling)+...+n^{th} tax rate*(n^{th} – (n^{th}-1)Tax Ceiling) (2)

Figure 6.3 illustrates the above formula. Tax rates are represented by the vertical axis, and tax ceilings (thresholds) by the horizontal axis. TBI as defined in equation 2 is the area under the line AB. In fact this area is the sum of areas of the set of n rectangles. The area of each rectangle is defined by the tax rate, and the income bracket corresponding to this rate. For example in Poland in 1997 the first tax rate was equal 20%, and all incomes not higher then 20 870 PLN a year were taxed according to this rate. This means that the area of the first rectangles was 20%*20,870 = 4174. The second tax rate was 32% and the second tax ceiling was 41,740 PLN. It means that all incomes higher then 20,870 and lower then 41,740 were taxed at 32%. Therefore the area of the second rectangle was 32%*(41,740-20,870)=6678,4. All further rectangles are defined in the same way, and the sum of all rectangles is the TBI.

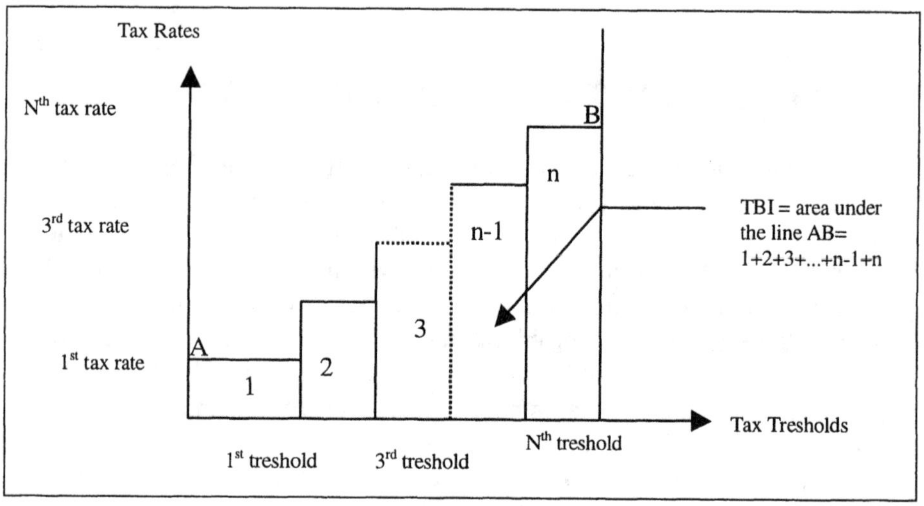

Figure 6.3. The definition of the Tax Burden Index (TBI)

There are two problems in the above definition of the TBI. The first is the way one calculates tax ceilings in order to make them comparable across countries. Clearly it would make no sense to calculate the TBI in the simple manner described in the above Polish example if one wanted to compare the TBI across countries.

The second problem is the nth Tax Ceiling. It has to be invented for the needs of this paper, since normally only the lower limit of the last tax bracket is defined. Thus, the nth tax ceiling does not exist and the area of the nth rectangle is infinite. It means, that the entire measure of the TBI could be determined by the last (highest) tax rate only. It would obviously make no sense in our case, since, as I have already mentioned, what we are trying to take into account are not only tax rates but the total tax burden i.e. the structure of tax rates and thresholds.

The first problem has been resolved as follows: tax ceilings have been calculated in every country as a percentage of GDP-per capita in a given year. For example, in 1997 in Poland the first tax ceiling was 20,870 PLN, and GDP-per capita was 11,490 PLN. Hence the first "normalised" tax ceiling was 20870/11490 = 1,82 (or 182%). Hence the area of the first rectangle was 1,82*20%=0,364 (of per capita GDP). This method of calculating tax ceilings and the TBI gives us measures that are comparable across countries.

The second problem is much harder to solve, since it requires decisions based on ad-hoc assumptions and calculations. The first assumption we make is that the upper limit of the last tax threshold should be set equal for all the countries analyzed, since if one set different limits for each country the measure would cease to be comparable. Choosing such a common limit would be quite easy if the lower limit of the last tax bracket (n-1th threshold) was similar across countries. In that case the nth tax ceiling could be set just "a little bit above" the n-1th threshold for all countries. Unfortunately this is not the case for the three countries analyzed, and the n-1th tax ceilings differ considerably.

Due to lack of other data, my choice of the last (nth) tax ceiling is based on the following information: in Poland only about 1% of taxpayers have incomes above the n-1th tax ceiling. This (n-1th) ceiling was, for example, 3.2 (320% of GDP/per capita) in 1993, and 4.33 (433% of GDP per capita) in 1992. These are the lowest and the highest numbers for Poland. In Hungary the n-1th tax ceiling was about 1.5 (150% of average GDP/ per capita) in the years 1992-97. Furthermore, about 10% of taxpayers paid taxes according to the highest rate in the years 1996-97 in Hungary and almost 20% did so in 1995. On the other hand in the Czech Republic the n-1th ceiling was about 11 (1100% of GDP/per capita) in some years. If one wanted to chose the nth tax ceiling for all the countries so as to take into account the ceilings in the Czech Republic in these years, the TBI in Hungary and in Poland would be completely determined by the highest tax rate. This is similar to the case of the "infinite nth tax ceiling". Therefore, considering all three cases, I have chosen to set the nth tax ceiling equal to 5 (500% of GDP/per capita) in all countries and for all years. This means that my measure does not take into account taxpayers whose incomes are more the 5 times as high as GDP/per capita in their countries. However, bearing in mind the Polish case, where an extremely low number of taxpayers had incomes higher then 400% of per capita GDP, I find this number reasonable.

This number lets to take into account all tax rates in both Poland and Hungary. In The Czech Republic during 1993-95 and in 1997 the last tax rate was excluded from calculations. However if one assumes that the percentage of taxpayers having incomes as high as 11*GDP-per capita is similar to that in Poland, this omission looks fair. (I do not have data on numbers of taxpayers in various income categories from the Czech Republic). For data on tax ceilings, tax rates, taxpayers and TBI see Table 6.1

Table 6.1. The Data Set

HUNGARY	1992	1993	1994	1995	1996	1997
hun-zero	0.35	0.29	0.26	0.2		
				16.22%		
hun-rate1	25	25	20	20	20	20
hun-cel1	0.7	0.58	0.35	0.28	0.22	0.28
hun-share1				9.69%	19.68%	32.00%
hun-rate2	35	35	25	25	25	22
hun-cel2	1.75	1.45	0.52	0.4	0.33	0.34
hun-share2				11.88%	15.44%	6.71%
hun-rate3	40	40	35	35	35	31
hun-cel3			0.89	0.7	0.57	0.57
hun-share3				23.67%	20.23%	22.27%
hun-rate4			40	40	40	35
hun-cel4			1.29	1.01	0.82	0.79
hun-share4				20.32%	20.53%	15.38%
hun-rate5			44	44	44	39
hun-cel5					1.34	1.25
hun-share5				18.22%	14.83%	14.03%
hun-rate6					48	42
hun-share6					9.29%	9.60%
hun-rev	6.7	7	6.5	6.5	5.9	6.12
TBI	175.45	179.7	198.257	203.003	224.147	197.191

POLAND	1992	1993	1994	1995	1996	1997
pol-rate1	20	20	21	21	21	20
pol-cel1	2,16	1,6	1,66	1,67	1,74	1,82
pol-share1	96,08%	91,25%	91,62%	92,70%	93,34%	94,57%
pol-rate2	30	30	33	33	33	32
pol-share2	3,17%	7,49%	6,82%	6,04%	5,49%	4,42%
pol-cel2	4,33	3,2	3,33	3,35	3,49	3,63
pol-rate3	40	40	45	45	45	44
pol-cel3						
pol-share3	0,75%	1,27%	1,56%	1,26%	1,17%	1,01%
pol-rev	7,7	9,2	9,8	9,8	9,2	8,85
pol_TBI	135,12	152,01	165,13	164,77	162,23	154,62

CZECH REP.	1992	1993	1994	1995	1996	1997
cze-rate1		15	15	15	15	15
cze-cel1		0,62	0,54	0,46	0,57	0,52
cze-rate2		20	20	20	20	20
cze-cel2		1,24	1,08	0,92	0,97	1,05
cze-rate3		25	25	25	25	25
cze-cel3		1,86	1,62	1,38	1,37	1,65
cze-rate4		32	32	32	32	32
cze-cel4		5,57	4,86	4,14	3,8	14,99
cze-rate5		40	40	40	40	39
cze-cel5		11,13	9,72	8,27		
cze-rate6		47	44	43		
cze-rev	7	4,3	5,3	5,5	5,3	5,32
cze_TBI		137,74	141,67	150,37	152,33	140,59

Source:
Share- share of taxpayers in tax bracket
Cel- tax ceiling
Rev-revenues from PIT as the percentage of GDP
TBI- Tax Burden Index
Rate- Tax rate

Nevertheless, part of the analysis has been done also with the TBI calculated for the nth tax ceiling set equal to 4 (400% percent of GDP/per capita) and also to 6 (600% of GDP per capita). The results have not been qualitatively different from those obtained when the TBI was calculated with nth ceiling set equal to 5. These results are presented in Table 6.8.

Most of the data for this chapter comes from Tomczyńska (1999). The data on shares of taxpayers in Hungary and in Poland is from the national Ministries of Finance, but, as has already been mentioned it has not proved possible to obtain similar data for the Czech Republic. The data on personal income tax (PIT) revenues for 1997 has been taken from OECD Revenue

Statistics 1965-97, and these are all estimated numbers. IFS-IMF CD-ROM XI'1998 was the source for the GDP and population figures.

3. DATA ANALYSIS AND ECONOMETRIC ESTIMATION

This section is divided in two main parts. The first is a simple study based on tables and graphs. The second part presents the results of some econometric analysis.

Table 6.2 presents coefficients from the following regression (run for each country separately):

$$\text{Revenue} = \text{constant} + \beta\text{TBI}$$

Table 6.2. Average revenues, TBI, and Tax Rates in the Czech Republic, Hungary and Poland, and coefficients of simple bivariate regressions of TBI on revenues in each country

	Coefficient β	REVENUE	TBI	TAX RATES
HUNGARY	-1.92	6.45	1.96	4.67
POLAND	6.49	9.09	1.56	3.00
CZECH R.	4.80	5.14	1.45	5.60

These coefficients are then compared to the following variables: average budget revenues from the PIT, the average TBI in every country and the average number of tax rates. We can treat the last of these as an approximation of the complexity of a tax system in a given country, and also as an additional measure of tax progressiveness, although the TBI itself also tries to measure this.[2]

In the case of Hungary the relationship between the TBI and revenues is negative. Hungary is also the country with the highest average TBI. On the other hand in Poland and in the Czech Republic the corresponding coefficients are positive. The TBIs in both countries are quite similar and much lower than in Hungary. At the same time the number of tax rates is much more stable in Poland and smaller than in the Czech Republic (see Table 6.1). One suspects this factor may explain the differences in the slopes of the relationship (the coefficient β) between in these two countries.

Obviously no strong conclusions can be drawn from such a simple analysis. However, it can be interpreted as *prima facie* evidence of the presence of some kind of Laffer Curve. Both an increase in tax rates above some critical point and a high level of tax complexity seem to result in a decrease in budget revenues.

The next step in the analysis is the inspection of graphs. Figure 6.4 presents the cross-plot of the TBI and revenues from the three countries analyzed. As one can see the cross-plot divides naturally into three parts, one for each country. Each part is labeled in the graph with the name of the corresponding country. In this way this cross-plot can be treated as a graphical representation of Table 6.2.

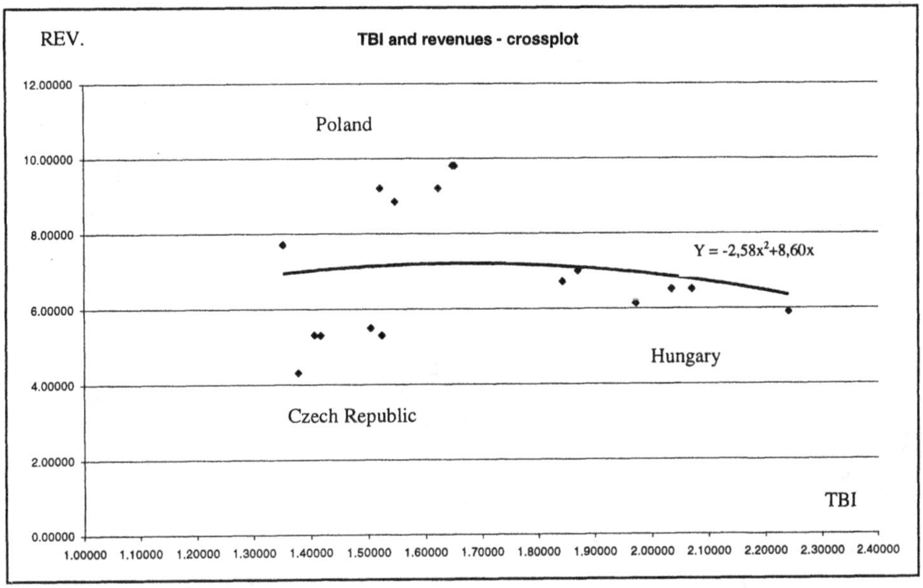

Figure 6.4. Revenues and TBI in the Czech Republic, Hungary and Poland. A Cross-plot.

However if one treats the data set as a simple cross section it is possible to fit a line, described by a second order polynomial function, illustrating the relationship between the TBI and revenues. Since by definition the Laffer Curve has an origin equal to zero, this restriction has been applied in this case.

The fitted line is concave, and this is the next indication of the existence of a Laffer Curve in the countries analyzed. Clearly, this does not prove much, especially taking into account that in all three cases points "belonging" to one country lie together on the same side of this line. This indicates that there are other important factors, specific to each country determining the PIT revenue independently of tax rates. This observation is consistent with earlier suggestions indicating an important role for the complexity of the tax system.

We now come to the econometric part of the analysis. Table 6.3 is an econometric extension of Figure 6.4. It presents the results of regressing revenues on TBI and on TBI squared without a constant term. As could have been expected, the results are the same as those on the graph, (slight differences observed are the result of rounding by the econometric software). However, as one can see, although the t-statistics on the estimated coefficients are significant the overall value of the estimation seems to be very questionable. The F-statistic, (bolded) indicates that the TBI itself is not able to explain differences in PIT revenues.

Table 6.3. Results of the cross section regression without intercept or Number of Rates

Dependent Variable: REVENUES				
Method: Least Squares				
Included observations: 17				
Variable	Coefficient	Std. Error	t-Statistic	Prob.
TBI	8.64	1.60	5.42	0.00
TBI^2	-2.59	0.89	-2.91	0.01
R-squared	0.09	Mean dependent var		7.00
Adjusted R-squared	0.03	S.D. dependent var		1.77
S.E. of regression	1.75	Akaike info criterion		4.06
Sum of squared residuals	45.68	Schwarz criterion		4.16
Log likelihood	-32.52	**F-statistic**		**1.42**
		Prob(F-statistic)		**0.25**

This situation changes after including the number of tax rates in the model as an additional variable. Results of estimation with this variable included are presented in Table 6.4. The improvement in the regression results is evident. The F-statistic shows that the probability of overall insignificance of the relationship is practically zero, also all t-statistics are significant as well. The positive coefficient on the TBI and the negative coefficient on TBI^2 suggest the existence of a Laffer-like relationship between the tax burden and budget revenues.

Table 6.4. Results of the cross section regression with Number of Rates

Dependent Variable: REVENUES				
Method: Least Squares				
Included observations: 17				
Variable	Coefficient	Std. Error	t-Statistic	Prob.
TBI	12.63	1.17	10.81	0.00
TBI^2	-3.39	0.53	-6.34	0.00
NUMBER OF RATES	-1.01	0.18	-5.56	0.00
R-squared	0.72	Mean dependent var		7.00
Adjusted R-squared	0.67	S.D. dependent var		1.77
S.E. of regression	1.01	Akaike info criterion		3.01
Sum of squared residuals	14.23	Schwarz criterion		3.16
Log likelihood	-22.61	**F-statistic**		**17.59**
		Prob(F-statistic)		**0.00**

However, the results also suggest also that the level of average taxes, although they are negatively correlated with budget revenues after some critical point, is not the most important factor determining revenues. In order to see this more clearly let us draw a graph with two lines corresponding to the function described by results from Table 6.4. For one of the lines the NUMBER OF RATES has been set at 3 (as in Poland), for the second one at 5 (similar to the Czech Republic and Hungary). As one can see (Figure 6.5), two bell shaped lines have been obtained. REVENUES (on the vertical line) are almost totally determined by the distance between these to lines, and not by their Laffer-type shape. Additionally, this function reaches its maximum when the TBI equals 1,86 (this number means that the average single personal income tax rate should be equal to 37%, to maximize budget revenues) i.e. a number only slightly smaller then average TBI in Hungary. This means that if the NUMBER OF RATES was the same in all countries, the Hungarian government would, on average, collect the highest revenues. But it shows also that cutting taxes a little bit, would not decrease, or could even increase revenues in this country. The issue looks quite different in both Poland and the Czech Republic. In both of these countries increasing taxes would result in an increase in revenues.

Obviously, interpreting the results of the above analysis in this way, one should not forget that the data set used was very poor, because of the short time series available, and the lack of other important information such as the number and size of tax-credits, as well as information on the effectiveness of tax collection. On the other hand, including such information in the analysis might be very difficult, because of incomparability of the data and the extremely short time series available. Thus, one cannot treat the lines in Figure 6.5 as point estimations of real Laffer Curves. They only illustrate certain general tendencies.

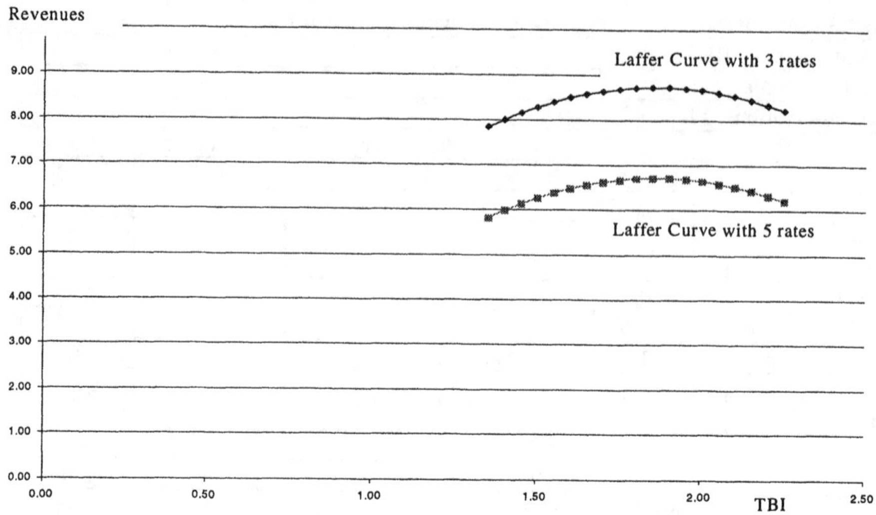

Figure 6.5. Estimated Laffer Curves with 3 and 5 Tax Rates

Treating a data set of this kind as a pure cross section is somewhat informal, so pooled data analysis has been also applied. Results of two pooled regressions, both of which calculated with the NUMBER OF RATES variable included, are presented in Tables 6.5 and 6.6. The results of the first regression, where all coefficients have been calculated as if they were common for all three countries, look very similar to the previous cross section estimation. This is because, like the previous (cross section) regression, this one also calculates an average relationship for all the countries.

Table 6.5. Results of the pooled regression with Number of Rates included

Dependent Variable: REVENUES				
Method: Pooled Least Squares				
Included observations: 5				
Total panel observations 15				
Variable	Coefficient	Std. Error	t-Statistic	Prob.
TBI	13.21	1.11	11.91	0.00
TBI^2	-3.47	0.49	-7.01	0.00
NUMBER OF RATES	-1.15	0.17	-6.77	0.00
R-squared	0.81	Mean dependent var		6.97
Adjusted R-squared	0.78	S.D. dependent var		1.88
S.E. of regression	0.88	Sum squared resid		9.32
Log likelihood	-8.90	F-statistic		25.82
Durbin-Watson stat	0.92	Prob(F-statistic)		0.00

In Table 6.6, on the other hand, I present results which try to take into account heterogeneity across our countries. Both the TBI and also TBI^2 are estimated as cross section specific variables. This means that the coefficients of both variables have been calculated separately for Hungary, Poland and the Czech Republic. The coefficient on NUMBER OF RATES is treated as common. It is not possible to treat this variable as cross section specific, since it has not been changed in Poland during the years analyzed. The result of the analysis suggests that, when one tries to analyze our three countries separately, the Laffer effect is detectable only in Hungary. In Poland and in the Czech Republic the coefficients on the TBI^2 are not statistically significant. This result is not surprising if we consider that Hungary is the only country, where the direct relationship between the TBI and revenues is negative. It means that Hungary is the only country in our group, where the Laffer Curve has really become apparent. Our very short time series does not let us detect evidence for that curve in the other two countries.

Table 6.6. Results of the pooled regression with the Number of Rates treated as the common coefficient, and TBI and TBI2 as the cross section (country) specific coefficients.

Dependent Variable: Revenues				
Method: Seemingly Unrelated Regression				
Included observations: 5				
Total panel observations 15				
Variable	Coefficient	Std. Error	t-Statistic	Prob.
Number of Rates	-0.28	0.02	-12.74	0.00
The Czech Republic - TBI	5.50	2.46	2.24	0.06
Poland – TBI	8.08	1.41	5.74	0.00
Hungary – TBI	8.07	0.18	43.79	0.00
The Czech Republic – TBI^2	-0.59	1.69	-0.35	0.73
Poland – TBI^2	-1.06	0.88	-1.21	0.26
Hungary – TBI^2	-2.08	0.10	-21.26	0.00
R-squared	0.98	Mean dependent var		6.97
Adjusted R-squared	0.97	S.D. dependent var		1.88
S.E. of regression	0.32	Sum squared resid		0.83
Durbin-Watson stat	2.10			

These results should not be over-interpreted, as they suffer from the same drawbacks as the earlier two. The number of cross-section and time series observations is very small, especially when compared with relatively large number of coefficients estimated.

All estimations thus far have been performed without an intercept. Absence of a constant term biases regression statistics and especially R^2, which becomes impossible to interpret, and also (in the case of pooled-regressions) the Durbin-Watson statistic. Therefore, the results of regressions with the intercept included, corresponding to those from Tables 6.3 and 6.5 are presented in Table 6.7. I have not tried to estimate the regression corresponding to Table 6.6, since it would mean estimating 10 coefficients with 15 observations. The pooled-data regression has been estimated by the fixed-effects method. Although the results do change slightly, they are not qualitatively different. Only the second cross-section equation shows that coefficients on the TBI are practically insignificant, and that the only factor that really matters for PIT revenues is tax system complexity (NUMBER OF RATES). Pooled-data regression does not confirm this result. Both the significance and the magnitude of the NUMBER OF RATES coefficient decreases in pooled-estimation. One can suspect that this variable has been "replaced" by fixed effects, which were not allowed earlier. Thus, both the shape, and the limited influence of the Laffer Curve effect on tax revenues has been confirmed.

Table 6.7. Results of regressions with intercept included

Dependent Variable: REVENUES			
Method: Least Squares			
Included observations: 17			
Variable	**Coefficient**	**t-Statistic**	**Prob.**
TBI	50.89	2.28	0.04
TBI^2	-14.48	-2.29	0.04
C	-36.63	-1.90	0.08
R-squared	0.27	Mean dependent var	7.00
Adjusted R-squared	0.17	S.D. dependent var	1.77
S.E. of regression	1.61	Akaike info criterion	3.95
Sum squared residuals	36.33	Schwarz criterion	4.10
Log likelihood	-30.58	F-statistic	2.63
		Prob(F-statistic)	0.11
Dependent Variable: REVENUES			
Method: Pooled Least Squares			
Total panel observations 15			
Variable	**Coefficient**	**t-Statistic**	**Prob.**
NUMBER OF RATES	-0.27	-1.89	0.08
TBI	19.37	2.59	0.02
TBI^2	-4.85	-2.42	0.03
Fixed Effects			
CZE_--C	-11.17		
POL_--C	-8.35		
HUN_--C	-11.47		
R-squared	0.98	Mean dependent var	6.97
Adjusted R-squared	0.97	S.D. dependent var	1.88
S.E. of regression	0.31	Sum squared resid	0.85
Log likelihood	23.47	F-statistic	255.82
Durbin-Watson stat	2.22	Prob(F-statistic)	0.00
Dependent Variable: REVENUES			
Method: Least Squares			
Included observations: 17			
Variable	**Coefficient**	**t-Statistic**	**Prob.**
NUMBER OF RATES	-1.05	-4.52	0.00
TBI	7.61	0.44	0.67
TBI^2	-1.97	-0.40	0.70
C	4.49	0.29	0.78
R-squared	0.72	Mean dependent var	7.00
Adjusted R-squared	0.65	S.D. dependent var	1.77
S.E. of regression	1.04	Akaike info criterion	3.12
Sum squared residuals	14.14	Schwarz criterion	3.32
Log likelihood	-22.56	F-statistic	10.99
		Prob(F-statistic)	0.00

Table 6.8. Results of cross-section regression with Number of Rates for the TBI calculated with the nth ceiling equal to 4 (400% of GDP/per capita) and 6 (600% of GDP/per capita).

The Nth ceiling = 4				
Dependent Variable: Revenue				
Method: Least Squares				
Included observations: 17				
Variable	Coefficient	Std. Error	t-Statistic	Prob.
TBI (with the nth ceiling equal to 4)	16.68	1.46	11.42	0.00
TBI^2 (with the nth ceiling equal to 4)	-5.83	0.85	-6.89	0.00
Number of rates	-1.03	0.20	-5.20	0.00
R-squared	0.69	Mean dependent var		7.00
Adjusted R-squared	0.64	S.D. dependent var		1.77
S.E. of regression	1.06	Akaike info criterion		3.11
Sum squared residuals	15.62	Schwarz criterion		3.25
Log likelihood	-23.40	F-statistic		15.40
		Prob(F-statistic)		0.00
N^{th} ceiling = 6				
Dependent Variable: Revenue				
Method: Least Squares				
Included observations: 17				
Variable	Coefficient	Std. Error	t-Statistic	Prob.
TBI (with the nth ceiling equal to 6)	9.77	0.97	10.04	0.00
TBI^2 (with the nth ceiling equal to 6)	-1.99	0.38	-5.20	0.00
Number of Rates	-1.04	0.17	-6.00	0.00
R-squared	0.74	Mean dependent var		7.00
Adjusted R-squared	0.71	S.D. dependent var		1.77
S.E. of regression	0.96	Akaike info criterion		2.91
Sum squared residuals	12.88	Schwarz criterion		3.06
Log likelihood	-21.76	F-statistic		20.17
		Prob(F-statistic)		0.00

4. CONCLUSIONS

It can be claimed that this simple analysis gives us some evidence for the presence of some kind of the Laffer-like relationship in the countries analyzed. It shows that the Laffer Curve for these three countries may be bell shaped. On the other hand this relationship does not seem to play an important role in determining budget revenues in this countries. It seems that differences in revenues between countries are more the result of other factors, specific to each country, and represented in our regressions by the number of tax rates. If, in spite of the poor quality of the data set and the simplicity of the analysis, one treated the obtained point estimate of the revenue maximizing TBI seriously, one would conclude that both the Czech Republic and Poland are still on the positively sloped part of the Laffer Curve, while Hungary is poised at the maximum. Simple correlations of the TBI and budget revenues calculated for these three countries seem to confirm this observation, although the correlation coefficient between NUMBER OF RATES and REVENUES in Hungary equals a very high – 0,96. This means that it is really possible that changes in the complexity of the tax system, and not changes it the TBI itself, which have determined the level of budget revenues in that country.

As far as policy implications resulting from this paper are concerned, it was important to find some evidence of the Laffer Curve in all three countries analyzed. However, taking into account the theoretical and empirical problems with this idea, estimating the maximum point of the curve for tax policy use seems to be extremely risky. Therefore, even if the main objective of a government were to maximize revenues, it should not pay too much attention to the Laffer Curve. It would do much better trying to make tax system as simple as possible, minimizing both incentives and possibilities for tax evasion and tax avoidance.

ENDNOTES

[1] Mirowski (1982) is the source of this diagram.

[2] It should also be mentioned that in the case of the Czech Republic all tax rates have been included, not only those taken into account when calculating the TBI.

REFERENCES

Borkowski R., Ostaszewski K. , *The Inflection Point of the Laffer Curve*, University of Luisville mimeo. (http://www.louiville.edu/~kmosta01/rafal.html)

Canto V., Joines D., Webb R., (Cited in Mirowski 1982) ,*Empirical Evidence on the Effect of Tax Rates on Economic Activity*, Proceedings of the American Statistical Assosiation Business and Economics Section, 1979

Hsing Y., (1996). *Estimating of Laffer Curve and Policy Implications*, Journal of Socioeconomics 25(3) pp.395-401

Kaufmann, D. and A. Kaliberda (cited in Kuzmin 1999), *Integrating the Unofficial economy into the Dynamics of Pos-Socialist Economies: A framework of Analysis and Evidence*, World Bank Kyiv 1995

Kloc K. (1998), *Szara Strefa w Polsce w Okresie Transformacji*, Raporty CASE nr.13

Kuzmin Y. (1999), *Structural Roots of Financial Crisis*, in M. Dabrowski ed. "Ukraine: Form Fragile Stabilization to Financial Crisis", CASE Sudies&Analyses Series no.158, , pp.63-71

Lindsey L. , *Estimating the Revenue Maximizing Top Personal Tax Rate*, NBER Working Paper 1761, (November 1985), 47 pages

Mariger R. , (1995), *Labor Supply and the Tax Reform Act of 1986: Evidence from the Panel Data*, Finannce and Economic Discussion Series, Federal Reserve Board, Washington DC,

Mirowski P. , *What's Wrong With the Laffer Curve*, Journal of Economic Issues Vol.XVI No.3 September 1982 pp.815-828

Malcolmson J., (1986), *Some Analytics of the Laffer Curve*, Journal of Public Economics 29 pp.263-279

Solow R. (cited in Mirowski 1982), letter dated 27 July 1978 in US Congress, Joint Committee on the Budget, *Leading Economists' Views of Kemp-Roth* (Washington DC, US Gov. Printing Office, August 1978 p.148)

Sultan K. , (1999), "Ukraine's Travail with Tax Reforms" in M. Dabrowski ed. *Ukraine: Form Fragile Stabilization to Financial Crisis*, CASE Sudies&Analyses Series no.158, , pp.53-62

Tobin J. (cited in Mirowski 1982) , letter dated 3 August 1978 in US Congress, Joint Committee on the Budget, *Leading Economists' Views of Kemp-Roth* (Washington DC, US Gov. Printing Office, August 1978 p.163)

Tomczynska M., (Warsaw 1999), *Comparative Analyses of Direct Tax Systems in Selected Central European Countries*, CASE Studies and Analyses Series no. 161

Van Ravenstain A., Vijlbrief H., (1988), *Wefare Costs of Higher Tax Rates: An Empirical Laffer Curve for Netherlands*, De-Economist 136(2), pp.205-219

Chapter 7

A LOOMING FINANCIAL CRISIS IN THE CZECH REPUBLIC?

Ondřej Schneider

and

Pavel Štepanek

INTRODUCTION: CZECH FISCAL MINEFIELD

This chapter analyzes Czech fiscal policy, its development, its outlook and its main flaws. We confirm the precarious condition of Czech public accounts. The share of revenues in GDP is lagging behind expenditures that are set to rise. The easy cuts in expenditures have already been made, social expenditures swell as the population ages, and past debts are slowly maturing. Moreover, hidden risks, implicit in the system of public finances during the transition period, are becoming ever more apparent. Since the financial capacity of the budget is overburdened by social commitments, governments try to find ways in which functions vital for the completion of the transition can be carried out without their financing taking the form of present cash outlays. All together, we foresee deficits of about 5% of GDP annually in the coming years. Public debt would therefore balloon to roughly 60% of GDP within a decade.

We then proceed with a more detailed discussion of the main revenue and expenditure programs of Czech budget, after which we propose forecasts as to how the budget may evolve in the medium term. As we have already indicated, growing importance is given to off-budget institutions and thus we enrich our discussion with a detailed description of their development and of their eventual impact on the public accounts. We conclude with a brief and admittedly incomplete reform proposal.

1. A BRIEF HISTORY OF TIME

Czechs thought that they could have the best of all possible worlds: falling taxes, balanced public budgets and a decent social security system. They knew it would take a miracle, as these were not mundane goals. When the first cracks in the economic facade began to appear, a sophisticated system of hidden, off-budget funds was built up. As the 1996 election approached, social security expenditures were stepped up. Now, the whole fiscal system is seemingly headed for a crash. What comes next? Looking at Czech fiscal policy, we cannot see any easy remedies, as the expected gap between revenues and expenditures stretches to 5% of GDP. In such times, tinkering at the edge of disaster offers little and fundamental reforms are needed.

What went wrong? The seeds of the current fiscal problems were planted in the early 1990s when the tax system was overhauled and a new social security system established. While tax revenues were tied to nominal GDP, expenditures have since moved more in tune with nominal wages.[1] This is a common feature of many tax systems in Europe and should not be particularly problematic. The Czech Republic, however, has become famous for its lax corporate governance, a feature of which was rapid wage growth as opposed to aggressive restructuring or layoffs. Thanks to the fiscal system, high wage growth has translated into collapsing corporate taxes, rapidly growing social expenditures and, eventually, to the growing gap between budget revenues and expenditures — see Figure 7.1.

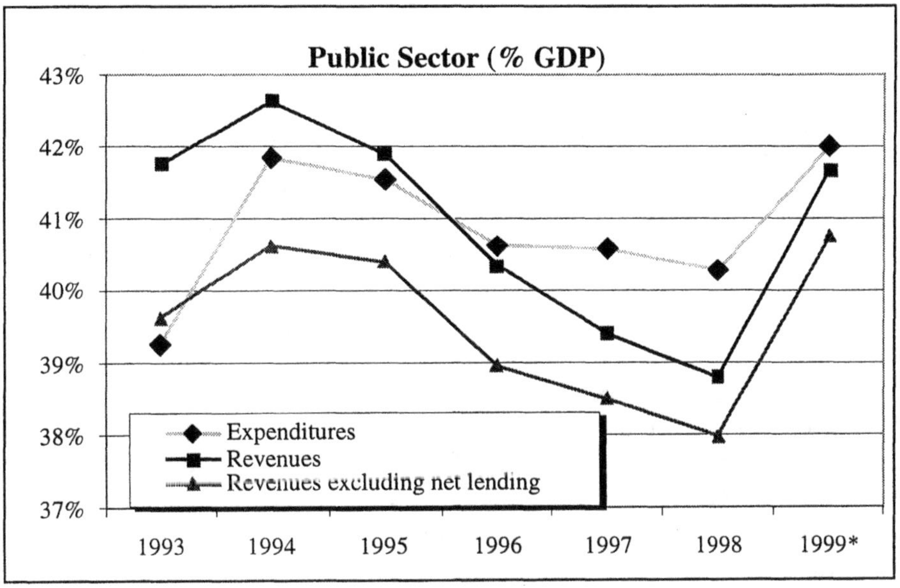

Figure 7.1. The Public Sector in the Czech republic

The sector public budgets in the first three years shown posted consolidated surpluses ranging from CZK 27 bn in 1993 to less than CZK 5 bn shown in 1995, i.e. from 2.6% to 0.4% of GDP. From 1996, however, the rate of deficit has been increasing gradually up to roughly CZK 31 bn in 1999, that is to say 2.7% of GDP.

The relatively small internal debt has resulted in a low cost of debt service. With GDP growth, officially published gross public debt declined from 19% in 1993 to 12.4% in 1999.

However, structural disproportions lurked behind these relatively favorable results. Surpluses of current revenues compared to non-investment expenditures were decreasing. A decrease was recorded also in the share of investment expenditures in both the total budget and in GDP. Significant problems started to accumulate in the state budget itself.

Table 7.1. Czech Republic: Official government debt, 1992-1999(in CZK billion)

	1992	1993	1994	1995	1996	1997	1998	1999
Total Debt	172	159	157	154	155	173	195	228
in % of GDP	21.7	15.8	13.7	11.2	9.8	10.3	10.6	12.4

Source: Ministry of Finance

Problems were kept under wraps for several years. In 1994 and 1995, budget revenues were supplemented by transfers from the National Property

Fund (about 1% of GDP). The fiscal system was further "augmented" by an excessive system of off-budget funds to which various expenditures had been tunneled without proper consolidation. The official government budgets have thus become very incomplete.

The system came under attack first in 1996 when the budget slipped into a deficit even when "surplus money" from 1995 was transferred to 1996 revenues. In 1997, the budget accumulated a deficit of CZK 16 bil. (1% of GDP), but only after an enormous effort was devoted to slashing budget expenditures by CZK 40 bil. (2.5% of GDP!).

Since 1997, a deficit on the so-called pension account has appeared, following a reduction in social insurance contribution rates. The growing share of social expenditures (mainly pension benefits) has started to create a budgetary debt trap. The inclusion of other mandatory items (such as expenditures related to the Czech Republic joining NATO) made the already limited space available to cover the remaining budgetary needs even narrower. Indebtedness of cities and municipalities accelerated. Declarations of budget discipline did not ensure actual fiscal discipline.

The 1998 budget was constructed as a restrictive one, and even though the economy contracted by 2.7%, the budget itself showed a deficit of "only" CZK 31 bil. (1.7% of GDP). We may consider 1998 as the last in a series of "conservative" budgets —when the government sought balanced budgets at almost any price and often played loose with economic logic toward that end. The government's share in GDP thus fell by two percentage points in two years. Since 1999, the driving philosophy has changed. A balanced budget is no longer seen as sacrosanct and, meanwhile, accumulated debts have begun to emerge. Combined with the aggressive spending plans of the new government, a combustible mix has been produced. Government expenditures' share in GDP began to grow again in 1999 and may edge upward in the future. The government deficit is expected to head toward 5% of GDP in the near future.

Until now the budgetary stance of the Czech Republic did not clash with the reference values of the Maastricht convergence criteria. Deficits have reached 2 - 3% of GDP in the Czech Republic, as opposed to the 3% limit. Indebtedness is at 13% of GDP officially, and although it is estimated at roughly double that figure when hidden debts are included (see below), this is still well below the 60% Maastricht requirement. Yet, open and hidden problems have manifested themselves more acutely since economic growth has ground to a halt, and the accompanying revenue slowdown has coincided with an undiminished demand for increased budgetary expenditures. The drastic budget cuts implemented in the 1997 austerity measures were a one-time solution that impacted most on the capital expenses chapter of the budget, with multiplier effects on slowing down economic growth. Deeper reforms with long-term effects were not carried out and they continue to present an unanswered challenge.

2. FISCAL POLICY ANALYSIS AND MEDIUM TERM OUTLOOK

Why do budget revenues under perform expenditures? We have analyzed the past patterns of the main expenditure and revenue items of state budgets. Table 7.2 illustrates the underlying trends: while current expenditures were growing faster than nominal GDP, revenue lagged by almost two percentage points. The most rapid growth experienced was in social security expenditures, whose growth exceeded nominal GDP growth by six percentage points. So much for radical neo-liberal economic reform in the Czech Republic.... Defense expenditures were slowest, they grew by a paltry 3.2% on average, and interest payments, which remained low due to the low level of debt.

The second part of the table dismisses the common notion that tax collection in the Czech Republic was ineffectual and that a shift occurred away from direct taxes. With the exception of corporate taxes, which were indeed collapsing, tax collection was quite efficient. Personal taxes grew by a robust 17% annually, as did social security contributions. Value-added-tax revenues lagged slightly behind nominal GDP growth, while excise taxes grew vigorously.

Table 7.2. The actual and projected rate of revenue and expenditure increase (in %)

Nominal GDP Growth	12.1%	9.5%
Expenditure programs	Average growth rate in 1993-1998	Expected growth rate in 1999-2005
Defense	3.2%	16.2%
Education	10.7%	9.5%
Health Care	12.9%	10.0%
Social Security	18.3%	10.7%
Capital Expenditures	10.1%	8.4%
Current Expenditures	**12.9%**	**9.6%**
Interest Payments	**4.0%**	**16.5%**
Revenues	Average growth rate in 1993-1998	Average growth rate in 1999-2005
Personal Income Tax	17.3%	13.2%
Corporate Tax	-5.1%	7.6%
Social Contributions	16.8%	10.6%
Value Added Tax	11.1%	8.4%
Excise Tax	12.6%	6.7% *(14.4%)*
Total Revenues	10.3%	9.2% *(10.0%)*

Source: Ministry of Finance and authors' calculations.

The future offers a similarly bleak picture. As social expenditure outpaces GDP growth, defense expenditure has to catch up in order to bring it to the level of 2% of GDP pledged by the government to its NATO partners. As the state debt will grow, interest payments will rocket by more than 16% yearly. Taken together, we estimate that expenditures will grow by 9.6% over 1999-2005, a shade faster than nominal GDP, slowly increasing the government's share in GDP from 42% in 1999 to 43% in 2005.

Budget revenues are expected to grow by 9.2% annually, due to the slow growth in corporate taxes and consumption taxes (VAT and excises). It is significant that personal income taxes represent the most dynamic portion of budget revenues, followed by social security contributions, even if we do not include future hikes in contribution rates as hinted at by the government.[2] Higher personal taxes and higher social security contributions of course project a further upsurge in the labor tax burden and in the rate of unemployment. Budget revenues may be boosted by an aggressive convergence of the Czech excises to the average European level (see numbers in parenthesis and discussion below).

Figure 7.2 provides the fiscal outlook for the government accounts in a nutshell and compares our forecast with a forecast published by the Ministry of Finance in 1999. The deficit jumped to almost 3% of GDP in 1999 and we expect it to rise further — even **if we assume no change in government policy**. As public debt increases each year, interest payments double from 1% in 1998 to almost 2% of GDP in 2005. This would stabilize the overall deficits at around 4.5% of GDP. In nominal terms, such deficits mean that central-government deficits would break the CZK 100 bil. (USD 2.8 bil.) mark in 2002, and reach almost CZK 150 bil. (USD 4.2 bil.) in 2005.

Although the numbers above do not differ significantly from the government's own figures, we are less optimistic that GDP growth will resolve the Czech fiscal conundrum. As long as expenses are correlated with wages and grow faster than revenues, the state budget will find it very difficult to meet its commitments.

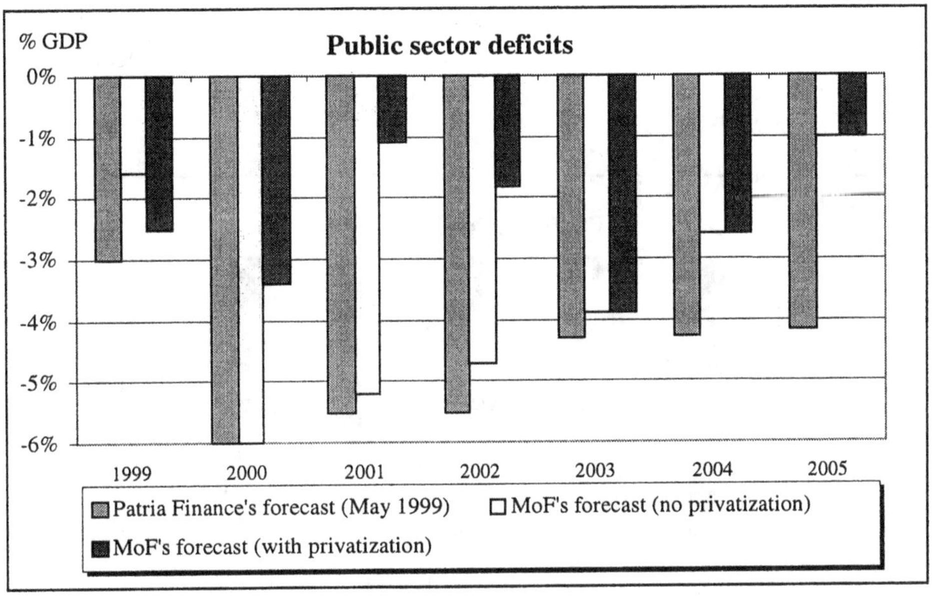

Figure 7.2. Budget deficits, 1999-2005

In our model we have not, thus far, foreseen any change in the government's policy. This is obviously too bold assumption. As we discuss below, the current budgetary rules in the Czech Republic are extremely weak and do not safeguard public budgets from operations that hinder long-term economic prospects. Therefore, to make our forecast more interesting, we have added two new features: First, we analyze a couple of new government initiatives that were approved in 1999. The Cabinet approved an "Agricultural Sector Strategy" that calls for increased state subsidies to the sector to the tune of 1.3% of GDP (currently these stand at 0.8% of GDP). Further, a "Medium Term Strategy for Transport" was approved. This implies new programs amounting to 0.5% of GDP. Also, the Ministry of Industry and Trade has had its soft-loan and subsidy package approved. These initiatives together increase the budget deficit by a combined 1.0-

1.5% of GDP, bringing it above 6% of GDP. It is interesting how easily and how stealthily the government has approved programs that so significantly deteriorate the fiscal outlook.

On the positive side, there seems to now be an agreement that excise taxes will be increased to European levels. Currently, they are about two thirds of the target value, therefore, they can be increased by 50% in the course of a few years. That could boost tax revenues by CZK 10 bil. in 2000, by almost CZK 50 bil. in 2003, and even by CZK 60 bil.-65 bil. in 2005, thus more than canceling the effect of the new spending programs described above. Even in such a case, the government deficit would stabilize at the fairly high level of 4% GDP.

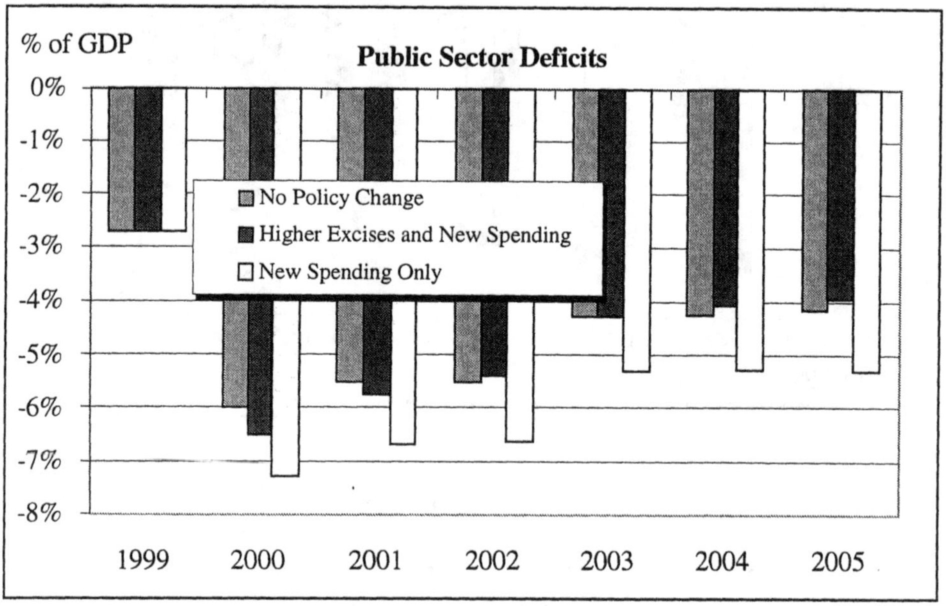

Figure 7.3. Influence of projected policy changes on the future fiscal outlook.

3. FORGOTTEN SINS – THE "TRANSFORMATION INSTITUTIONS"

The current Cabinet must, moreover, one day face the legacy of previous governments, which have accumulated so-called "hidden debts," which according to the World Bank amount to about CZK 220 bn (12% of GDP).[3] The debts consist of the outstanding liabilities of the government's off-budget funds and of government-guaranteed loans. Public debt would, in fact, double to 25% of GDP, if we added the hidden debt to the officially recognized debt.

There are four main so-called "transformation institutions" that have been created in the Czech Republic to address some of the outstanding issues of the economic transition. These are:

- the National Property Fund, an agency, primarily founded to carry out the technical operations needed to channel state owned assets to private investors according to privatization decisions approved by the government;
- the Consolidation Bank (Konsolidační banka), primarily founded to extend the maturity of and reduce the interest charged for loans, which had been issued in the past to finance part of the working capital of enterprises;
- the Czech settlement unit (Česká inkasní), designed to improve the structure of risk weighted loans at the CSOB (Ceskoslovenska obchodni banka – The Czechoslovak Commercial Bank, originally specialized in foreign trade financing and in the foreign financial activities of the government);
- the Czech financial unit (Česká finanční), designed by the central bank to assist in the stabilization of small banks in the Czech Republic.

All of these institutions enjoy the implicit guarantee of the government. The impact of their activities on the budget has two dimensions. First, for a given year, net public spending by "transformation institutions" includes cash outlays on new programs in the form of directed credits and asset purchases and interest expenditures, i.e. it is adjusted for debt collection and other revenue from programs and for interest revenue. Second, state guarantees reflect the amount of hidden subsidies and the default risk of the guaranteed loans.

There have been two distinct periods in the life of the "transformation institutions". Until 1993, off-budget programs had mainly dealt with pre-transition problems inherited by the banking sector. These programs had been financed through Konsolidacni Banka, which was capitalized by the National Property Fund, and borrowed from the Czech National Bank. In 1995, the Ministry of Finance established Ceska Inkasni, a non-banking financial institution, to clean-up the portfolio of CSOB. Covered by a guarantee issued by the National Property Fund, Ceska Inkasni took a credit from CSOB and used this credit to purchase CSOB's bad assets at face value.

The second phase relates to years 1996-1998, when the new bank consolidation and stabilization program was launched in order to deal with the newly emerging problems of the banking sector. In order to implement these programs, the Czech National Bank established Ceska Financni, also a non-bank financial institution.

Aside from the bank rescue operations, Konsolidacni Banka and, less directly, the National Property Fund have also financed government programs to support troubled insurance companies, public hospitals and the Czech Railways, to build infrastructure, and to clean up industrial enterprises before privatization. The National Property Fund has partly financed these programs from privatization revenues but partly also from the issuance of bonds.

The troubling fact is the rapidly increasing level of contingent public liabilities, which have been accumulated outside the budgetary system mainly by the "transformation institutions", as they had to borrow in order to finance their activities. Table 7.3 shows approximate levels of contingent public liabilities connected with their existence.

Table 7.3. Contingent Public Sector Liabilities (CZK bn)

	1993	1994	1995	1996	1997	1998
Konsolidacni Banka (KOB) (net of provisions and reserves)	79	81	79	70	86	98
Ceska Inkasni (CI) (net of provisions and reserves)	20	27	25	17	8	7
National Property Fund (NPF)	29	33.	40	22	17	15
State guarantees (risk adjusted guarantees outstanding)	3	3	6	28	74	107
Contingent public liabilities (net of provisions and reserves)	**131**	**144**	**150**	**137**	**185**	**226**
Contingent public liabilities (% of GDP) (net of provisions and reserves)	**13.1**	**12.1**	**10.8**	**8.7**	**10.9**	**12.4**
Provisions and reserves of KOB and CI	19	24	42	59	71	84
Gross hidden public liabilities (not adjusted for provisions and reserves)	150	168	192	196	256	310
Reported gross government debt	159	162	154	155	173	194
Reported gross government debt (% of GDP)	15.8	13.7	11.2	9.8	10.3	10.6

Source: Polackova-Brixi (2000).

Off-budget programs, such as guarantees and support extended through Konsolidacni Banka, the National Property Fund and other agencies impose costs on taxpayers with a delay but with no discount. Off-budget programs contribute only marginally to achieving the main policy objectives of the government and, in some instances, may even undermine these objectives. A brief overview suggests that many off-budget programs, such as the bailing-out of banks and health insurance companies, have done rather the latter. Sometimes, programs, which did not qualify for budgetary support (for example, an additional subsidy to the Railways) did qualify for assistance outside the budget (such as a very risky guarantee extended to the Railways). Moreover, these programs have often implied that government will help again in case of future failures, and thus generate moral hazard among market agents, reducing their incentives to improve productivity and competitiveness.

"Transformation institutions" serve the government as the channel for pursuing restructuring programs without much parliamentary or other public scrutiny and in a costly manner (compared to budgetary decisions). Since the government guarantees its obligations, for example, Konsolidacni Banka is able to borrow in the markets and finance as many programs as requested even though it is unable to repay its debts without future support from the budget.

The problem with policies, which are not incorporated into the state budget, lies in the low transparency of their costs and final fiscal consequences. This manifests itself at five levels.

The first level involves a macroeconomic problem - that is the sustainability of public finances over the medium term; this is also a problem of the clear identification of the goals and instruments of fiscal and monetary policies and their consequences. At the second level there is the political problem of the decision-making process regarding the priorities of spending public money. Decisions regarding state intervention and programs implemented outside of the official budget need not necessarily be based on a thorough evaluation of their costs and effects.

The third level involves the high costs of implementation and financing programs outside the state budget. This is connected with the problematic supervision of the economic activities and management of the "transformation institutions" and bears on the likely greater costs of their refinancing in comparison with the state debt. At the fourth and possibly the most important level, there is the problem of the moral hazard to which the conduct of the banks, enterprises, and other entities is subjected. Finally, at the fifth level, the methods of financing such government policies have varying monetary impacts.

At all five levels, there is the problem of incomplete legal and institutional frameworks, which define the adoption, implementation, and financing of government policies outside of the state budget. Therefore, solving the problem of hidden state debt must necessarily involve the creation of such a legal and institutional framework, which would prevent the further development of such state interventionism, the increase of potential state obligations, and its financing outside of the framework of the official budget process. This is necessary not only for the support of the long-term stability of public finances, but also for the correct evaluation of the cost of individual government programs, facilitating public control of government policies, supporting the efficiency of management of quasi-budget institutions that implement such programs, and creating healthy stimuli for other economic agents.

3.1 Government guarantees issued by public authorities

Guarantees represent a very dynamic component of the Czech fiscal system and have been a much favoured instrument of government since the mid 1990s when the fiscal balance came under pressure. The system of guarantees issued by public authorities is quite complicated, as many different authorities at different levels of the public administrative structure (both within central government but also municipalities) issue guarantees. Guarantees are also issued by the off-budgetary funds attached through the balance of their activities to the budget, and while there is at least some specification of the purpose and limits of state guarantees issued by the central government in the law, lower tiers are in this respect not regulated at all. Given the complicated financing channels used by different "transformation institutions", there exists an equally complicated system of mutual and multiple guarantees, issued occasionally by those same institutions or the state itself. Table 7.4 lists the main government guarantees issued so far.

Table 7.4 List of State Guarantees

Type of guarantee	Year	Outstanding amount (CZK billion, as of 1998)	Probability of state payment
Power Plants Desulfurization	1992	11.9	Nil
Temelín Nuclear Plant	1996	15.9	Low
Lease of new fleet by ČSA	1993	2.2	Low
Prague Airport Terminal	1995	6.3	Low
Railway tracks	1996/7	45.5	High
Railway modernization	1996/7	1.4	High
Highway system	1996/7	8.9	High
Military airplane production	1996/7	23.8	Medium
Loans to hospitals	1997	2.4	High
Prague Congress Center	1998	2.0	High
Flood damages relief fund	1998	7.5	High
Česká spořitelna guarantee	1995	4.1	High
PGRLF	1993-8	60+	Mixed

Source: Ministry of Finance, Ministry of Agriculture

The system of guarantees is not well regulated and represents an area, through which a government may avoid the disciplining pressure of the need to balance fiscal activities. Almost no statutory and regulatory procedures guide the government's exposure to such risks. The government of the Czech Republic has very broad authority to issue state guarantees and accept other off-budget obligations. With respect to state guarantees, the law authorizes the government to extend state guarantees "designed to finance government-approved development programs" without requiring estimates of future potential budget claims and, more broadly, without any public policy framework.

This shortcoming has created an incentive for the spending ministries and budgetary institution that are unable to secure the desired level of state assistance through the regular budget to seek state assistance through loan guarantees. The additional state assistance provided via guarantees is perceived as cost free and is not included in the overall financial support provided to a given sector (e.g., agriculture and transport). In some cases, guarantees are even extended for purposes that are not authorized under the broad authority of the law. They do not in fact cover development programs as the law requires, but aim at stabilizing the financial situation of the beneficiary.

The amount of guarantees issued is not subject to meaningful limits. The law sets out that the sum of installment payments due within a calendar year cannot exceed 8 percent of expected state budget revenues. This limit is extremely high and not very meaningful. For 1999, the limit allowed for about Kc 47 bil. of installment payments, compared to the scheduled Kc12 bil. Other EU applicant countries place much tighter limits on guarantees, such as the one percent of budget revenues as a limit for new guarantees issued in a given year in Hungary.

The guarantee approval process is weak. Proposed guarantees are presented to the Ministry of Finance by the spending ministries. Then the Ministry of Finance analyses the viability of the proposed project and the borrower's potential ability to repay the proposed guaranteed loan. However, no mechanism encourages the Ministry of Finance to assess a high-risk project as non-viable. Once a project is determined to be viable, it has to be approved by the government. In this process, guarantees are often extended as a result of emergencies and political pressure rather than as a result of a strategic decision to support certain outcomes at a given price and against other competing claims on public resources.

The government requires almost no risk sharing by the lending institution that extends the guaranteed loan, which creates a moral hazard problem. As a result of the government's acceptance of virtually all credit risk, the role of the private lending institution is reduced to that of a loan distributor. The lender disregards the credit quality of the borrower. Borrowers also tend to neglect the risks of projects, which are covered by government guarantee. In the case of default, the borrower negotiates with the government rather than the lender, because the lender does not have a stake in the loan performance. Risks are not properly monitored. The Ministry of Finance provides only limited oversight of outstanding guaranteed loans.

No reserves are set-aside in advance for expected guarantee claim payment. Each year the Ministry of Finance estimates the expected claim payments in the upcoming year. Given the pressure to present a balanced budget, incentives are created to make an optimistic estimate of expected claims in the upcoming year.

The lack of reserves to cover future guarantee claims results in "shocks" to the state budget. As guaranteed loans default, resources must immediately be found within the state budget, potentially requiring substantial and unexpected reductions in other state programs.

The lack of a requirement to establish loan loss reserves allows loan guarantees to avoid the discipline of the budget process and creates tremendous incentives to issue guarantees, because they do not require budgetary resources in the current year. As a result, substantially higher budgetary resources may be required in future years to pay for defaulted guarantees. Therefore, the current guarantee structure distorts the decision making process and encourages policy makers to make decisions today that may severely limit the options of future policy makers.

According to the Ministry of Finance, the hidden debt will be eventually securitized, so future budget expenditures would incorporate servicing the costs of this debt and would be more predictable. If we estimate conservatively that the government will service only the interest and never retire the debt as such, then budget expenditures would be increased by approximately 1.5% of GDP as from 2000. As interest payments remain flat in nominal terms, their share in GDP slowly declines and the yearly overall budget deficits stabilize at around 5% of GDP.

4. LIVING BEYOND ONE'S MEANS OR REFORM?

The trends and underlying factors in the evolution of public budgets that we have identified suggest that the tendencies to deficits will not be resolved solely by the restoration of economic growth. A true reform of public finance in the Czech Republic is needed. To be successful, it should include a reform of the tax system aimed not at rising the tax to GDP ratio but at such a change in the structure of taxation that would lead to an increased elasticity of tax yields to economic fundamentals and, consequently, to the improved operation of the tax structure as an built-in stabilizer.

A successful reform, however, must include a reform of spending programs as well. For this purpose, a public expenditure review will have to be conducted with the goal of limiting/eliminating those spending programs where the purposefulness and efficiency of the funds spent is not demonstrated. Such a reform must focus on a comprehensive analysis of spending programs and accept only programs and projects comprising a calculation of effects, costs and a clear definition regarding the sources of their financing, whether by savings in existing spending programs or by proposing new resources. The reform process must also introduce measures preventing the introduction of new spending programs that work against the reforms already started or against the need to harmonize spending policies with those of the EU.

Regarding public expenditure reforms, particular attention will have to be paid to the area of mandatory spending and more specifically to the pension system. The Czech Republic faces the same issue of aging populations as many countries in Europe. Despite that, the budget is still burdened by an increasingly expensive and unsustainable PAYG system that has been only marginally reformed. It is therefore necessary to be concerned about the looming demographic time bomb that will destabilize the current parameters of the pension system and to initiate, at once, changes in the pension system to make it sustainable.

To meet the above targets, it will be necessary to develop a comprehensive and well-articulated medium-term fiscal strategy. Over the medium term, the development of a medium-term fiscal framework, with the inclusion of contingent liabilities and off-budget activities within the budgetary process is needed. Part of the process will have to be a reassessment and redefinition of the legal and institutional framework for governmental budget activities (the so-called budgetary rules).

5. CONCLUSION

As we demonstrated, Czech fiscal policy is headed for substantial deficits in the future. Deficits will occur if the government simply extends the current policies and they will be even higher if it adopts some of the recently proposed measures. Moreover, off-budget institutions will, in all likelihood, continue to generate substantial losses in the future. As they are explicitly or implicitly guaranteed by the state, the government budget should better prepare for high and unpredictable expenditures, similar to the CZK 30 bn required by Konsolidacni banka in 1999. Therefore, all of our estimates should be taken as optimistic.

It has been often noted that the Czech Republic has ample room for deficit financing, as its debt is relatively low, even if we allow for the so-called hidden debts. A strategy of aggressive deficit financing would, however, be quite risky. As debt is accumulated, servicing costs balloon, and the government will find it increasingly difficult to slash other expenditures to stabilize deficits. Indeed, as Figure 4 shows, state debt rises relentlessly in all scenarios. If we disregard the "hidden debts" and do not change current policies, public debt reaches almost 50% of GDP in 2010, as compared to a mere 13% in 1999. However, as the "hidden debts" cannot be hidden forever and the government has pledged to increase spending on some programs, this scenario is far from certain. If, at the other extreme, the government acknowledges the hidden debts, increases spending according to its latest proposals and brings excise taxes to European levels, public debt will expand from 30% to more than 60% in the same period.

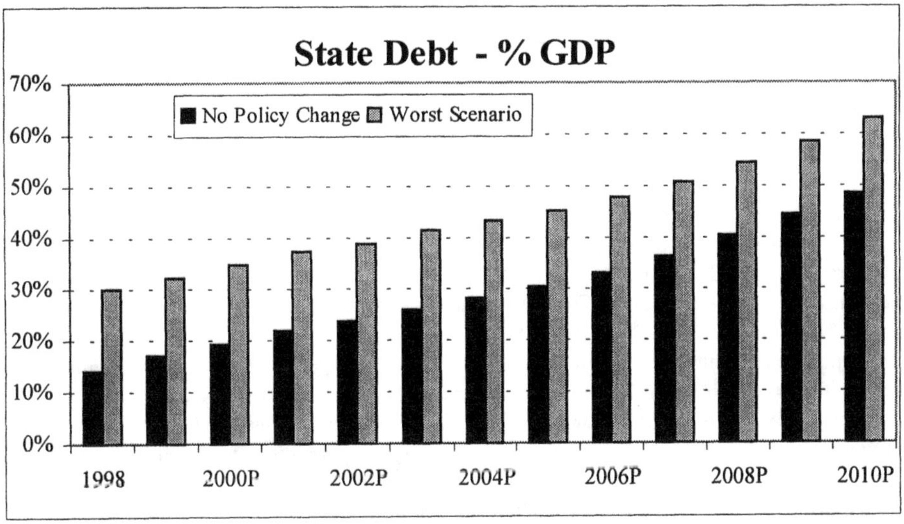

Figure 7.4. Possible scenarios for public debt in the Czech Republic.

The fiscal outlook of the Czech government is thus very worrying. Even though our quantitative analysis has left out the future annual deficits of all "transformation institutions" — and we have not even contemplated pension reform — we have identified deficits of about 5% of GDP each year that are already in the pipeline. Such a relaxed fiscal policy would accumulate debt amounting to 50-65% of GDP in just a decade. The experience of other countries (e.g. Belgium and Italy) shows that this would certainly lead to higher costs in the future, when the interest has to be paid, without necessarily improving the economy's competitiveness or the welfare of its citizens.

ENDNOTES

[1] Bezdek and Stiller (2000) estimate that while expenditures grow faster than nominal wages by a factor of 1.4, budget revenues lag behind nominal wage growth by 15%.

[2] Here we assume a more favourable development than Bezdek and Stiller's (2000) results would suggest, as we rely on a simplified estimate of revenue elasticities that yield a slightly more optimistic budget revenues.

[3] See Polackova-Brixi (2000).

REFERENCES

Vladimír Bezděk a Vladimír Stiller, (2/2000), *Modelování hlavních daňových příjmů české rozpočtové soustavy*, (in Czech), Finance a uver, Prague

Drabek, Zdenek and Schneider Ondrej, (2000), *The Size Of Public Sector, Contingent Liabilities And Structural And Cyclical Deficits*, (1997), The Czech Case, 1993-1999, mimeo

Jelinek Tomas and Schneider, Ondrej, *Time for Pension Reform in the Czech Republic; Pension Trouble Is Brewing in the Visegrad Countries*, Prague, Transitions, 4

Patria Finance,(May 1999), *Czech Fiscal Policy Outlook*; Prague: Economic Focus

Polackova-Brixi, Hana, (3/2000), *Fiskalni rizika nejsou jen v deficitu*, (in Czech), Finance a uver, Prague

State Budgets 1993 - 2000, Ministry of Finance, Czech Republic

Symansky Steven, (1999), *Czech Republic: Medium-Term Fiscal Policy, Projections and Analysis*, Background Paper for the 1999 Article IV Consultation with the Czech Republic; Washington, D.C.: IMF

Schneider Ondrej and Krejdl Aleš, (3/2000), *Strukturální schodky veřejných rozpočtů v ČR* (in Czech), Finance a uver, Prague

Chapter 8

FROM TRANSITION TO ACCESSION - AGRICULTURE IN THE CZECH REPUBLIC, HUNGARY AND POLAND AND THE COMMON AGRICULTURAL

Katarzyna Zawalińska

INTRODUCTION

The assimilation of Central and East European Countries (CEECs) into the Common Agricultural Policy (CAP) of the EU should be somewhat easier now than before the latest CAP reform of March 1999. EU member states have at last accepted a financial framework for the years 2000-2006 and set guidelines for the development of the CAP over the next few years. Thus, the CAP is no longer a moving target for CEECs. The likely amount of annual transfers to current members has become clear. The main instrument of the CAP - price supports – which has raised most EU prices above world prices (leading to both overproduction and highly subsidised exports), is gradually being replaced by direct payments. Rural development has become more important, and is now the second pillar of the CAP.

The most important external pressures for the latest CAP reform have come from the World Trade Organisation, the U.S., and uncertainty over the future size of the EU. Apart from that, internal pressures have also conditioned CAP reform. First, the budget costs of the CAP needed to be controlled by overall budget constraints; second, the CAP needed to adopt broader rural and social aims, such as environmental protection, health and income distribution.

If we compare the accession of the Czech Republic, Hungary and Poland (CEC-3) with previous accessions, we see that it is not as "untypical" as is sometimes stressed. In terms of population growth, it would be very similar to that of the accession of Greece, Spain and Portugal in the 1980s (see Table 8.1). Population growth would actually be smaller (59.1 million or 15.9%) than after the 'western enlargement' to the UK, Ireland and Denmark in 1973 (64 million people or 31% of the EU's population at that time). Also the increase in agricultural area after the accession of the CEC-3 would not be a revolution, since after the enlargements in 1973 and in the 1980s these indicators grew twice as much as they will in the case of the CEC-3. Farm population will rise by 4.6 million, which is comparable to the accession of Greece, Portugal and Spain, but much higher than in previous enlargements. However, it is usually thought that the employment figures for CEC-3 are inflated by hidden unemployment in rural areas. This is especially true of Poland, where during recent years employment in agriculture has grown, bringing some people in from urban areas.[1] The largest difference between the 'eastern enlargement' and previous ones lies in the poverty of the CEC-3, since GDP per head in these countries is on average 58% lower than in the EU (see Table 8.1).

Table 8.1. Changes in area, population and welfare after successive enlargements

Enlargement:	1973 (UK, Ire., Den.)	1980s (Gre., Spain, P)	1995 (Austr., Fin., Sw)	200?* (Cz., Hu., Pol.)
Increase in population (Mio)	64	58	22	59,1
Percent population increase	31%	21%	6%	15,9%
Increase in agric. Area (Mio ha)	27	41	10	29
Percent agric. Area increase	41%	41%	7%	21,2%
Increase in farm population (Mio)	1,1	4	0,6	4,6
Percentage difference in GDP per head	-10%	-33%	6%	-58%

* Based on data of 1996

Source: Based on Josling T.E., Pearson S. R., (1981)

For CEC-3 farmers, entering the CAP will be a great opportunity to improve their financial and social situation since, the so-called "Common

Organisation of the Market" (COM) in the CAP guarantees prices for more than 60% of EU agricultural output. However, the scale of costs and benefits from this accession for both parties (the EU and CEC-3) will depend on many factors, which are analysed in this chapter.

The main goal of this chapter is to present the conflict of interests between the three applicants in relation to their participation in CAP. The next section of the chapter is of an informative character and briefly describes elements of CAP history, instruments and mechanisms. It begins with a short review of literature on the eastern enlargement of the CAP. Section 1 presents the current agricultural situation in CEC-3 and compares it with the situation in some other CECs considered to be first-wave countries[2] (Slovenia, Estonia), and in the present EU-15. Section 2 considers the fiscal and other consequences of the eastern enlargement of the CAP for the CEC-3 as well as for the EU-15.

1. THE COMMON AGRICULTURAL POLICY

1.1 The Impact of the Eastern Enlargement

The literature addresses the problems connected with the accession of the CEECs to the European Union, and particularly stresses the issue of costs for an extended EU. Quantitative analyses of the agricultural impact of EU enlargement are typically performed in either a partial equilibrium or a general equilibrium framework. However, there are significant differences among the models applied as well as in their results.[3]

The lowest estimate of the costs of EU enlargement to the CEC-3 plus Slovakia is about EUR 4 billion per year (Brenton and Gros, 1993), while the highest is EUR 37 billion per year (Anderson and Tyers, 1993) – see Table 8.2. However, we should remember that these early analyses showed the possible effects of the Pre-Agenda 2000 CAP on agricultural markets and the budget, and therefore they tend to overestimate the costs of CAP enlargement at present. What is more, they are based on output levels and prices that have already changed very much in the CECs. Over the last few years, the price gap between the EU and CEEC has decreased substantially.

Table 8.2. Estimated CAP costs of Eastern enlargement for CEECs

STUDY	COSTS (billion ECU)
Anderson and Tyers (1995)*	37
Tyers (1994) for CE-3**	34
Brenton and Gros (1993)	4-31
Mahé (1995)	6-16
Tangermann and Josling (1994)***	9-14
Slater and Atkinson (1995)	5-15
Tangermann (1996)	13-15
R. Baldwin, J.Francois, R. Portes (1997)*	10
Bojnec et.al (1998)*	9-15

* For CE-4: The Czech Republic, Hungary, Poland and Slovak Republic.
Further calculations, made after the Agenda 2000 proposal (from 1997 on) compare accessions taking into account a reformed CAP (Münch and Tangermann 1998, Banse and Münch 1998, Bojnec et.al. 1998, and Münch 1999).
**For CE-3: Czechoslovakia, Hungary, Poland
*** For CE-3 + Romania and Bulgaria
Source: R. Baldwin, J.Francois, R. Portes (1997), Nielsen Ch.(1999)

Münch 's (1999) paper, which is one of the latest and most comprehensive works devoted to the subject, focuses on the market and budgetary effects of CAP accession for five CECs, i.e. the Czech Republic, Estonia, Hungary, Poland and Slovenia (CEC -5). He uses the European Simulation Model (ESIM) to analyse the effects on the five acceding countries and the EU of the enlargement of the CAP. The analysis is based on five scenarios:

- The MEMBER scenario assumes that although CEC-5 are in the EU, at first they do not participate in the Common Agricultural Policy;
- In the AGENDA scenario, the CEC-5 are assumed to be integrated into the CAP and the Single Market from 2003. In that year a complete alignment of policies, prices, tariffs and other measures takes place. Therefore all CAP measures apply to the Central European members from that date, except direct payments. Quotas for sugar and dairy products and export measures on the pork, poultry and egg sectors are defined in such a way that WTO export competition constraints are met;
- The third scenario (AGENDA+DIR[4]) assumes that the CEC-5 will become eligible for direct payments for dairy and beef cattle as well as for arable crops. The cattle payments take into account the constraints arising from the abundance of small producers (90 animals per enterprise) and the constraints on dairy cow numbers arising from the milk quota system;
- In the above scenarios technical progress occurs at conventional rates such as 2.3 percent per annum for corn yields. The scenario AGENDA+DIR +TP varies this assumption and sets yearly rates of technical progress 50 percent higher from 2006. Rapid growth in yields in CEC is very likely especially for crops and intensive livestock

production. This development may be caused by increased investment due to greater availability of capital, lower risk in contracting and increasing competition in downstream sectors and structural change.

- The last scenario AGENDA+DIR+NQ varies the policies applied to the sugar and the dairy sectors. The Agenda 2000 proposal does not include the sugar regime, which consequently remains one of the most protected crops in the CAP. Moreover, the question of future milk quotas after 2006 is still open. This scenario analyses the effects of lifting these quotas.

As far as budget implications are concerned, ESIM generates projections for net expenditure on trade measures, i.e. export subsidies minus tariff revenues, as well as on compensatory and headage payments. The budgetary expenditures are illustrated in Figure 8.1.

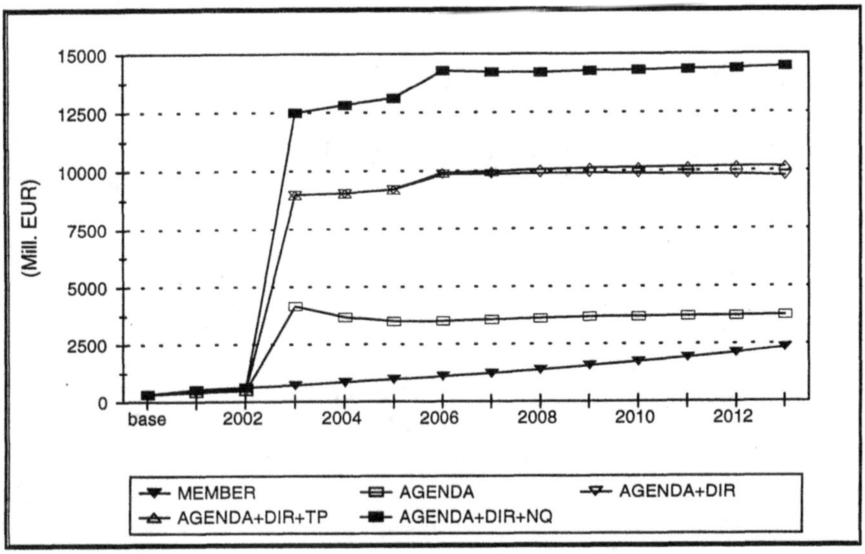

Figure 8.1. Development of Budgetary Expenditure for Market Guarantee.

In the MEMBER scenario, national government spending on CEC agriculture gradually rises to EUR 2.5 billion in 2013 (in the baseline projection). This is a result of growing net exports and increasing protection due to appreciating real exchange rates. Integration into the EU under the AGENDA scenario in 2003, i.e. without direct payments, would result in EUR 3 billion spending in 2013. Strikingly, this is only EUR 500 million more than the expenditure expected from national policies under the MEMBER scenario.

The complete introduction of the Agenda 2000 measures in AGENDA+DIR increases the costs to close to EUR 10 billion by the end of the simulation period. The bulk of the spending results from direct payments for arable area. The spending in AGENDA+DIR+TP is only somewhat higher if technical progress is 50 percent higher than in the other scenarios. This is different in the AGENDA+DIR+NQ scenario, in which the milk and sugar supplies are able to expand freely and react to price developments. In this case, expenditure would amount to EUR 15 billion.

Münch also estimates the share of each CEC-5 in the expenditures of the EU under the AGENDA+DIR scenario in 2006. The two small countries, Slovenia and Estonia, have a share of less than 2 percent of total *additional* EU spending. A larger share goes to the Czech Republic and Hungary. However, the bulk, 60 percent of expenditure for agricultural policies, falls to Poland, which has the largest agricultural sector, the largest amount of arable land and cattle and a large share of higher protected commodities in total production.

1.2 The future evolution of the CAP

The European Commission in its "Agenda 2000", highlighted the need for a further evolution of the CAP. The need for the reform was explained by various factors 'foremost internal in nature'.

- First, the current level of prices in the Union is still too high. If this is not corrected, the consequences will be growing surpluses and, consequently, costs. The Union will gradually lose its position on both the world and internal market, not only in agricultural products but also in processed goods. This would have an adverse effect on employment as well.
- **Second, the CAP has had a number of negative effects, which were only partially corrected by the 1992 reform. The support it provides is distributed unequally and is concentrated on regions and producers who are not the most disadvantaged. This is having a negative effect on regional development planning and rural communities, which have suffered badly from the decline in agricultural activity in many regions. At the same time, other regions have seen the development of excessively intensive farming practices, which often have a serious impact in terms of the environment and animal diseases.**
- Third, the current way the CAP operates was designed for a Community of six and has not been changed much since. It is not suited to a Union of fifteen, which is to welcome further members.

These internal factors, which would have been enough to justify reforming of the CAP are strengthened by external challenges:

1. The need to adapt EU agriculture to an increasingly competitive international context characterised by further moves towards trade

liberalisation. New multilateral trade negotiations started in 1999 in the second stage of the Uruguay Round. The Union needs to cut border protection, reduce export subsidies and reshape internal support instruments. There is also a need to introduce environmental and social standards at the international level and to take consumers' requirements into account (e.g. food safety and quality).

2. The second big challenge relates to EU enlargement to the Central and East European countries, which could potentially add over 100 million consumers, whose average purchasing power is one third of that of the current consumers in the Union. Agricultural area could be expanded by 50% and the agricultural labour force could double.

The latest decisions on the future shape of CAP reform were made in Berlin in 1999. Eventually, an agreement was reached, with however less ambitious goals than had been proposed in Agenda 2000. Nevertheless, the agreement fully endorses the philosophy of Agenda 2000 and its main principles: (1) to reduce price intervention and replace it with direct payments; and (2) to increase support for environmental and structural measures within the EU.

The following technical adjustments were accepted[5]:

1. Lower institutional prices in the cereal, beef, and dairy sectors (by 15%, 20%, and 20% respectively).[6]
2. Making rural development a second pillar of the CAP. This second pillar of the policy is to be guided by a multi-functional, integrated approach to rural development. On the one hand, it recognises that farming plays a number of roles, including the preservation of the rural heritage. On the other hand, it recognises that the creation of alternative sources of income must be an integral part of rural development policy.

The guiding principles for rural development policy are those of decentralization of responsibilities and flexibility. It is for EU member states to come forward with proposals for rural development programs.

1.3 CAP Instruments and Institutions

The CAP is implemented through the Common Organisation of the Market (COM) and financed by the European Agricultural Guarantee and Guidance Fund (EAGGF).

The plans for the creation of a common agricultural market were set out in the 1950s, at time when Europe was a net importer of most food products. The EEC member states were differently organised at national level. Although they intervened in one way or another to ensure the income of their farmers and stable supply for their consumers but the systems of intervention varied from one country to another. Hence, there was a need for a common organisation of the market. The **Common Organisation of the Market** was created to remove obstacles to intra-Community trade and assure common protection at frontiers. The intervention systems can be divided into two main categories: **direct income support** for farmers, which prevailed in the UK before its entry to the Community, and the **system of price support** on the internal market combined with external protection. The later represented 80% of the total public support to agriculture in OECD countries and was chosen by the EEC. The *price support system* seemed less expensive at that time, as Europe was a net importer of food, so that the income from import levies was greater than expenditure on export subsidies. Furthermore, higher prices stimulated agricultural output and productivity. They also tended to guarantee self-sufficiency in basic agricultural products and foodstuffs, which was another point in their favour. If they were set too high, however, they could naturally lead to production surpluses, which is what happened.

The **Common Organisation of the Market (COM)** takes different forms for different products. Based on a single market, it guarantees prices for more than 60% of agricultural output. There are four main types of COM:

1. Direct aids[7] to producers linked to factors of production such as land and livestock. Aid is based on reference periods and on the existence of production control mechanisms. This covers: cereals, oilseeds, protein crops, sheep meat and beef;
2. Assistance that is proportional to production levels. This covers: olive oil, tobacco, cotton, certain processed fruit, and vegetables such as citrus fruit, tomatoes and prunes, and to a certain extent, table wine.
3. Income support for producers of dairy products and sugar.
4. The fourth type allows the market itself to adjust to fluctuations in supply and demand with little intervention. This applies to fruit and vegetables, quality wines, pig meat, poultry meat, eggs and honey.

The European Agricultural Guarantee and Guidance Fund (EAGGF) is made up of two sections: the Guarantee section and the Guidance section.

The Guarantee Section finances Community expenditure under the policy on prices and markets, including compensatory payments under the reform of the CAP, and accompanying measures. About 90% of the EAGGF goes on this, of which 70% is spent on direct payments to farmers.

While the Guarantee Section is the consequence of market policy, the **Guidance Section** implements structural policy. It contains the Community resources allocated to aid for the modernization of holdings, the installation of young farmers, aid for processing, marketing, diversification and so on. It should be mentioned that, together with the European Regional Fund and the European Social Fund, it also finances rural development. Planning and execution of these measures is fairly decentralized, in co-operation with the individual Member States or regions, and the principle of co-financing applies. The Guidance Section's share in the total farm budget is usually 10%. The Guidance Section is broken down by the following objectives: Objective 1 (for underdeveloped regions), Objective 5a (for agricultural structure in all regions), Objective 5b (for rural development in certain limited areas), Objective 6 (for Nordic regions). It is to be noted that, as a proportion of the EU budget, the EAGGF is on a downward trend - from 70% of the total EU budget in 1980 to around 57.4% in 1998, and supposedly less than 50% in the period 2000-2006.

Rural development

Since the mid-1980s, the European Union has been focusing to an increasing extent on the development of rural areas. The aim of rural policy is to meet the challenges posed by the depopulation and abandonment of many areas. The Maastricht Treaty, which came into force in 1993, mentions rural areas specifically in the context of economic and social cohesion, i.e. the Union's policy of assisting the peripheral, lesser-developed regions to catch up. In the period 1994-1999, one third of the EU budget - ECU 141 billion at 1992 prices - was devoted to this policy of economic and social cohesion. Concerning rural development, the principal objective is to maintain viable rural communities. A competitive agricultural sector is an essential element in this process. In addition, however, diversification of the rural economy is a key element. In this context, the Union is concentrating on developing small and medium-sized businesses, exploiting new technology in favour of rural areas, rural tourism and so on.

2. THE AGRICULTURAL SITUATION IN THE CZECH REPUBLIC, HUNGARY AND POLAND

2.1 The share of agriculture in the economies of CEC-3

In terms of area, contribution to GDP, and share in total employment agriculture is still relatively more important in the CEECs than in the EU. Only in the Czech Republic, Slovakia and Slovenia are the relative sizes of agriculture comparable to the EU average. The share of agricultural production in GDP has declined in the CECs since 1989, but is still much higher than the EU-15 average in the case of Hungary and Poland (see Table 8.3). The share of the total workforce employed in agriculture is particularly high in Poland where, unlike the Czech Republic and Hungary, it has increased. The Czech Republic's relative share of agriculture in the economy is much smaller than Hungary's and Poland's. In 1997 the contribution of agriculture to GDP was 2.1% - down from 6.2% in 1990. The share of employment in agriculture dropped by more than half - from 9.6% in 1990 to 4.0% of total employment in 1997 (Table 8.3). In Hungary, agriculture is still of major importance to the national economy. In 1997, agriculture accounted for 5.7% of Hungary's GDP and employed 7.7% of the working population (down from 17.5% in 1990). During the recession of 1990-1993, agriculture suffered more than the Hungarian economy as a whole: the cumulative fall of agricultural GDP amounted to 31%, against 18% for the rest of the economy. However, recovery has been visible since 1994, and has been faster for agriculture than for the economy in general.[8]

Table 8.3. Share of agriculture: in total labor force and GDP, in EU and CEEC (selected years)

	Share in total labor force (%)				Share in National Output (%)				Productivity gap (%) ***	
Countries	1955	1975	1990	1997	1955	1975	1989	1997	1990	1997
Belgium	9,3	3,8	2,6	2,7	8,1	3,2	2,4	1,1	8	59
Czech R.	26*	14,9	9,6	4,0	-	-	6,3	2,1	34	48
Denmark	25,4	8,9	5,6	3,7	19,2	7,4	4,2	2,4	25	35
France	25,9	10,7	5,5	4,6	12,3	5,6	3,3	1,9	40	59
Germany	18,9	7,8	4	2,9	8,5	2,9	1,7	0,8	58	72
Greece	52*	36,6	22,9	19,9	-	19	16,5	5,9	28	70
Hungary	38*	22	17,5	7,7	-	-	15,6	5,7	11	26
Ireland	38,8	22,2	14,3	10,9	29,6	18,1	10,5	3,4	27	69
Italy	39,5	15,5	8,6	6,5	21,6	8,7	4	2,5	53	62
Luxem-bourg	25	6,6	3,6	2,4	9	3,5	2,4	0,7	33	71
Netherlands	13,7	6,2	4,5	3,5	12	4,7	4,6	2,6	-2	26
Poland	48*	34,2	27,5	26.7**	-	-	11,8	5,1	57	81
Portugal	44*	28,8	17,8	13,3	-	7,3	5,5	2,4	69	82
Spain	42*	22	11,9	8,3	-	-	4,7	3,3	61	60
UK	4,8	2,7	2,2	1,9	5	1,9	1,5	0,7	32	63

Source: El-Agraa Ali M., (1990), WDI 99,European Commission, Directorate for Agriculture (GD VI), (1998a),
* in 1960
** in 1996
*** 100 - (agri share in national output/agri share in total labor force)*100

In Poland, agriculture also plays significant role. The contribution of agriculture to total GDP is still relatively high at an estimated 5.1% in 1997 (Table 8.3), in spite of a "transition recession" similar to the Hungarian. The agricultural labour force is officially 26.7% of total employment (there are 4.13 million farmers). However, only 31% of all agricultural households produce mostly for market purposes. The lowest labor productivity of agricultural production is in Poland, and between 1990 and 1997 the "productivity gap" between agriculture and the rest of the economy increased from 67% to 81%. In the Czech Republic the gap fell from 68% to 47%, while in Hungary it increased from only 11% to 26%, but remained the lowest among CEC-3 (Table 8.3). However, in the case of Poland and Hungary these changes in the "agricultural productivity gap" are due rather to rapid growth in the rest of the economy. At 67% the agricultural productivity gap in the EU was significantly higher than in Hungary or the Czech Republic in 1996.

2.2 The structure of land ownership

In the Czech Republic and Hungary, nearly all cultivated land in the pre-transition era was in hands of state farms (Poland was the major exception, since private agriculture dominated even during the central planning period). The main objectives of the structural reforms were therefore the decollectivisation of agriculture and re-establishment of private property rights. In the Czech Republic and Hungary, the average size of the biggest (previously state-owned) farms has decreased significantly, while the size of family farms has started to increase slowly. The maintenance of this tendency may contribute to an increase in efficiency, as the larger units become more manageable and the smaller ones acquire more land and benefit from economies of scale. In Poland, the structural reforms were less rapid, with many small and fragmented private farms, struggling with efficiency and financial problems.

The privatization of Czech agriculture, which in the pre-transition period was dominated by very large scale collective and state farms, has led to the emergence of three new forms of farming: *the transformed coops*, *joint stock or limited liability companies* and *family farms*. The major part, 43%, of agricultural land is still in hands of the *co-operative farms* – see Table 8.4, although their average size has decreased from over 2,578 ha in the pre-transition period to around 1,447 ha. The *joint stock and limited liability companies*, which have been created from the previous state farms and from property withdrawn from the former coops, farm about 32% of agricultural land and cover on average 690 ha (compared to an average size of the former state farms of over 9,000 ha) and specialize in animal production (pigs, poultry and eggs).[9] The remaining quarter of agricultural land is farmed by *individual producers*, often on very small plots of less than 3 ha, producing mainly for own consumption and local markets. In contrast to larger farms, family farms significantly increased their profitability in recent years. Of the individual farms exceeding 3 ha, the average size is above 30 ha, with quite a number of larger farms of over 100 ha operating on leased land and with hired labor. Still pending is the sale of around 500,000 ha of state owned land, which are held by the Land Fund. For the time being this land (about a quarter of all farmland) is being rented out.[10]

As in the Czech Republic, in Hungary the process of reforms resulted in a rather fragmented structure of land ownership. However, Hungary has carried out a much more successful privatisation of agricultural land. The 1,200 Hungarian collective farms have been almost completely privatised. Of the 120 state farms, the majority has been privatised, one third have been liquidated, and a quarter is still under state ownership (Table 8.4). As for land use, 1.2 million individual farms use more than half the agricultural land area (54%) and ensure nearly 60% of the output. Only 5% of these farms are full time holdings. Co-operatives and other corporate farms occupy respectively 28% and 14% of the land.

Table 8.4. CEC-3 farm structure according to land use

	cooperatives*		state farms**		other corporate farms***		private/individual farms****		last census
Share in total agricultural area (%)									
	pre-transition	current	pre-transition	current	pre-transition	current	pre-transition	current	
Czech R	61	43	38	2	-	32	0	23	1995
Hungary	80	28	14	4	-	14	6	54	1996
Poland	4	3	19	7	-	8	77	82	1996
Average size (ha)									
	cooperatives*		state farms**		other corporate farms***		private/individual farms****		
	pre-transition	current	pre-transition	current	pre-transition	current	pre-transition	current	
Czech R	2578	1447	9443	521	-	690	5	34	
Hungary	4179	833	7138	7779	-	204	0,3	3	
Poland	335	222	3140	620	-	333	6,6	7	

* collective pre-transition, transformed into private (producer) cooperatives/associations currently

** state farms pre-transition, remaining state farms and state held/controlled enterprises currently

*** joint stock, limited liability companies and other business entities currently

**** household plots pre-transition, individual (part time)farms currently

Source: European Commission, Directorate for Agriculture (GD VI), (1998a)

Changes in the structure of land ownership in Poland are the least impressive of the three countries. Average farm size increased only by 12.9% over eight years from 7.0 ha in 1988 to 7.9% ha in 1996. The number of individual holdings went down by 6% to a total of 2.04 million (Table 8.5). There is a visible polarisation in the structure of private holdings, which is partly due to the liquidation of state farms. As a result, the share of family holdings of over 10ha in agricultural land use has increased by over 11 percentage points, with all the gains among holdings of over 20ha, which accounted for only 1% of land use in 1988, and now represents 24%.

However, a significant obstacle on the road to efficient cultivation of land is the fragmentation of farms into small plots. Only 16.5% of farms own their land in one piece. Although little state owned land has been privatised, much of it is now rented to private farmers so that the land farmed by the state sector has been reduced from around 20% in 1989 to 7% in 1996.

Table 8.5. Number and size of holdings in 1988 and 1996 in Poland

DISTRIBUTION OF FARMS ACCORDING TO FARM AREA							
Total number of farms			1-5 ha	5-10 ha	10-20 ha	20-50 ha	>50 ha
1988	000 farms	2 168	1 159	637	372	na	na
	%	100%	53%	29%	17%	-	-
1996	000 farms	2 041	1 130	521	307	75	9
	%	100%	55%	26%	15%	4%	0%
DISTRIBUTION OF UTILISED AGRICULTURAL AREA ACCORDING TO FARM AREA							
Total land area			1-5 ha	5-10 ha	10-20 ha	20-50 ha	>50 ha
1988	000 farms	15 280	3 731	5247	6302	na	na
	%	100%	24%	34%	41%	-	-
1996	000 farms	16 141	3 403	4237	4650	2249	1602
	%	100%	21%	26%	29%	14%	10%

Source: European Commission, Directorate for Agriculture (GD VI), (1998d)

2.3 Agricultural trade

The Czech Republic, Hungary and Poland are the largest exporters in value terms among all CEECs in the first wave. Poland and the Czech Republic are also large importers and Hungary is the only net exporter of food in recent years in the group. The most important agricultural trade partner for most CECs is the EU, in particular on the import side, having a share of between 40% and 55%, although this has declined somewhat since 1995, as trade among the CECs themselves has increased. The EU is also important as an export destination.

The EU, as the Czech Republic's biggest trading partner, takes around 50% of Czech agricultural imports and around 35% of Czech exports of, although both have declined in the last three years. Among the CEC-3 Hungary is the only net exporter of agricultural and food products. In the first years of transition, agricultural exports accounted for 24% of total exports, and agricultural imports for 8% of total imports. However, in recent years the contribution of agriculture and food processing to overall Hungarian exports has decreased to 15% (in 1997). Hungary's main trading partner by far is the EU, with 47.4% of agro-food exports and 43.1% of imports (1996). Within Polish foreign trade, agricultural products represented 13% of exports and 9% of imports in 1997. At the beginning of the transformation the agricultural trade balance was positive but since 1992 it has been negative. Poland's main agricultural trading partner is the EU.

2.4 Agricultural support and rural policies

In most CEECs agriculture was quite heavily supported in the pre-transition era. Under the initial price and trade liberalisation, at the beginning of Transformation, support for agriculture either dropped drastically, as in Hungary and the Czech Republic, or even turned into net taxation of this sector as in Estonia and Poland. After the initial liberalisation shock, measures were introduced to stabilise the agricultural sector and more recently there has been a tendency in the CEC-3 countries to increase support again as indicated in Figure 8.2.

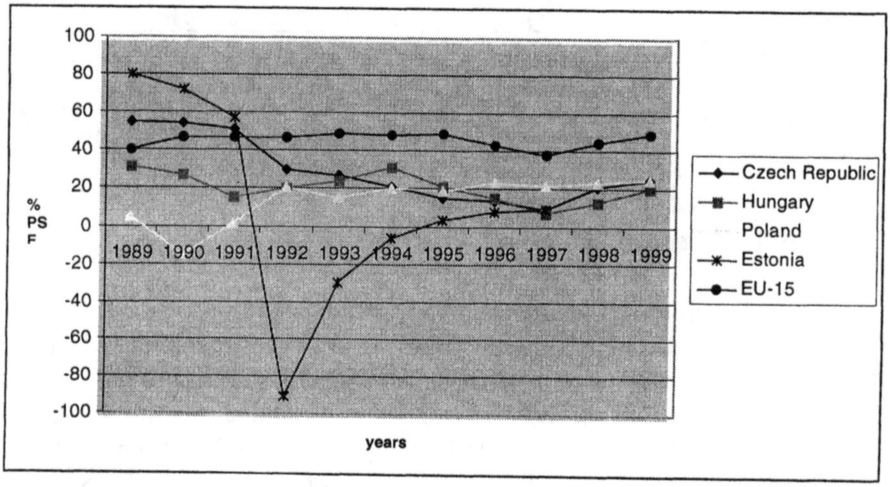

Figure 8.2. Percentage PSE CEECs-EU

As measured by the percentage producer subsidy estimate (PSE)[11] support for agriculture in the Czech Republic has been declining since the early 1990s. The trend was reversed after 1997, and the level of support increased to 21%, as a result of increases in market price support (mainly for pigmeat and sugar) and in direct payments (area and headage payments). However, in 1998 support was still half of the pre-transition level. In Hungary, the situation was similar. Support to agriculture increased in 1998 as a result of increases in market price support (mainly for poultry and oilseeds) and to some extent in budgetary transfers to agriculture. However, as in the Czech Republic the level of support did not reach that of the pre-transition period. Only in Poland has support, measured by %PSE, increased compared to the pre-transition level, and it has almost doubled compared to the early 1990s.

Despite the fact that support for agriculture has increased in the CEC-3, the overall support level measured by the OECD's producer subsidy estimates is much lower than in the EU. In 1998 the EU PSE was 45%, compared with 21% in the Czech Republic, 13% in Hungary and 23% in Poland - see Figure 8.2.

Across the CEECs, agricultural policies use a wide range of support instruments: from market price support (import protection, and/or domestic floor prices) to several types of direct input subsidies, investment expenditure, and tax exemptions. Generally, agricultural policies in the CEECs have not been very stable, with frequent changes in instruments and in the range of commodities and activities covered. The main market price support instruments applied are border measures (tariffs, import/export licensing and export subsidies) and intervention in the market to underpin minimum or floor prices. The countries apply domestic floor prices for several of the main commodities, particularly for livestock products, but generally at lower or much lower levels than in the EU. The gap has become smaller in recent years due to increase in support prices and real appreciation of domestic currencies. The changes in price support, world market developments and some recovery in domestic demand have led to an increase in producer prices, somewhat more for crop products than for animal products. Thus price gaps at farm gate level with the EU have tended to decline over time. However, in most cases support prices are still lower than in the EU, although for cereals, in particular wheat and barley, CEEC producer prices exceed or have come within 20% of EU levels. On the other hand, for maize farm gate prices are still generally somewhat lower and for sugar beet about half the EU level (Figure 8.3)

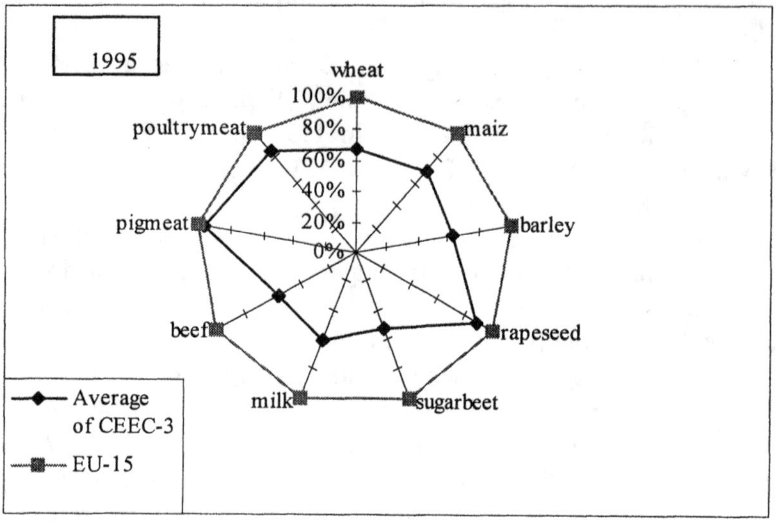

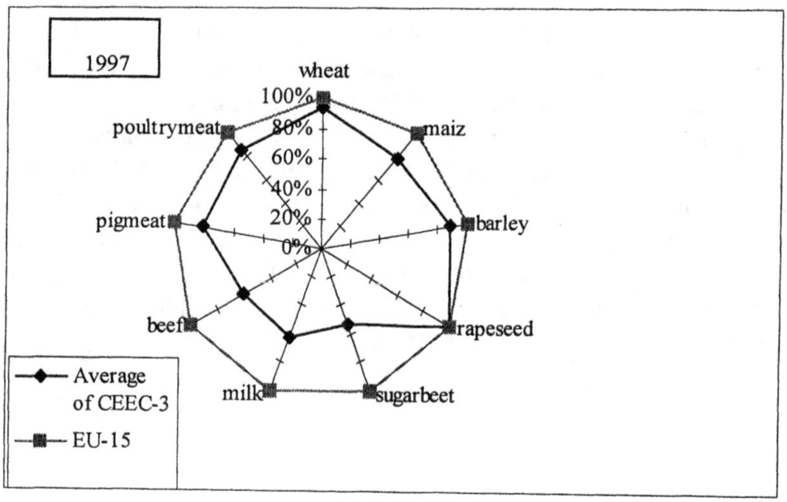

Figure 8.3. Comparison of prices between CEC-3 and the EU in 1995 and in 1997

The most expensive policy is found in Poland, but in terms of expenditure per farmer, the most was spent by Hungary (Figure 8.4). In Poland the expenditure was EUR 3.4 billion, EUR 821 per farmer (around 2/15 of the EU level). In Hungary, the agricultural budget for 1997 amounted to EUR 477 million or EUR 1,716 per farmer. In the Czech Republic budget expenditures amounted to around EUR 315 million which was EUR 1,491 per farmer.

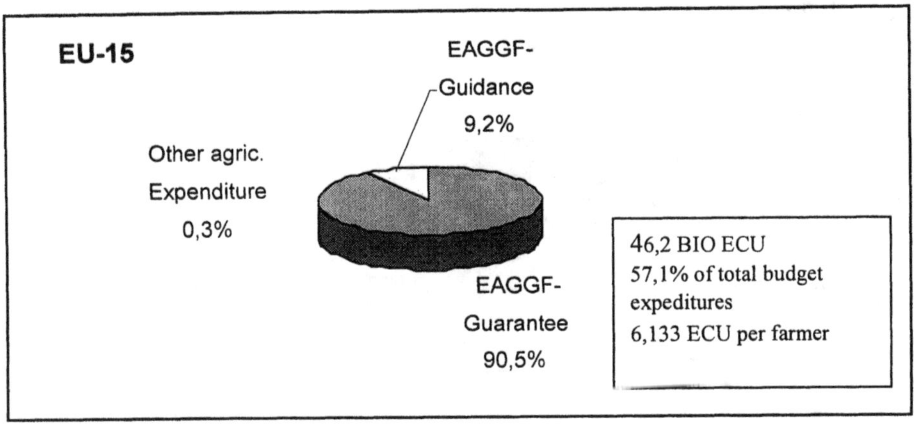
EU-15
EAGGF-
Guidance
9,2%
Other agric.
Expenditure
0,3%
EAGGF-
Guarantee
90,5%
46,2 BIO ECU
57,1% of total budget
expeditures
6,133 ECU per farmer

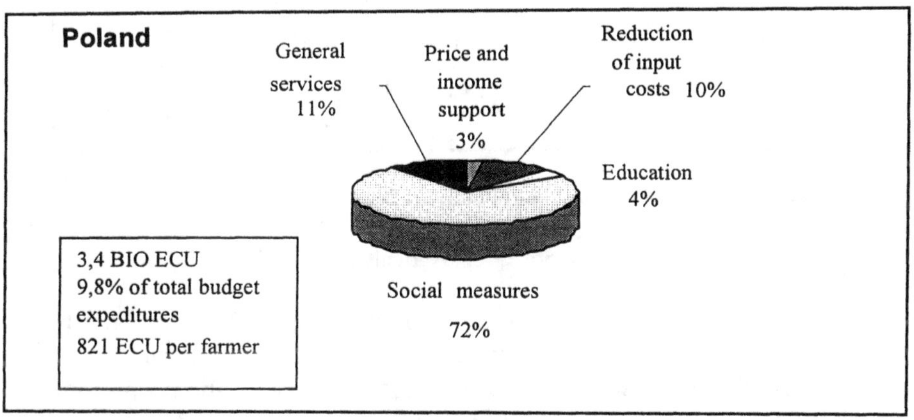
Poland
General
services
11%
Price and
income
support
3%
Reduction
of input
costs 10%
Education
4%
Social measures
72%
3,4 BIO ECU
9,8% of total budget
expeditures
821 ECU per farmer

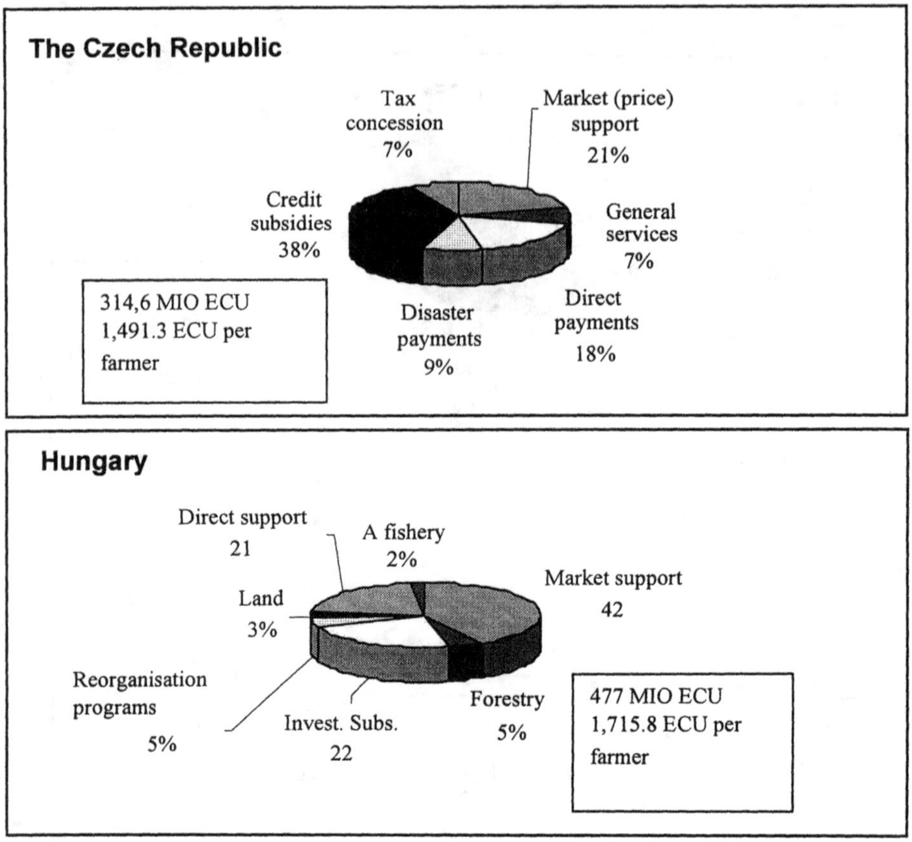

Figure 8.4. Agricultural expenditures in the EU and CEC-3 in 1997

Source: European Commission, Directorate for Agriculture (GD VI), (1998a),(1998b), (1998c), (1998d)

Budgetary expenditures on agriculture also differ significantly among the CEC-3 when expressed as a percentage share of GDP. In the Czech Republic, expenditures constitute 0.7% of GDP, which was about one third of agriculture's contribution to GDP in 1997. The agricultural budget in Hungary represented around1.2% of GDP, while agriculture's contribution amounted to 5.7% of GDP. In Poland, expenditures amounted to 2.8% of GDP in 1997, while budget expenditures for the agricultural sector amounted to 9.8% of total budget expenditures. However, this number does not reveal all relevant expenditures, since there is also an implicit fiscal loss connected with tax exemptions for Polish farmers[12], equivalent to 0.25% of GDP.[13] That gives total agricultural expenditures in Poland of about 3% of GDP, which is half of agriculture's contribution to GDP. Poland spends the highest share of GDP on its agriculture. Also comparing expenditures with the contribution of agriculture, Poland is in the worst position: agriculture consumes half of its contribution to GDP, while in the Czech Republic it consumes one third and in Hungary one fifth of its contribution. However, if 'social measures' in the Polish fiscal accounts were classified outside the agricultural budget (as in the case of the Czech Republic and Hungary) then budgetary expenditures on agriculture would come closer to their counterparts in the other CEC. They would amount to 2.46% of total budget expenditures, instead of around 10%. Including tax exemptions they would reach 0.95% of Polish GDP, instead of 3% - which means more than in the Czech Republic but less than in Hungary. Hence, budgetary expenditure on Polish agriculture would be one fifth of agriculture's contribution to GDP, a similar level to that in Hungary. Of course, with their smaller agricultural populations, the Czech Republic and Hungary spend less on social measures for farmers than Poland does. Nevertheless, it is not clear to what extent such expenditures should be thought of as going to agriculture as opposed to the poor and old, who also happen to be farmers.

3. FISCAL ASPECTS OF THE ENLARGEMENT OF THE CAP TO THE CZECH REPUBLIC, HUNGARY AND POLAND

3.1 Pre-accession fiscal adjustment

Countries, which formally apply for EU membership, usually receive pre-accession aid from the EU. Poland, Hungary and the Czech Republic will also get such aid in the field of agriculture and will be able to benefit from it until they formally become EU members and start to participate in the Common Agricultural Policy and structural Funds. During the period 1999-2006, agricultural expenditure for the applicant countries would comprise *pre-accession aid* and *expenditure related to the accession of the new Member States*.

Pre-accession agricultural aid, amounting to EUR 520 million per year (at constant 1999 prices), will be granted from the year 2000 (Table 8.6).[14] This will be provided in areas such as the improvement of (1) market mechanisms and technical infrastructure (to make them compatible with the single market), (2) marketing channels and (3) food quality control. These measures will be implemented on the basis of national programs co-financed by the EU. That is around one sixth of the agricultural budget of Poland.[15] The applicant countries really start to participate in agricultural transfers only after joining CAP. Thus, pre-accession agricultural aid from the EU is likely to have little direct budgetary effect. More important for budgetary expenditures are the national pre-accession policies adopted by the countries.

Table 8.6. The EU Financial Framework for 1999-2006 (selected positions and years)

EUR (million)	1999	2002	2006	EUR (million)	1999	2002	2006
Agricultural expenditure for EU-15	40 400	46 965	48 760	Agricultural expenditure for the Applicant Countries	0	2 250	4 500
Reformed CAP (Market Measures)	37 800	42 035	43 670	Pre-Accession Aid*	0	550	600
Accompaning Rural Development and Horizontal Fisheries Measures	2 600	4 830	4 990	Estimated Expenditure for Accession:	0	1 700	3 900
Veterinary and Plant-health Measures	100	100	100	CAP Market Measures Rural development measures		1 100 600	1 400 2 500

* It makes 520 million EUR at constant 1999 prices
Source: Based on The European Commission, (1999)

Generally, each of the applicant countries has to choose its path to the CAP. The most desirable objectives for all the countries seem to be improvement in agricultural productivity and improvement in the agricultural to non-agricultural income ratio. As W. Orłowski (1996) shows, there are several policy instruments that could be used to obtain these objectives, but they differ as to their budgetary implications. *Investment in rural development* to increase value added per unit of production (through better agricultural product processing and better production structure). This policy satisfies both of Orlowski's objectives and EU objectives[16], and its costs are relatively easily controlled. *Surplus management* policy stimulates production growth but is very costly and satisfies only one objective - improvement of the agricultural to non-agricultural income ratio, and does not help productivity. *Price support* would be counterproductive, since the resulting short-term increase in farmers' incomes and apparent higher productivity due to artificially higher prices would reduce economic incentives to modernise agriculture and to reduce employment. Greece, which obtained much greater transfers for price support policy than Portugal or Spain, (Greece got 2,8% GDP while Portugal only 0,2% GDP and Spain 0,4%GDP in 1990) has experienced the slowest outflow from its agricultural sector. This amounted to -2.1% a year on average during 1981-1993, while

Portugal and Spain achieved –5.5% and –4.1% outflow respectively. Wrong signals sent to producers through the distorted price structure would lead agricultural producers to invest in areas where no real comparative advantage exists and would result in an excessive increase of output and surpluses. The misallocation of resources would have a detrimental impact on the overall growth of the economy, while inflation would increase due to a faster rise in food prices. Such policy then, would lead to large economic costs (related to implementing tariffs) mainly paid by consumers and partly by the budget (in the form of export subsidies). In the case of *direct payments* to farmers all the costs are borne by the budget. Although the policy is very costly, it guarantees, at least theoretically, most effective (in relative terms) use of funds, since it improves the income ratio, while maintaining pressure for increased productivity, without encouraging over-production. The last policy variant is *reduction in agricultural employment*. This satisfies both objectives and its costs seem easier controlled than those of surplus management, price support or direct payments policy.

We can see that the best pre-accession policies should be based on investment in rural development and reductions in agricultural employment. In addition, such policies are consistent with the objectives defined by the EU for pre-accession agricultural aid, so the expenditures will be partially co-financed. The least effective policies for satisfying the objective of employment reduction, are those concentrated on social payments as in Poland, where the greatest part of the agricultural budget (72% - 76%) is devoted to social measures (see discussion in Section 2.4 and Figure 8.4). Investment in rural areas is more effective. In the Czech Republic 38% of the agricultural budget is spent on credit subsidies (supporting investments in infrastructure) and Hungary, 22% is spent on investment subsidies.[17]

3.2 Post-accession fiscal adjustment

There are no direct contributions from member countries to the CAP. First the countries contribute to the EU general budget and then part of these resources is transferred to the CAP, namely to the EAGGF. The proportion of the contribution from the overall EU budget to the EAGGF has been decreasing gradually. In 1994 total agricultural expenditures amounted to 59.6% of the total EU budget, in 1998 the figure was 55.9%, and in 2006 it is projected to be 49.4% of total EU expenditures. The member states' contributions to the EU budget come from four (national) *own resources*:

1. VAT revenues
2. national percentage contributions
3. custom duties
4. agricultural levies

The VAT contributions' rate amounts to 0.5% of national VAT revenues.[18] This contribution is derived from a hypothetical harmonized VAT rate and is not based on the individual countries' VAT revenues. National contributions are proportional to the shares of national GDP in total EU GNP. At first, the CEC-3 will probably pay less than their GDP shares – as was the case of the Mediterranean countries. Custom duties and agricultural levies depend on the trade structure of the country. 90% of custom revenues from imports from outside the EU go to the EU budget (10% are allowed for collection costs). The overall EU budget, financed by the system of own resources, has a ceiling of 1.27% of the EU GNP.

Now, let us look at the funds received by the countries due to CAP. The CAP is financed from the European Agricultural Guarantee and Guidance Fund. The Guarantee section amounts to 90,5% of the total EAGGF. One third of this section is spent on Market Support (refunds on exports to third countries and intervention to stabilise agricultural markets) and two-third is spent on direct payments to farmers. The Guidance Section amounts to 9.2% of the total EAGGF. These resources are spent on rural development (objectives 1, 5a, 5b, 6).

The benefits to CEC-3 will crucially depend on whether the countries will receive direct payments. EU officials have several times questioned the possibility of participation of CEC-3 in direct payments, on the grounds that these are compensation for limiting previously attained production levels. CEC farmers are likely to face maximum output quotas that are higher than current production levels (see next section), and therefore, according to the EU, need not be compensated for the imposition of these quotas. The CEC view is that the quotas will prevent their farmers from producing as much as they would at CAP prices, and that they should therefore be compensated for this loss. In any event, the amount of transfers budgeted for the post-accession period (between EUR 1.7 billion in 2002 and EUR 3.9 billion in 2006), reveals that the EU has not budgeted for direct payments. The *expenditures relating to the accession of new member states* would be at least twice as high.[19] Direct payments for Poland alone have been estimated at around ECU 2.3 billion.

The introduction of direct payments will raise the expenditures of the EU in CEC (see Section 1.1). According to Münch (1999) the largest part of the extra expenditure on direct payments would fall to arable crops. The crop sector is the one with no EU limits on production so if crop producers from CEC obtain higher prices they will have incentives to increase production. Thus, direct payments for crop producers would be the only way to exercise control over their production as the producers would then be involved in the obligatory and voluntary set aside system. The EU, instead of buying the crop surpluses (coming from increased production), would pay the crop producers directly to compensate them for not producing. Such a policy might even be cheaper for the EU. However, whether it is depends primarily on the difference between EU and CEC prices, and on headage of cattle and acreage of arable land in each country at the moment of accession. If the price gap is large it may trigger a significant increase in production, and then buying the surpluses may be more costly than providing direct payments (Figure 8.5).

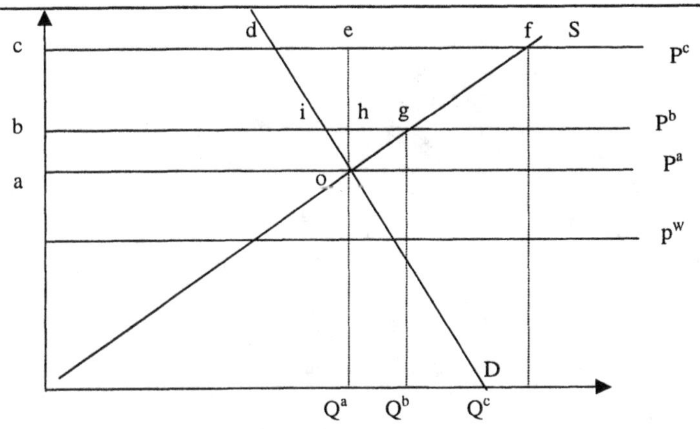

For simplicity, let us assume that each of the CEC-3 has balanced trade in agricultural products * and produces Q^a for a price P^a. We then analyze various levels of the price gap between the EU and CEC and their consequences for direct payments.
If: (1) the EU price is high (e.g. P^c), and (2) the production of the commodity in question is not limited by quotas under the CAP, then the area aofc indicates the value of additional income of CEC farmers after accession, due to increased production and the higher price. If direct payments equal the value of this area, then the EU will gain if direct payments (of the amount of aofc) are less than the cost of buying the increased production (Q^c - Qa) for the amount of Q^aefQ^c ** and selling it outside the EU for p^W.
The net gain from the new prices to CEC, in the absence of quotas, is aofc – aodc (the loss of consumer surplus). The smaller the gap between CEC and EU prices (e.g. P^b - P^a), the smaller the amount of direct payments needed to compensate CEC farmers for not increasing production, because of the lower price gap itself and smaller quantity effects.
* Such assumption does not change the logic of the analysis.
** If the production cannot be sold on the market the EU is obliged to buy it for the intervention price P^c.

Figure 8.5. Consequences of direct payments for the EU and CEC depending on different variants of price gap.

Such reasoning is applicable to all products for which (1) there are no quotas, and (2) prices are much lower than in the EU. These are mainly crops: barley, maize, wheat[20], oilseeds, and beef – see Figure 8.6. However, the products that have the lowest prices relative to the EU are highly protected in EU and have their output limited by quotas. In the case of such products (e.g. milk or sugar) direct payments to CEC producers are pure transfers without additional effects on production. Pig-meat, is not included in supply policy (quota limits) or income policy (direct payments), and as such does not constitute any burden for the EU budget. Thus, the EU is unlikely to agree to direct payments for milk, sugar or pigmeat.

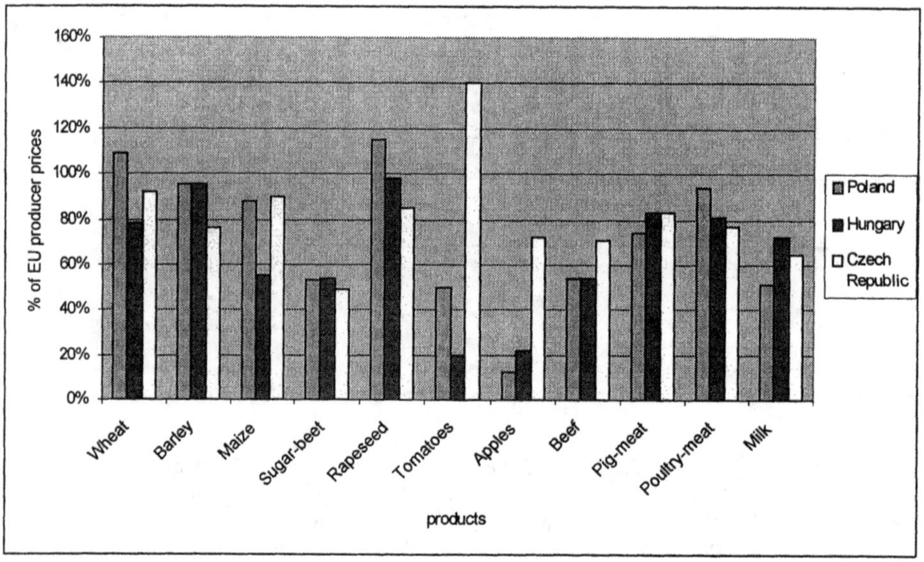

Figure 8.6. Comparison of producer food prices between EU and CEEC-3 in 1997

Source: European Commission, Directorate for Agriculture (GD VI), (1998a),(1998b), (1998c), (1998d)

Now, let us analyze the consequences of implementation of direct payments from the CEC point of view. After CAP accession farmers will gain from 1) the increase in prices of some products (indicated above) as well as from the 2) increase in production (in the case of products with no supply controls or for which negotiated quotas will be higher than current production). It seems that, with or without direct payments, the net increase in the producer surplus after accession should be positive in CEC-3[21], and the net gain for the CEC-3 should also be positive, if EU prices are higher than CEC prices – Figure 8.5. However, it seems likely that at the moment of accession the price gap will be either insignificant or CEC prices may even be higher for many products (see discussion in Section 4).

Nevertheless, whatever the price gap, CEC farmers should receive direct compensatory payments. This is because compensatory payments are not only compensation for reductions in support prices, but they are also play a general income support and pay for environmental services provided by farmers.[22] The deprivation CEC-3 of direct payments would cause an uneven playing field for competition between EU and CEC-3 farmers after accession. This is because EU farmers would have the advantage of additional transfers per unit of production and per capita.

Furthermore, if CEC farmers do not achieve EU quality norms for their products they will not be able to sell them at all on EU market, yet shortage of finance makes the achievement of the quality requirements difficult. Direct payments would allow this "poverty-low quality" trap to be avoided. Direct payments could have positive effects for modernization of farms and rural development in CEEC. Farmers understand the need for modernization of their farms, consolidation in groups of producers, repaying old debts to banks, consolidation of land, quality improvement etc.[23] However, they indicate a lack of resources as the main reason why they cannot deal with these problems. If they had resources from direct payments they could modernize.

4. EFFECTS OF ACCESSION ON AGRICULTURAL PRODUCTION AND FOOD PRICES

As was clarified in the previous section, the differences in levels of food prices between the CEC-3 and the EU will be the most important factor determining the impact of integration on the agricultural sector and the EU budget. However, these differences are gradually decreasing, and this process is accelerating. Therefore, after integration CEC-3 should not experience a radical change in the path of food prices. The reform of CAP will also contribute to this convergence, as well as real appreciation of the CEC currencies due to pre-accession capital inflows (Orlowski 1998). So far the widest gap in food prices between CEC-3 and EU is for those products which are the most protected in the EU: sugar, beef, and milk (Figure 8.6).

Producer prices in the Czech Republic have generally moved up in recent years - somewhat more for crops than for animal products - but in most cases they have not kept up with general inflation. Expressed in EUR domestic price rises have been to some extent mitigated by the depreciation of the Koruna. Nevertheless, price gaps at farm gate level within the EU have tended to decline. Thus in the arable sector, Czech prices for cereals and oilseeds have moved to about 80-90% of the average EU level, although sugar-beets are still at only half of the EU level. In the fruit and vegetable sector Czech tomatoes are relatively expensive, while apples are at around 70 % of the EU level. In the livestock sector Czech dairy prices have moved to around 65% of the EU level, while beef prices have gradually increased to over 70% of the EU level. Despite the still existing differential in cereals prices, Czech pig-meat prices are close to what could be considered normal EU prices, while poultry prices, at 70-80% of the EU level reflect, more or less, the difference in feed costs (Figure 8.6).

In Hungary also, producer prices are generally about 30 percent lower than EU prices, although for cereals, (except maize), pork and poultry, prices are already close to EU levels, for oilseeds, prices are similar. After EU accession, the gap for cereals and dairy products will close further and for beef it will close significantly. The sugar price gap will probably remain wide, but the introduction of quota regimes could limit market impact at accession time.

In simulations made for Poland by SAEPR/FAPA (Piskorz, Guba, et al.,1998) three scenarios were taken into consideration: (a) Polish agricultural policy will not change and Poland will not join the EU untill 2010, (b) Poland will join the EU in 2003, but the CAP remain unreformed, c) Poland will join the EU in 2003 and the CAP will be reformed according to Agenda 2000. The resulting prices are summarised in Table 8.7.

Table 8.7. Food prices in Poland: three scenarios for 2005-2010

Products				Prices (PLN/t) in:			
				2005		2010	
	Base period (1994-1996)	w.o. Akcession	Accession and CAP unchanged	Agenda 2000	w.o. Akcession	Accession and CAP unchanged	Agenda 2000
Wheat	421	358	439	421	369	456	446
Rye	375	342	414	392	330	425	416
Rapeseed	894	968	783	773	982	796	786
Sugar	1 556	1 563	2 423	2 423	1 824	2 403	2 403
Milk	624	639	1 238	1 104	639	1 228	1 095
Butter	4 858	4 969	13 380	11 949	4 969	13 273	11 854
Beef	6 189	7 097	9 469	7 475	7 799	9 394	7 811
Pig-meat	4 777	5 190	4 811	4 781	5 310	5 035	5 011
Poultry-meat	5 291	5 555	3 848	3 830	5 616	3 750	3 736

Source: Piskorz W., Guba W., et al., (1998)

Thus, according to SAEPR/FAPA, after joining the CAP *crop prices* in Poland may rise 20-30%. As a result crop production will rise and demand for feed stuffs will decline. In the *sugar sector* prices will rise nearly by half. As a consequence, domestic sugar consumption should decline and more sugar will be directed for export (either within or outside the EU). Simulation results suggest that *milk* and *butter* prices will rise significantly. Integration will also cause also a rise in beef prices, which are around 60% lower in Poland than in the EU. Pig-meat prices will not rise significantly after Polish accession, while poultry-meat producers will face lower prices under both accession scenarios.

The conclusion is that food prices in the Czech Republic, Hungary and Poland are not expected to increase significantly after joining EU because the price gap is not as big as it was a few years ago and is still declining, and CAP is undergoing gradual liberalisation. Therefore, the expected impact of CAP instruments on the supply side of the CEEC-3 economies will be much lower than has been presented in some previous estimates (e.g. Anderson and Tyers 1993, and Piskorz et al. 1995, etc.).

Such a conclusion is also consistent with the experience of the Mediterranean countries, which joined the EU in the 1980s. None of the countries experienced a quick increase in food prices in the year in which they joined the EU. In Greece (1981) and Portugal (1986) food price inflation even decreased in the year of accession. Spain (1986) experienced increased food price inflation but it was a very small change. Common to all three countries, was the fact that they kept their food price inflation at the same level (Portugal) or even lower (Greece and Spain) during the years following accession. There was an increase in food price inflation in all three countries in the 1990s but this was 3 years after Portugal and Spain joined and eight years in case of Greece. So the conclusion is that changes in prices need not occur immediately as a consequence of joining the EU.

5. CONCLUSION

The experience of the EU and CEC-3 in reforming their agricultural sectors suggests that this is a long and difficult process from a social and political point of view. The beginnings of the CAP were considered as a great success because agricultural production grew and the EEC reached self-sufficiency at reasonable prices. However, after a decade high costs from overproduction and storage of costly surpluses arose. There have been four major attempts to reform the CAP, but the changes have come very slowly. After 30 years, the policy still has the same problems: high support prices, costly surpluses, high expenditures on EAGGF (the CAP is the most costly among EU policies although agriculture accounts for only around 5% of total employment and contributes only 1.7% to GDP). As for the Czech Republic, Hungary and Poland, they also have many problems which are similar to those that were characteristic of the EEC in the 1960s: (1) low productivity (especially in Poland); (2) over-employment together with hidden unemployment; (3) a fragmented structure of land holding and underdeveloped infrastructure in rural areas, (4) lack of alternative job opportunities; and (5) poverty. However, a lot has already changed in CEC-

3. The Czech Republic and Hungary have a share of agriculture in the labour force at the one-digit level. All CEC-3 have carried out reorganisation and privatisation of a significant part of their agricultural area. They have also undertaken attempts to liberalise and expand their agricultural trade. However, the smallest changes have happened in the ownership structure and in infrastructure development. Finance matters, and common financing of agricultural policy in the EEC helped the relatively less developed regions to catch up with more developed ones. On the other hand, the way of spending the funds also matters. For example, in Poland the bulk of the agricultural budget is spent on social measures, not for structural change, education or job creation in rural areas - goals, which in the long run would bring better results than social support.

Both CEC-3 and EU farmers may benefit from accession. On the one hand, CEC-3 farmers will obtain higher incomes (due to an increase in the prices and quantities of some agricultural products) and significant support for structural changes. On the other hand, the EU farmers may benefit from CEC accession, because of expansion of the free-trade Single Market, particularly if many CEC-3 farmers fail to satisfy EU quality standards, and are therefore excluded from the market. The price gap between the EU and CEC-3 will also be crucial. For the CEC-3 it would be better to keep prices in the pre-accession period low (since price support would be counterproductive) and hence to maintain a wide price gap. On the other hand, the EU is interested in lowering its prices (in order to improve competitiveness) and in decreasing the price gap (in order to avoid production incentives for CEC-3 farmers after accession). Therefore, the accession is a difficult process with many conflicts of interests. The first is about when CEC-3 will be allowed to adopt the CAP and on what conditions.

In order to prepare their own farmers for competition with the EU counterparts, the CEC-3 should concentrate their pre-accession policies mainly on two matters: (1) investment in rural development; and (2) other means reducing employment in agriculture. Such policies guarantee improvement of agricultural productivity and improvement of agricultural incomes compared to non-agricultural incomes.

Investment in rural development in CEC-3 should be directed mostly at: creating new job opportunities in rural areas (especially in Poland), restructuring the collective farms (especially in Hungary and the Czech Republic), and changing patterns of farm size inherited from the socialist period (all CEC-3). Furthermore, investment in rural development should also focus on: providing technical and social infrastructure; providing better access to education; agricultural marketing (enhancing the marketing chain, development of the private marketing co-operative sector, strengthening the wholesale marketing infrastructure); services to infrastructure (by promoting the transfer of employment between agriculture and its service industries); improving access to financial markets for projects in agro-industry: streamlining quality controls.

Employment reduction in agriculture is a much more difficult policy to implement than investment in rural development, at least from a social point of view. Some new jobs will be available due to investment in rural development but the low level of education will restrain the process of employment reduction. Early retirement schemes although seemingly the quickest instrument are also the most costly. In Poland for example 72% of the agricultural budget is already spent on social services for farmers[24] (not including tax exemptions). In future, the imposition income tax on Polish farmers is planned, which may cause some outflow from agricultural activities. Nevertheless, the process is slow and we should not expect radical changes in agricultural employment over the next few years.

The pre-accession agricultural aid from the EU has little or no direct budgetary effects. However, because it is in the form of co-financing it hopefully will assure a more effective use of funds and the sharing of responsibility between the applicant country and the EU. What is more, this aid will be directed toward structural change – a very desirable aim from both the applicants' and the EU's points of view.

A very important issue is whether CEC-3 will benefit from CAP equally with other EU members. Especially important is the outcome of the debate on the participation of CEC-3 in direct compensatory payments. The deprivation CEC-3 of direct payments would cause an uneven playing field for competition between EU and CEC-3 farmers after the accession. EU farmers would obtain a larger income for the same production sold.

APPENDIX – FARM SUPPORT SCHEMES IN THE CZECH REPUBLIC, HUNGARY AND POLAND.

The agricultural policies in CEC-3 differ considerably as to their expensiveness and the instruments they use. In the Czech Republic, as in Hungary, the main categories of support to agriculture are 1/ *market price support*, 2/ *direct payments* and 3/ *credit subsidies*. The main instruments for *market price support* in the Czech Republic, are border measures (tariffs, import/export licensing and export subsidies) and direct (through the state agency) or indirect (through market agents) intervention in the market. The main institution for market support is the State Fund for Market Regulation (SFMR). Its stated objective is to stabilize agricultural markets (i.e. to prevent large price movements either downwards or upwards, supposedly in the interest of both producers and consumers) by purchasing/exporting surpluses and selling/importing in the case of shortages. Its council, chaired by the minister of agriculture, decides on the products to be regulated and the mode of intervention. Expenditure on market support has tended to grow over the last couple of years. In 1997 it amounted to 21% of the overall total agricultural budget while in 1998 it amounted to 36% (Figure 8.4). This was due in particular to increased expenditure on cereals. Protectionist measures, which strengthen market support, are to a large extent limited by the Czech Republic's Uruguay Round commitments on market access and export competition. Most Czech tariffs are considerably lower than the EU-15 ad valorem equivalents with the exception of poultry, potatoes and oilseeds, which enjoy higher protection, and of pig meat, which has a similar level of protection.

In Hungary, as in the Czech Republic, the largest part (35%) of the agricultural budget goes to the market support policy (the breakdown of expenditure is set out in Figure 8.4). Market support is mainly provided through export refunds and, for a limited number of products, by direct price support. Although Hungary's agricultural policy has traditionally been export-oriented and rather liberal (reflecting Hungary's long-standing membership in the GATT and the efficiency of its agriculture even in Habsburg times) since 1994, Hungary has taken a more interventionist approach, adopting different elements of the EU's Common Agricultural Policy, albeit with much lower support prices, and also increasing import protection. Between 1997 - 1998 expenditure on market support decreased from 42% to 35% of total expenditures on agriculture and the significance of direct subsidies increased. Since January 1998 agricultural policy started to be reshaped with a view to future EU membership, with export subsidies continuing to play a major role.

Recently, both the Czech Republic and Hungary have increased expenditure on *direct payments*, and hence these have become the second largest agricultural expenditure categories in these countries. In the Czech Republic, direct payments were introduced in 1995 in the form of area payments to encourage specialized beef production in less favored areas (LFAs). The share of direct payments increased in the Czech Republic from 18% in 1997 to about 29% in 1998, overtaking credit subsidies as the largest structural expenditure item. In Hungary direct subsidies include credit subsidies, support for the use of poor land and, since 1998, a subsidy designed to encourage farm employment. They have increased from 21% to 27% between 1997 and 1998. As can be seen, in spite of our preference for direct payments as a form of support for agriculture, a number of these items are efficiency reducing.

In the Czech Republic, *credit subsidies* and *loan guarantees* took third place in the agricultural budget, amounting to about 23% in 1998. In Hungary, it was investment subsidies which ranked third in importance, with a share of 24% in 1998. As far as structural policy in agriculture is concerned, the Hungarian government developed various instruments, mainly support for investment and support for the use of poor quality land. Unlike in the Czech Republic, but as in Poland, Hungarian farmers with revenue of up to 1 million HUF per annum are exempt from income declarations and taxes. Farmers with a revenue of between 1 and 2 million HUF were not obliged to keep accounts but had to pay taxes at a personal rate (up to a maximum of 42% in 1997). Farmers with gross revenue above 2 million HUF (about $10,000) had to keep accounts but could pay taxes at corporate rates (18% of net income). Co-operatives pay corporate tax, while their members pay income tax on their personal income. Land tax was eliminated in 1995. Farmers benefit from a refund of 85% of the fuel excise tax. In practice, most individual farmers do not pay taxes at all and do not provide statistical information to the tax authorities, even though this means they forgo the right to receive subsidies.

The Polish agricultural budget differs significantly from those of the Czech Republic and Hungary. First of all, by far the biggest part of the agricultural budget (76% in 1998) is spent on the farmers' social security system. These expenditures constitute an increasing and hardly manageable burden. Second, market intervention has a much smaller share, about 2% to 3% only. As for other policy instruments, such as export subsidies and direct payments, their importance has recently been rather low (although the significance of direct payments has been increasing). While in the pre-transition period Poland's agriculture and food exports were quite highly subsidised, since 1990 export subsidies have rarely been applied and are limited to sugar, butter and pork.[25] Direct payments have always been insignificant.

ENDNOTES

[1] Nevertheless, the fears of large-scale emigration of Polish rural inhabitants to other EU countries after accession are unfounded. Even if the rate of unemployment in rural areas is underestimated, there are still many obstacles to such movement (low educational attainment, no knowledge of foreign languages, fear etc.) We would expect migration to be first visible from rural to urban areas within Poland, but such migration has not as yet been observed. Therefore, it seems likely that rural unemployment will remain a local Polish problem.

[2] First-wave countries are those which are expected to enter the EU first.

[3] For detailed overview of the quantitative models and literature dealing with the EU enlargement see the survey done by Nielsen (1999).

[4] This scenario seems to be the most likely at the moment.

[5] See EU (1999)

[6] *Cereals*: 15% price cut (instead of 20% suggested in Agenda 2000) in two steps of 7.5% in 2000/2001 and 2001/2002, with compensatory aid rising in two stages from 54 to 63 EUR/t (multiplied by historic regional yields). A decision on any further cut from 2002/2003 onwards will be taken in the light of market developments with the same 50% compensation formula applied. The base rate for compulsory set-aside will be set at 10% for the whole 2000-2006 period. The arable area payment from 2003 will also apply to oilseeds.

Beef regime: 20% price cut (instead of 30% proposed in Agenda 2000). Effective market support should be gradually established at a level of 2.78 EUR/ton, over the period 2000-2003. It should be possible to stabilise market prices around or above this level through border protection, export measures and the introduction of a private storage regime, as already exists for pig meat. Direct income payments should gradually increase and should be still paid per head of cattle. Intervention purchases will be initiated at a lower price level, i.e. when market prices fall to 60% of the intervention price.

Dairy: 15% price cut of milk in powder and butter (instead of 10%) but over 3 years, starting from 2005/2006. Compensation will be paid per liter of quota, and 1.5% linear increase in dairy quotas is expected. The agricultural package did foresee a mid-term review of the dairy sector in 2003.

[7] This system causes subsidies to benefit domestic rather than foreign consumers. Additionally, direct income support causes less market distortion than the price support system, and can be more tightly controlled from the fiscal point of view.

[8] Deabatisse (1999)

[9] In the Czech Republic farming is characterised by relatively high indebtedness resulting from the privatisation process. Large-scale farming sector owes the government for non-

land privatized property. This debt represents sometimes up to 20 percent of the assets of farms.

[10] Csaki, Debatisse and Honisch (1999)

[11] PSE (Produces Support Estimate) measures support to farmers from consumers (through higher commodity prices), and from taxpayers (through budgetary transfers). Support expressed as a percentage of gross farms' receipts (%PSE), shows the amount of support to farmers irrespective of the sectoral structure of a given country. For this reason, the %PSE, developed by the OECD, is the most appropriate indicator for comparisons of support across countries, commodities and time.

[12] In the Czech Republic farmers are not exempted from taxes and in Hungary tax concessions are included *explicite* in the agricultural budget as a separate position. Therefore, in these countries all expenditures on agriculture are covered in agricultural budgets and therefore, they can be derived directly from the official figures. In Poland, tax exemptions are not included in the budget and therefore in order to calculate all agricultural expenditures one must additionally estimate these exemptions.

[13] The calculation of the value of income tax exemptions for farmers is presented in Koronowski A. (1997). Budget revenue is only 94% of possible revenue – there is 6% loss due to tax exemptions for farmers. In 1996 this loss amounted at 2.128 million PLN or 2% of real budgetary revenues.

[14] Apart from the Czech Republic, Hungary and Poland, also Slovenia, Estonia, Romania, Bulgaria, Slovakia, Lithuania and Latvia may participate in this pre-accession aid.

[15] The Polish agricultural budget in 1997 amounted at ECU 3.4 billion but excluding KRUS it was only ECU 952 million.

[16] Objectives defined for EAGGF Guidance Fund: Objective 1 - development of regions lagging behind, Objective 5a – adaptation of farm structures, Objective 5b – development of rural areas.

[17] For more precise discussion on CEC-3 agricultural expenditures and their efficiency see Section 2.4 and the Appendix.

[18] This has declined from 0.75% after the latest reform

[19] However, there is still a hope that the EU while discussing its long-term budget program (in 2002 or 2003) will agree direct payments to CEC's farmers. On the other hand, such re-budgeting will be difficult because the EU has postulated accession without any increase in the expenditures on CAP.

[20] With exception of Poland where wheat prices are above the EU level.

[21] Although consumers will loose as a result of higher prices, and they will not necessarily be compensated by the improved quality of the products. If in relatively poor nations such CEC the consumers are forced to buy higher quality food and pay higher prices than they otherwise would pay, then this implies a welfare loss for them.

[22] Fore detailed discussion on reasons behind direct payments for CEEC see Buckwell and Tangermann (1999)

[23] See for example research on Polish farmers done by Institute of Public Affairs (1999)

[24] In spite of dire warnings over the last 30 years about the ageing of the rural population in Poland, the share of people over 65 in the rural population increased only by 1 percentage point between 1990 and 1997. The number of people of working age (particularly those between 18-25 and 40-49) increased significantly. In the overall population the share of people over 65 increased by 1.5 percent, i.e. by more than in the countryside. So in no way can we claim that rural society is ageing.

[25] However, export undertaken by the Agricultural Market Agency (ARR) on the basis of intervention purchases, are partly carried out with losses and can therefore be regarded as a form of indirect export subsidy.

REFERENCES

Agenda 2000, *European Commission*, Strasbourg, 15 July 1997.

Anderson K. and Tyers R, (1993), *Implications of EC expansion for European agricultural policies, trade and welfare*, Centre for Economic Policy Research, Discussion Paper No. 829

Baldwin R.E, Francois J.F, Portes R., (April 1997), *The Costs and Benefits of Eastern Enlargement: the Impact on the EU and Central Europe*, Economic Policy,

Bojnec S., Munch W., Swinnen F.F.M. (1998): *Exchange Rates and the Measurement of Agricultural Price Distortions in CEEC and the Costs of CEEC-EU Accession*, in Brockmeier M., Francois J.F., Hertel T.W. and Schmitz M.P. Schmitz (eds) *Economic Transition and the Greening of Policies : Modelling New Challenges for Agriculture and Agribusiness in Europe*. Proceedings of the 50th European Seminar of the EAAE, October 1996, Wissenschaftsverlag Vauk Kiel KG, Kiel.

Buckwell A, Tangermann S, (1999), *The Future of Direct Payments in the Context of Eastern Enlargement*, Economic Policy in Transition Economies, Vol 9, No 3, Special Issue "Agricultural Transition and European Integration", Kluwer Academic Publishers.

Brenton P., Gross D., (1993), .*The budgetary implications of EC Enlargement,* CEPS Working Document No. 78, Centre for European Policy Studies, Brussels

Csaki C, Debatisse M., Honisch O., (1999), *Food and Agriculture in the Czech Republic. From a Velvet Transition to the Challenges of EU Accession*, The World Bank Technical Paper No. 437

Deabatisse M A., (1999), .*Successful Agriculture and Food Economy in Constant Search for Higher Competitiveness*, ECSSD Environmental and Socially Sustainable Development, Working Paper No. 9, The World Bank

El-Agraa Ali M., *The Economics of the European Community*, Redwood Books, 1990,

European Commission, Report on Implementation of the Commission's Work Programme for 1996, 1996.

European Commission, *Commission Communication to the Council and to the European Parliament on the Establishment of a new Financial Perspective for the Period 2000-2006*, 1996.

European Commission, DG VI, *Budgetary Expenditure on the Common Agricultural Policy*, 1997.

European Commission, Directorate for Agriculture (GD VI), *Financing of the CAP in 1996*, Extract from the Report, The agricultural situation in the European Union, 1996.

European Commission, Directorate for Agriculture (GD VI),), *Agricultural Situation and prospects in the Central and Eastern European Countries*, Summary Report, 1998a.

European Commission, Directorate for Agriculture (GD VI),), *Agricultural Situation and prospects in the Central and Eastern European Countries: Czech Republic*, 1998b.

European Commission, Directorate for Agriculture (GD VI), *Agricultural Situation and prospects in the Central and Eastern European Countries: Hungary*, 1998c.

European Commission, Directorate for Agriculture (GD VI), *Agricultural Situation and prospects in the Central and Eastern European Countries: Poland,* 1998d.

FAOSTAT Data Base, htttp://apps.fao.org, FAO 1990-1990.

Institute of Public Affairs, (November 1999), *Rolnicy i mieszkańcy wsi o przyszłości polskiej wsi i rolnictwa w obliczu integracji z Unią Europejską*, Warszawa

Josling T.E., Pearson S. R., (1981), *.Developments in the Common Agricultural Policy of the European Community*, United States, Department of Agriculture, Washington,

Koronowski A., (1997), *Problemy opodatkowania rolnictwa*, Sejmowe Biuro Studiów i Ekspertyz, Informacja nr 567

Münch W., (1999), *Effects of CEC-EU Accession on Agricultural Markets in the CEC and on Government Expenditure*, Research project (No. FAIR1-CT95-0029) funded by DG VI of the EU-Commission

Nielsen, Ch., (1998b), *Enlargement of the European Union. A Survey of Quantitative Analyses*, Danish Institute of Agricultural and Fisheries Economics, Report No. 106, April 1999.

OECD, Data Base,

Orłowski, W.M., Prspektywy polityki dezinflacyjnej w Polsce, Conference Paper presented at the CASE seminar 21-22.12.1998

Orłowski W. M., (1996b), *.Droga do Europy. Makroekonomia wstepowania do Unii Europejskiej*, Warszawa

Piskorz W. et.al., (1995), *Konsekwencje wspólnej polityki rolnej EU dla polskiego rolnictwa. Wyniki analizy symulacyjnej.*, Fundacja Programów Pomocy dla Rolnictwa (FAPA), SAEPR

Piskorz W., Guba W., et.al., (1998), *Konsekwencje wspólnej polityki rolnej EU dla polskiego rolnictwa. Wyniki analizy symulacyjnej.*, Fundacja Programów Pomocy dla Rolnictwa (FAPA), SAEPR

SAEPR/FAPA, (Marzec 2000), *Potencjalne skutki integracji z Unią Europejską dla sektora rolnego w Polsce*, SAEPR (FAPA)

UN Commodity Trade Statistics, (1997)

WDI, The World Development Indicators (The World Bank Data Base), 1999

WDI, The World Development Indicators (The World Bank Data Base), 1998

WIIW, *Handbook of Statistics1997*, Chapter 4, pp.200-205.

Chapter 9

THE FISCAL IMPACT OF HEALTH CARE REFORMS IN CENTRAL EUROPE

Peter Mihalyi

and

Ryszard Petru

INTRODUCTION

The chapter provides a perspective on recent developments in heath care reforms in three fast-reforming transition economies: the Czech Republic, Hungary and Poland.* The first two countries have been implementing reforms since the early 1990s, while Poland started its reform only on January 1, 1999. But the reforms are not over - in all three countries further changes are envisaged. The objective of this chapter is to assess the current situation from a fiscal perspective. This, of course, is not the only possible criterion, but it is still vital enough to deserve careful analysis.

All three countries have opted for a mandatory social insurance system – the so-called Bismarckian model. In Hungary, the monopolistic health insurance fund is now under full government control, but a competitive multi-player insurance system is envisaged after 2002 at best. In the Czech Republic, initially there were as many as 20 funds, but the state-controlled General Health Insurance Company now receives about 80% of total contributions. In Poland, there are 17 newly created funds, 16 of them regional controlled by representatives of local parliaments and one occupational insurance fund for specially privileged groups of workers. Private funds will be allowed to compete in Poland only from 2002 on.

The health care systems in all three countries are contractual systems with a clear separation between financing and provision. Financing is made through the health insurance companies (funds). On the supply side, primary health care is organized at municipal level. Hospitals, outpatient health care centers and physicians sign contracts with health insurance companies for the provision of services. Hospitals are generally owned by municipalities, only a few hospitals are private.

The payment scheme in the Czech Republic is based on fee-for-service principle. The fee-for-service system stimulated a considerable growth in services provided by hospitals and outpatient health care centers. Hungary applies three different payment systems at different levels of health care, the Polish model is still under construction.

The reforms so far have led to different financial consequences. In the Czech Republic, the share of health expenditures relative to GDP rose quite sharply, while the direction of change in Hungary was just the opposite. It is too early to guess what will happen in Poland. But the issue is very important, since 2-4 per cent of GDP is at stake!

1. HEALTH CARE AS AN ECONOMIC PROBLEM

One of the most striking features of modern medicine is its diminishing rate of return. If the output of health care is measured in increased life expectancy – as it is often the case in international comparisons -, this rule seems to hold in virtually all developed economies. This means that – *ceteris paribus* – more money to buy more doctors, more machines and more medicaments will not yield a proportional rise in life expectancy. Quite interestingly, this fact was first noticed by demographers in the late 70s. They were surprised to notice that life expectancy in the Soviet Union was shorter only by 5-7 years, as compared to the United States, although per capita dollar expenditures were 20 times higher in the United States than in the Soviet Union.

At a high level of abstraction, the diminishing rate of return in health care can be explained by the following factors:

- The rise in the number of doctors tends to increase the number of doctor patient encounters. At an earlier stage of development, where doctors are in short supply, both doctors and patients are more selective. Patients

with smaller complaints do not go to doctors. Doctors concentrate on those patients, who need care most.
- At a lower development level, the extensive growth of the hospital network leads to significant health gains. Hospitals are very efficient in fighting communicable diseases and in reducing infant mortality. The upgrading of an existing hospital network cannot yield really significant health gains in terms of life years gained.
- The most efficient tools of modern medicine, such as vaccination or antibiotics are relatively inexpensive. Once a country is well supplied with them, more money cannot buy equally powerful weapons to fight diseases.
- Modern medicine is based on high level specialization. If this is not combined with an effective system of the division of labor in order to eliminate overlaps, the cost of health care can grow infinitely.
- With the expansion of the health care system, some positive features can turn into negative (self-medication, unnecessarily frequent use of medicaments (*polipragmasia*), and iatrogen diseases).

From an economic perspective, it is also important to understand that the definition of „illness" is not a 'hard' scientific matter. First, the meaning of illness has a very strong historical, sociological and economic component. With the progress of economic well being health care needs rise continuously. Aging is an additional factor creating demand. Life style problems (e.g. allergies), smaller pains, psychological disorders, which remained largely unnoticed at an earlier stage of development or were treated in the family, are now medicalized. Second, large segments of health care have become businesses, where strong marketing skills are used to boost consumption.

Needless to say, the Czech Republic, Hungary and Poland are not able to escape the consequences of such changes. The problem is that health policy experts in these countries are not fully aware of these dangers. It is widely believed in medical circles that health care needs can be and should defined through a scientific procedure. And once this is done, it is the governments' duty to guarantee the "necessary" financial resources.

2. MAIN TYPES OF HEALTH CARE SYSTEMS

There are four major ways of financing and providing health care.

1. Tax financed, government controlled system
2. Mandatory social insurance

3. Voluntary health insurance
4. Case-by-case financing.

1. The first category can be subdivided into two, depending whether there is a separation between the payer and provider of medical services or not. In the United Kingdom, the National Health Service (NHS) is based on the principle that the providing and financing of services should be separated. All citizens are covered; the system is financed from taxes, but the NHS contracts services on behalf of citizens by negotiating the cost of services with hospitals and physicians. To a large extent contracting takes place at the level of regions to ensure that local differences in needs are taken into account. It is generally believed, that this system is providing satisfactory services at low-cost, though access to state-of-the art specialized care can be difficult. A similar system is used in the Nordic countries. Both in the UK and in the Nordic countries quantitative rationing is used to contain demand. The other type of budget-financed system was common in Central & Eastern Europe before the collapse of communism, and was, till the end of 1998 in place in Poland. Both financing and health care facilities were managed by the state. In other words, supply and demand were simultaneously controlled by the same administrative apparatus. The main problem with this system was that financial resources were often allocated regardless of local needs and spent in an extravagant manner.

2. The social insurance system, also known as the 19th century Bismarckian model, is based on a strong link between the world of labor and social services of different kinds. At that time Germany used health care and old age pension insurance as ways to build solidarity among citizens nation-wide. The idea was to force low-income workers in industry to pool a fraction of their wage in a common financial fund to finance health care, sickness pay and old-age retirement. In the course of the 20th century, some West European countries (e.g. Belgium, Switzerland, and France) emulated this model, but not in its original form. The most important change was that health care provision was extended to the family members as well. The logic of the Bismarckian model tends to support the rise of several insurance companies – typically industry specific companies (occupational health funds). Due to the increased burden of administration - and more recently: the increased costs of marketing, the Bismarckian system provides a high level of services at a relatively high cost. The post-1990 health insurance reforms introduced this modified Bismarckian system in the Czech Republic, Hungary and in Poland. In all three countries, the original reform blueprints made a strong commitment to competition in health care insurance, although the scope, the modalities and the deadlines for introducing competition have varied from country to country.

In retrospect, the choice of these countries can be explained by several factors:

- In some ways, all three countries knew the Bismarckian model prior to Word War II. Workers in certain industries, as well as civil servants had the privilege of Bismarckian health care, accident and pension insurance. Therefore, it was natural to restore the pre-war system and gradually expand it to the entire population.
- Policy makers in the three countries are watching each other closely. This explains why Poland has just recently re-introduced the Bismarkcian model. It seems that over 10 years of preparation it has become increasingly burdensome to postpone further the decision on health care financing.
- It is equally important to note that the multilateral agencies, such as the WHO and the World Bank, didn't push the three East European countries towards the acceptance of the Bismarckian model. In particular, the advisors of these organizations warned against the dismantling of the unified health care financing system. On the other hand, German policy advisers were quite active in promoting the Bismarckian system – at least in two countries (Hungary, Poland).

3. The voluntary health insurance system is characteristic for the US. The majority of the population, about 74 per cent, is covered by private health insurance provided by more than 1000 companies. Those under 65 years of age (and their dependants) obtain private health insurance either through their employers (61%) or by direct purchase of non-group health insurance (13%). Approximately 12-14% has no insurance at all. Although this sounds strikingly high, the majority of the uninsured is only temporarily uncovered for the period between two jobs.

4. In virtually every country, health care is *partially* financed through non-insurance based techniques.

- User fees. In this scheme the patient pays a certain fee to the provider for the service rendered. Historically, such fees were always present in the private health care sector. In the public sector it is very rare that significant user fees are required. Usually, they exist in the form of co-payment. The standard criticism of co-payment is that it disproportionally hampers low-income people to access medical care.
- In some countries, including Hungary, governments „earmark" a certain tax specifically for health expenditures. Examples are taxes on alcohol and tobacco. The major disadvantage is that these taxes are regressive and mostly hit people on low-income.
- Under-the-table payments. In all three countries, health care workers – and medical doctors in particular – routinely receive gratuity payments

from their patients. More recently pharmaceutical companies have started to "sponsor" medical doctors in order to direct prescription habits into the "desired" direction. Both types of payments are untaxed, illegal, and - consequently - statistically unrecorded.

There are very few countries in the world where the financing schemes described above exist in their pure forms. In the UK, the NHS is complemented by a well-developed private insurance sector. The home country of the Bismarckian system – Germany – has also developed its own private insurance system that serves high-income groups above a certain statutory income. In the US health care for the elderly (over 65 years of age), the disabled and certain groups of very poor people is directly financed from the budget (MEDICARE, MEDICAID).

To complete the picture, it is noteworthy to briefly describe two schemes of financing that elude the classifications used above. In Canada, there is the National Health Insurance system, which covers the whole population. The revenues come from general taxes and payroll taxes. Both federal and provincial governments finance the National Health Insurance. Patients may choose providers freely (both in outpatient and inpatient care). In Singapore the system of financing is based on so-called MEDISAVE. Every citizen has his or her personal Medical Savings Account (MSA), where money is regularly deposited. The saving is compulsory and covers the costs of hospital care. The savings may be used for medical expenses only. Inheritance law also applies to MEDISAVE. In order to cope with payment for rare and very expensive services – such as cancer, AIDS or Alzheimer-disease - a publicly funded catastrophic insurance has been established. If the patient decides to use the private outpatient service - he or she has to pay the full amount. In the case of the private inpatient care (or a higher standard in public hospitals) - the patient pays the difference between the cost of private and public provision (deductible).

In a similar vein, the Czech, the Hungarian and the Polish systems cannot be regarded as pure Bismarckian regimes. In all three countries, important segments of health care are financed from the tax revenues of the central government (e.g. preventive programs, certain high cost treatments, certain medicines, etc.); local governments bear their share, too. In addition, patients pay doctors and a part of their medicine-bills directly.

3. HEALTH STATUS AND HEALTH CARE RESOURCES

Over the past two decades, a number of scholarly studies have made attempts to establish quantifiable links between economic development indicators on the hand and health outcome on the other. In a worldwide sample, the correlation between health outcome indicators – such as life expectancy or child mortality - and GDP levels is strong. However, if countries with similar GDP levels are sampled, the correlation is weak or nil. The correlation is similarly weak between health expenditure – measured as % of GDP – and health status. Different countries with different health care regimes produce identical health outcomes, irrespective to the percentage share of health expenditures in GDP. The direction of causation appears to work more strongly in the opposite direction. Countries with higher GDP per capita levels tend to spend a relatively higher fraction of their GDP on health but this is not necessarily reflected in better health outcomes. There is no clear correlation between *changes* in GDP and health outcome indicators, either. In some countries of Central and Eastern Europe, the post-communist transition shock – i.e. the sharp decline of GDP – was associated with a drop in life expectancy (e.g. Hungary, the Czech Republic), but in other countries this drop did not occur, although the output fall was deeper than in Hungary or the Czech Republic (e.g. Romania, Slovakia).

While it remains true that higher GDP levels do tend to be associated with lower infant mortality (Table 9.1), there is virtually no correlation between GDP levels and life expectancy or the overall health status of the population (Tables 9.2 and 9.3). In fact, there are quite striking counter-examples. Life expectancy in Albania is higher in than in Hungary (the "advantage" of Albania is 4 years for men and 2 years for women).

Table 9.1. Infant mortality under 1 year per 1000 live born.

Country	1990	1991	1992	1993	1994	1995	1996	1997	1998
Hungary	14.8	15.6	14.1	12.5	11.5	10.7	10.9	9.9	9.9
Czech R.	7.7	7.0	6.2	5.7	4.7	4.9	3.8	...	...
Poland	19.3	18.1	17.5	16.2	15.1	13.6	12.2	10.2	...

Source: GUS (1998); Potucek (1998), Hungarian Statistical Office

The difficulty of establishing causal links between economic and health outcomes is partially explained by the fact that better health outcomes are associated with better education and higher incomes. This is true both at aggregate and individual levels. Life chances within one country improve with income (and education), as exemplified by several US and UK studies. Both longer life and higher education means higher health expenditures during one's lifetime. International experience also shows that 50 per cent of the differences in health outcomes are explained by life-style factors, while wealth and associated socio-economic factors account for 30 per cent only. The volume of preventive and curative health accounts for 10 per cent and environmental risks for another 10 per cent. Unfortunately, there is no comparable study to test these findings for the three Central European countries. But there is no question that people in these three countries have failed so far to adopt responsible health behavior. High cholesterol, high blood pressure and obesity are prevalent. The population has a traditionally permissive attitude to the consumption of alcohol and tobacco.

Table 9.2. Life expectancy at birth (1997 estimates)

Country	Years
Slovenia	74.93
CZECH REPUBLIC	73.86
Croatia	73.45
Slovakia	72.91
POLAND	72.47
Bulgaria	71.65
HUNGARY	70.48
Romania	70.11
Lithuania	68,70
Belarus	68.40
Estonia	68,38
Latvia	66.91
Ukraine	65.77
Moldova	64.25

Source: NERA (1998)

Table 9.3. Overall health ranking of European countries *

Ranking	Country	Ranking	Country
1	Sweden	18	Belgium
2	Finland	19	Ireland
3	Norway	20	Portugal
4	Italy	21	Albania
5	Switzerland	22	POLAND
6	Slovenia	23	Croatia
7	Austria	24	Macedonia
8	Greece	25	Yugoslavia
9	France	26	HUNGARY
10	Netherlands	27	Lithuania
11	Slovak R.	28	Bulgaria
12	Spain	29	Romania
13	CZECH REPUBLIC	30	Turkey
14	UK	31	Estonia
15	Germany	32	Belarus
16	Iceland	33	Latvia
17	Denmark	34	Ukraine

* Ranking takes into account 14 different health indicators, including life expectancy, infant mortality and death rates from a number of diseases.
Source: Economist Intelligence Unit

Under the system of central planning, policy makers evaluated health care by the number of medical staff and hospital beds (Tables 9.4 and 9.5). In such comparisons, the former socialist countries generally fared very well. In fact, The Czech Republic and Hungary have **too many hospital beds and too many specialists**. The Polish situation is more in line with that country's relative development level. In all three countries little attention was paid to increase financing per medical staff or per hospital bed, although technical progress required this. As a result, the condition of the infrastructure deteriorated, with much needed reconstruction postponed and the standard of technology lagging behind the West. Wages of doctors were also kept low by international standards, although the discrepancy was not so striking within the wage structure of the socialist countries themselves. The insufficient number of nurses – particularly in Hungary and Poland – is also a question of wages.

Table 9.4. Health sector employment in Hungary, Czech Republic and Poland (1997)

Indicator	Hungary/Czech Republic/Poland	OECD average
	Per 1,000 of population	
All health-care workers	16.0 21.9 n.a.	23.9
Physicians	4.2 2.9 2.4	2.7
Specialist	2.7 2.2 n.a.	1.3
General practitioners	0.7 0.7 1.8	0.8
Nurses	4.9 8.1 5.6	7.7

Source: OECD

Table 9.5. Hospital beds in Hungary, Czech Republic and Poland (1997)

Indicators	Hungary/Czech Republic/Poland	OECD average
	Per 1,000 of population	
In-patients care beds	9.3 9.0 5.5	7.8
Acute care beds	6.4 6.9 n.a.	4.4
Nursing home beds	1.0 0.6 0.0	2.7

Source: OECD

During the 1950s and 1960s, the rapid increase of hospital beds was justified by public health concerns. Hospitals were very effective in the battle against communicative diseases and of reducing infant mortality. As morbidity patterns changed, hospitals have lost their comparative cost-effectiveness. Furthermore, as medical technology developed, hospitals were forced to accumulate a large pool of different machines. In Hungary – for example - hospitals with their barrack buildings dispersed in a large campus like territory, became hopelessly cost-ineffective. This is one of the most difficult policy tasks that Hungarian health planners face today. Everybody agrees that the country has far more hospitals and hospital beds than needed, but at the same time many hospitals are unsuitable for providing cost-effective treatment, and they need to be replaced by newly built hospitals.

Strangely enough, patients in the Czech Republic and Hungary are not aware that their countries' vast health care network allows for a luxury that few other countries can afford. If compared to virtually *any* West European country, Czech or Hungarian patients have a better chance to be seen by a doctor (Table 9.6) and operated instantaneously, rather than waiting for weeks or even months. (In the UK, for example, the number of people waiting for hospital admittance is around 1,5 million and growing!). As noted, the situation in Poland is much less favorable, since the number of inpatient beds remains well below the OECD average. Poland has fewer doctors, as well.

Table 9.6. Doctors' consultations (Number/head) in 1996*

UK	Sweden	Germany	USA	Poland	Hungary	Czech Republic
5.9	2.9	6.4	6.0	5.4	14.8	14.7

* or latest available
Source: OECD and. WHO (1996)

4. HEALTH CARE REFORMS - LEGAL FRAMEWORK

The first post-communist country that started to dismantle Soviet-type, state-run health care was Hungary. As early as 1989, a government decree on private social and health enterprises authorized private health practices. (Note, however, that some doctors had the privilege of running a private practice throughout the communist period.). In the following year, the system of consensus management was introduced through a decree on the election of hospital directors by the doctors themselves. The 1990 Local Government Act transferred ownership of health care facilities and responsibility for health care provision to municipalities. These two latter developments were – of course – in contradiction to each other. Very soon, the right of nomination (i.e. hiring and firing hospital directors) was granted to the local authorities.

In 1991 further changes were introduced, when the Act on Self-governance of the Social Insurance Funds divided the former social insurance fund into a Pension Fund and a Health Fund. The act regulated the tasks, organization and financing of the funds. A parliamentary resolution set the main directions of development of health insurance. The year 1992 brought further fine-tuning of the system. Groups entitled to compulsory health insurance were specified, and the services covered by the health insurance scheme were defined. These included curative and preventive care, maternity care, subsidies for medication, sick leave, invalidity pensions and maternity support, i.e. virtually everything, except cosmetic surgery and alike. Privatization of primary health care practices started in the same year.

With hindsight, it can be safely said that these changes were largely cosmetic. There was no intention to curtail eligibility substantially or to limit the scope of health care services. From the patients' point of view, the situation is the same as before 1989: every Hungarian citizen is entitled to receive any treatment free of charge. In theory, health care is provided on an insurance basis. In reality, care is extended to all citizens irrespective of payments and the benefit package remains contractually and/or legislatively undefined.

Reforms in the Czech health care system were introduced piecemeal. The year 1990 saw the privatization of primary doctors' practices and the decentralization of the ownership of hospitals. The main set of regulations shaping the financing system was passed by Parliament in 1991-92. They included Laws on General Health Insurance and the General Health Insurance Company, the establishment and functioning of professional associations (the medical, the dental and the pharmaceutical chambers of the industry), the creation of Branch, Local and other Health Insurance Companies and on Non-State Health Care Facilities. From 1993, the separation of providers of care from funders of care has been complete. Funding is now mainly the responsibility of various health insurance funds, which make contracts with providers of services.

Poland was the latest in introducing reforms. However, it is important to stress that before 1989 the Polish government also allowed for some degree of private sector participation in health care provision (individual practices and co-operatives), mostly in dental care. Starting form 1989, the most visible impact of liberalization was the "spontaneous self-privatization" of dentists and pharmacists. Today nearly 100% of dentists and pharmacists run private practices. The first major breakthrough in the organizational framework of health provision was Law on local governments of 1990 (amended in 1996) that gave a local community (*gmina*) competencies in health care provision and funding. The decentralization that started in 1990 was a success. In 1995, Parliament passed a Law on large cities (urban *gmina*), which received competencies to run and finance health care institutions (as a result of which they virtually took over primary health care). A Law on Health Care Institutions (HCIs) was passed in 1991. It allowed for HCI-s (outpatients' centers, hospitals, etc.) to become independent units with legal personality. It is the strategic goal of the reform that all HCIs become autonomous in terms of financial management, staffing, and salary policy. (For comparison, note that in Hungary such legislative actions are just planned for 2001 or 2002!) The ownership of Polish HCIs passed from the State to local authorities, a process, which was completed in 1998. The debate on the financing the health care started in late 80s, but the Health Insurance Act was only passed in February 1997 (amended in 1998). Some changes reforming the health care system as regards private practices were introduced before 1999 but the main part of the reform started only on January 1, 1999. The Common Health Insurance bill of 1997 (with amendments in 1998) introduced 16 Regional Health Insurance Funds, a National Union of Insurance Funds and an Office of Health Insurance Supervision. Patients have the possibility of choosing their physicians, specialists, nurses and other medical personnel. The same principles of free choice apply to their choice of hospitals and clinics.

5. CURRENT STATE OF HEALTH CARE SYSTEM

The health care systems in the Czech Republic and Hungary are contractual systems with a clear separation between financing and provision. Financing is made through health insurance companies (funds), which are under the supervision of government bodies. Hospitals are generally owned by municipalities, with only few private ones. The health insurance companies are independent bodies responsible for contracting health care facilities. In the Czech Republic contracts are short (1-2 years), in Hungary the contracts are – for all practical purposes - open-ended. Although in theory, the Hungarian National Health Insurance Fund (NHIF) has the right to select among providers, in reality the existing contracts are automatically renewed year after year. The problem with this practice is that it is extremely difficult for a newly established private venture to be accepted by the Fund. In Poland, the health care system was financed from the state budget and the hospitals were mainly owned by the state. The whole system has changed as of January 1, 1999.

5.1 Insurance funds

Today, health insurance funds (HIFs) are the cornerstone of the system in all three countries. They collect payroll contributions from their members and contract medical services with appropriate medical suppliers. HIFs are non-profit organizations. The number of HIFs in a country ranges from 1 in Hungary to 23 in the Czech Republic. The Hungarian HIF operates throughout the whole country. Poland has just created 16 regional HIFs - one in each of the new regions. There is also a so-called Branch Insurance Fund for the staff of the Ministry of National Defense and the paramilitary and police-type formations of the Ministry of the Interior.

In the Czech Republic the number of HIFs was not arbitrarily set by the authorities - they could be set up with the permission of the Ministry of Health and the Ministry of Finance. Several years ago there were as many as 27 HIFs but some of them went bankrupt as a result of competition. In 1996 there were 23 HIFs but two of them were nearly bankrupt, and it is expected that the number of HIFs will decrease further, until it settles at about 15. It is possible to switch between HIFs every three months. By far the biggest fund is the General Health Insurance Company (GHIC), which covers 80% of population and its solvency is guaranteed by the state. The relative strength of the company comes from the fact, that it insures all non-wage earners. Those insured in bankrupt HIFs are automatically moved to GHIC, unless they decide otherwise. HIFs are permitted to set their own range of services available to their clients but recent bankruptcies of companies that tried to do so, discourage others from following them. In the case of financial difficulty, only limited assistance is available from the state but the insured are protected from loss of insurance by the existence of the GHIS safety net. Children and pensioners can register with any health insurance company but most of them are registered with GHIC. At the same time, HIFs were organized by various ministries. The Ministry of the Interior and the Ministry of Defense set up their own health insurance company (in other words: an occupational health fund) for their staff. Thus fund owns a number of health care facilities which have contracts with all the other health insurance companies and are available to the whole population. The remaining insurers are generally organized around certain categories of employees (such as miners or bank employees) or very large companies.

The Ministry of Finance and the Ministry of Health jointly monitor these insurance companies but in practice this control is fairly weak. In case of financial difficulty only limited assistance is available from the state budget. Managing directors of each of the GHIC's 76 branches are accountable to supervisory boards. These consist of 3 employers' representatives, 3 representatives from municipal councils or representatives from Parliament, and representatives from the Ministry of Finance and the Ministry of Health and Social Affairs (appointed by Parliament).

The new health insurance system in Poland is based on 16 regional health funds that operate in 16 regions due to the new administrative division of the country. According to the Act, it is possible for a health fund to operate on territory consisting of more than one region, but in practice this is unlikely to happen. The Branch Insurance Fund which operates nation-wide has come into being as a result of political bargaining between forces representing general health policy interests and those of defending existing privileges of certain social groups. On the other hand, it is worth noting that the Branch Insurance Fund has the potentials to become a competitive institution *vis-à-vis* the regional funds.

During the first 9 months of 1999, the Plenipotentiary of the Government for implementation of the health insurance reform was responsible for setting up and monitoring the system. In September 1999, regional councils (*Sejmik Samorzadowy* – the legislative branch of the regional self-government) designated members of the health fund councils. This body consists of *Sejmik* members and people from outside the Sejmik. The term of the council is 4 years. The council will appoint the management board that will act similarly to the board of a partnership or joint stock company (as in the Commercial Code), with the difference that a health fund is the not-for-profit institution. So, there is a clear and close link between local government (on the regional level) and governance of the fund.

The Polish health care reform has also created the Office of Health Insurance Supervision. This is a central government body, and its president is nominated by the Prime Minister. It controls funds' financial situation and has authority to impose temporary administration. It also oversees legality of HIFs' and National Union of Insurance Funds' activities and can impose financial punishment, if the law is infringed.

In Hungary, the relative financial independence of the NHIF, together with the political independence of its ruling body, the so-called Health Insurance Self Government (HISG) has been heavily criticized since 1993. Between 1992-98, the NHIF had an elected board of 48 non-paid officials, who were representatives of three stakeholder groups: associations of employers, associations of employees and the associations of local governments. It turned out that political independence induced moral hazard. Since neither the NHIF, nor the HISG were constrained financially, the annual budgets of NHIF were repeatedly violated both in absolute terms, as well as in the details. The moral hazard stemmed from the fact that these budget overruns were automatically re-financed by the Treasury at the expense of the central government's regular budget. When the 1998 elections brought in a new government, the independence of the health insurance system was abolished. First, the Prime Minister's Office was in charge of the health insurance system, later this responsibility was transferred to the Ministry of Finance.[1]

5.2 Health care facilities

The delivery system is organized in similar way in all three countries. The gatekeeper of the system is a "family doctor" (the general practitioner or

GP) whom patients are free to choose. He provides primary care, refers them to specialists and hospitals, writes sickness certificates to justify absence from work. Hospitals sign contracts with HIFs for the provision of medical services. Various forms of ownership in the health care system are considered to be legally equal. The majority of institutions are now owned by the municipalities. This change of ownership took place in the Czech Republic and Hungary early on, while in Poland only on January 1, 1999. This ownership structure creates a "free rider problem". The municipality in which a hospital is located is obliged by law to finance repairs and investment, although the hospital provides services for neighboring areas as well. Quite often, the municipality burdened with a large hospital doesn't want to support these costs alone. By contrast, university teaching hospitals and Specialized Health Institutes (so-called "centers of excellence") are owned by the central government in all three countries. Some hospitals - usually smaller ones - are operated by churches that deliver services primarily in the field of long-term nursing care of the chronically ill, as well as hospice care. In the Czech Republic, spas and sanatoria are in private hands and function as for-profit companies. Schemes of financing the different levels of health care treatment differ, however, considerably between the three countries.

In Hungary spending caps are built into payments for family physician services, outpatient care and hospital care. Payments to GPs depend on the number and age of the patients served by them as well as on the number of patients with chronic conditions under continuous care. Prior to 1990 all family doctors had been in public employment with an obligation to provide in-area care to the inhabitants, which had been assigned to them. Currently the entire population is covered by family practices that have an obligation to provide in-area health care. People can freely choose from the pool of family practitioners. Between 1993 and 1996, practically all citizens took advantage of this opportunity.

The prime objective of establishing a family practitioner's system was to deliver continuous, personal and possibly definitive health care, including preventive care close to where people live. Through the financing system and the free choice by patients it was hoped to create incentives for providers to deliver high quality care that is fully tailored to the needs of patients. Efforts were aimed at improving the quality of care through increasing the number of practices and decreasing a number of people on the lists of individual practices. Although the municipalities are responsible for the provision of primary health care, they can meet this obligation not only with a family physician employed as a doctor in public service. They can also contract out the service to a private doctor, or more precisely to a limited partnership owned and managed by a qualified doctor. As the financing arrangements provide strong incentives to family practitioners to work as private entrepreneurs, the proportion of privatized practices increased to about 80% by 1996 (and continued to rise later on).

Outpatient specialists are financed on the basis of a points system. The value of points is calculated to reflect the complexity (professional and technical difficulties) involved in a given treatment. In-patient care is financed by a system of DRGs[2], whereas chronic care is paid for by the in-patient day.

There is general agreement, that outpatient specialist services will play an ever-greater role in the modernization of the health service. They relieve some of the burden on hospitals by taking over pre-admission work and follow-up care. Other important and developing areas include outpatient services, 1-day surgery, non-invasive and micro-invasive diagnostic and therapeutic procedures that are able to replace in-patient care. During the past decades, the hospital system was grown into the most developed sector within the health service in Hungary. It provides high standard medical care, however, with its size and cost, it endangered the operation of the entire health care delivery system. The very high bed/population ratio decreased by 25% between 1990 and 1999. Rather than aiming to merely shrink the total bed volume, this measure was implemented to decrease unjustified geographical differences and for the distribution of medical specialities, so as to better fit the morbidity patterns of each region.[3] In the 1990s medical facilities were supplied by a variety of new state-of-the-art equipment. The number of units of specialized equipment (such as CT scanners, MRI) increased two to threefold during 1990-96. However, no resources were left to replace and upgrade conventional X-ray machines, though radiography is required in the treatment of a number of conditions. A short-lived program to overcome this shortage was launched only in 1998.[4]

In the Czech Republic, the District Health Department is responsible for primary health services in its area. Citizens register with a primary health care physician and can re-register with another doctor every 6 months. By 1998, more than 95% of Czech physicians were in private practice. Almost all primary health care physicians work in health centers. Centers are owned by municipalities and run by directors. Private health care physicians who are in private practice pay rent for using the facilities of the centers. Primary care physicians are rather underused – a large part of their work involves the certification of absence from work, and referral rates to specialists are high. Like in other countries, they are orientated towards curative rather than preventive services.

Both physicians and hospitals are paid on a fee-for-service principle, but the system is capped. Certain fixed points value is attributed to each activity from a list of about 4500 services. As there is a ceiling on the total amount of point payments, the value of points decreased in previous years with increased activity levels. The value of each point differs between health insurance companies, as those with higher income can offer higher payment per point. In 1994, the value of a point was 0.52 CZK in GHIC and 0.70 CZK in both Zeleznicni and Bankovni Health Insurance Companies - a difference of over 30%. As patients can change insurance company every three months, there are incentives for the doctors to encourage patients to move from one company to another. The point-based payments are supposed to cover all operation costs and include allowance for capital expenditures. In practice, it is believed that it overestimates the costs of several specialities compared to others. It also does not take into account the fact that labor costs differ significantly between regions and are higher in big cities.

Hospitals also paid with points for each day spent by a patient in their facilities. Since the end of 1994 the payments have been made on a decreasing scale to reduce the length of stay. Recently the point system has been modified and some aspects of lump-sum payments were introduced. Hospitals get money straight from the GHI, without calculating the points earned. The points system continues for GPs and outpatient clinics.

There is a difference in earnings between private physicians and state physicians. The state physician gets permanent salary, which roughly corresponds to the nation-wide average wage level. Those in private practices are paid on a fee-for-service basis and earn at least twice the incomes of salaried doctors. Wage increases for physicians in recent years were 30% higher than increases in the average wage. It is common for physicians to bill for more than one hundred hours per week, which is hardly reasonable. Surgeons in private practice bill for 25% more points than those working in government hospitals. A similar pattern existed in charging for supplies. The fee-for-service system stimulated a considerable growth in services provided by hospitals and outpatient departments. In the next phase of the reforms a combination of capitation fee and fee-for-service reimbursement is being considered in order to contain the costs.

In Poland, health care institutions have to be registered in the court as autonomous entities in order to be eligible to contract medical services with health funds. This legal change has not yet been followed by an effective change in management, restructuring of hospital beds, staff reduction and quality improvement. Patients' first contact is the family doctor (GP), whom the insured are entitle to select. The maximum number of patients a GP may enroll is 2500. A family doctor authorizes referrals to specialists, diagnostic tests and hospital treatment. In some cases, however, direct access is allowed (e.g. dentists, dermatologists, oncologists, and psychiatrists). In addition, the insured may turn directly to specialists for substance abuse services (e.g. tobacco, alcohol, and psychotropic drugs addiction). The health insurance act gives certain groups of people direct access to specialized care, e.g. those infected with HIV or TB and veterans. In case of emergency the insured is allowed to access necessary treatment without prior authorization.

The health insurance act gives the health funds and providers freedom of choice to agree on the payment scheme for the medical services (e.g. GPs are paid on capitation basis and some hospitals on per admission basis). This payment scheme determines to a large extent the behavior of the provider (i.e. under-service with capitation and over-service in fee-for-service mechanism). This certainly gives more flexibility when negotiating contracts but, on the other hand, it poses some risk that the payment scheme selected may lead to a sharp increase on the demand side.

The year 1999 was a transitional period. Health funds contracted medical services with all providers (which met certain criteria). Starting January 2000, selective contracting is permitted and, hopefully, will lead to competition and quality improvement on the provider side.

The system of universal co-payment that was proposed by the Ministry of Finance has not been adopted by Parliament. Therefore, only some services will require co-payment from the patient (e.g. drugs, „hotel fees" in long-term care facilities, transportation if not in emergency). The patient will pay in full for certain services, e.g. plastic surgery other than due to congenital failure, trauma, disease or treatment of it, acupuncture, some stomatological services not included in the basket of services guaranteed by the health fund, emergency care other than that due to accidents, traumas or life threatening situations. As stated before, certain high-cost procedures and drugs will be financed through general taxes (from the central budget). Theses include – *inter alia* - tertiary care and oncology drugs.

6. FINANCING THE SYSTEM

Health insurance funds are financed from payroll contributions collected from the insured and his/her employer. The level of contributions varies significantly among the three countries. As a general principle, contributions are levied on gross salaries. In some cases, pensions and unemployment benefits and other types of personal incomes are also liable for contributions. Another problem of comparison is that in the Czech Republic and Hungary both employers and employees are charged with an additional insurance fee for income replacement in case of sickness. In these two countries, the contribution is not linear, as the percentage fee indicates. The burden is capped for employees (but not for employers). Czech workers hit the ceiling at 600% of the average wage. In Hungary the ceiling is fixed in absolute terms. In 1999, its level corresponded approximately to 200% of gross average wages. To make comparisons even more complicated the rate of contribution and its detailed method of calculation change in Hungary virtually every year.

The second source of health care financing comes from the central budget. The budget contributes on behalf of certain social groups - mostly those without incomes (in the Czech Republic children and student, in Poland the unemployed not receiving benefits). It also finances health care directly. The central budget co-finances investments in facilities in Hungary, and is supposed to take care of financing the most expensive services in the Polish system. Co-payments are required in all three countries, primarily as cost sharing in payments for drugs and in outpatient care.

Table 9.7 Health care premium in % levied on gross salary.

Country	1992	1993	1994	1995	1996	1997	1998	1999
Poland	-	-	-	-	-	-	-	7.5
Hungary*	27.9	26.3	26.3	24.8	24.8	23.2	22.5	20.9
Czech Republic**	13.5	13.5	13.5	13.5	13.5	13.5	13.5	13.5

Notes: Although it is frequently done, the percentage wise expressed contributions of employers and employees cannot be simply added (as shown in our table), since the first one is levied *on* the gross wage, while the second is deducted *from* the gross wage. Quantitatively, however, the distortion arising from this problem is not significant.

* These figures are estimated by one of the author, taking into account the totality of employers' contributions (linear rate, flat rate, contribution to rehabilitation), but excluding the burdens of direct sickness payments and the accident insurance payments rendered by self-employed.

** Excluding sickness contributions paid by both employers and employees, because these sums are not included in the revenues of the health insurance funds. Sickness payments and other health related cash expenditures (e.g. maternity leave) are covered by the state financed social insurance fund (i.e. the pension fund).

When splitting the social insurance fund into a pension fund and a health insurance fund in 1993, the Hungarian authorities decided to divide the 54% payroll tax levied on gross salary into two parts: 23.5% went to health and 30.5% to the pension fund. The employees contributed 4% and 6% respectively, and employers 19.5% and 24.5%, respectively. In subsequent years the employer's contribution to health insurance was reduced year after year. The employees' rate fell by 1 percentage point in 1993, then in 1998. For those people who are of working age, but self-employed the compulsory health contribution is 11.0 % (11.5 % in 1998) of the statutory minimum wage. Since 1997 there is also a fixed health contribution paid by the employer. At first, this was defined as 2100 HUF /month/employee (10 USD). In the subsequent year, the fixed sum was increased more or less along side with CPI inflation. Pensioners and children do not pay contributions at all.

The high rate of contribution caused increased incentives for the evasion of payments. The economic downturn in the 1990s resulted in growing unemployment, an extensive black economy and a worsening of the financial standing of many state and private companies. Evading health insurance contribution enabled companies to defer insolvency or bankruptcy. The arrears resulting from unpaid contributions in 1994 exceeded 20% of the total annual revenues of the NHIF. As contributions were insufficient to cover expenditures, the central budget has to come in with transfers every year. What is worse, contributions did not increase with GDP; thus, the professedly self-financing system is in a chronic deficit. As can be surmised from the above, the Hungarian health care system operates on the basis of dual financing. Major investments like equipment purchases and construction or maintenance are financed by local governments or co-financed from the central budget. Only the recurring expenditures on daily operations are financed by the NHIF.[5]

With an ongoing systemic deficit, the NHIF is facing a tricky task. Since the actual funding of the NHIF deficit is part of the general government deficit (*ex post*), the incentive to contain costs is weak. Furthermore, the NHIF has been under constant reform since its interception and there is still no political/professional consensus about its role. Several experts argue for a shift towards an UK-type state-financed, state-controlled organization, while others would like to push the system towards a more competitive structure with 4-6 participants. Decisions on these questions were promised in 1999, but these debates never ended. Another aspect of the public debate concerns the question of revenue collection. Until 1998, the NHIF collected the contributions with half of its staff being tied up in this work. The new government, elected in May 1998, followed the suggestion of its predecessor and took away this task from the NHIF. Thus, from January 1999, the Tax Authority collects the contributions on behalf of the NHIF. This was an important step towards a more focused health-care financing activity within the NHIF itself.

Co-payments in the Hungarian system can be requested in exceptional cases for specific health services, for example, if the insured wants higher standard of accommodation or referral to a provider other than suggested his GP or a lower-level specialist. In practice, however, this happens very rarely, if at all. Exceptional treatment is honored by the patient through illegal payments, the so-called gratitude money. The levels of subsidies for prescribed medicines in the out-patient system are 100%, 95%, 80%, 50% and 0% - depending on the class of the drug. For certain drugs, a fixed amount of subsidy is applied for all drugs with identical ingredients, regardless of their price. This move is intended to encourage the use of low cost generic drugs. In 1993 about 78% of expenditures on pharmaceuticals was covered by the insurance, the rest was co-paid by the population in out-of-pocket payments. By 1999, this level dropped to 65 per cent. The charges for therapeutical aids and therapeutical services (such as spas) are also subsidized by the NHIF. Drugs used in hospitals are not billed separately. These costs are incorporated in the DRG system.

The problem of health insurance contribution arrears also faces the health care system in the Czech Republic. It stems mainly from unpaid contributions by the self-employed, due to weak control of the system. The contributions are defined as a percentage of income before tax: employees pay 4.5% and employers 9%. The self employed pay the same proportion (13.5%) but it is levied on only 35% of their profits. The Ministry of Finance contributes 13.5% of 80% of the minimum wage on behalf of the unemployed, pensioners, students and children.

About 60% of contributions' fees collected by health insurance are redistributed by the GHIC according to a capitation formula. For insured over the age of 60 three times the standard capitation rate for those being under 60 is allocated. This weighting probably exceeds the true average costs of health care for those over 60, so the redistribution tends to favor the GHIC, which insures most of the elderly population.

It was proposed at the beginning of the transformation process that there should be a multi-source system of financing. As yet the system is fully financed from public funds. Co-insurance is in its infancy and covers mainly travel abroad, cosmetic surgery or special kinds of dental care.

Cost sharing is used mainly for selected drugs, dental services, and some medical aids. There are small co-payments for outpatient care. Co-payments represented some 5% of total health care expenditure in 1995 and about 10% in 1997. Under-the-table payments (gratitude money) seem not to be important anymore.

Table 9.8. Main groups of insured and their contributors

Country	Farmers	Unemployed	Self employed	Employees	Children	Students	Pensio-ners
Hungary	Farmers	Labor Market Fund from contributions of employers and employees	Self employed	Employees and employers	Automatically insured by their parents at no extra charge	Automatically insured by their parents at no extra charge	State budget until 1997
Czech Republic	N/A	Central budget	Self employed	Employees and employers	Central budget	Central budget	Central budget
Poland	Central budget	Central Budget or Labor Fund (for those receiving cash benefits)	Self employed	Employees and Employers	Automatically insured by their parents at no extra charge	Automatically insured by their parents at no extra charge	SIF[6]

Source: Reforma (1998); WHO (1996).

In Poland statutory health contribution premium amounts to 7.5% of gross incomes. It is deducted from income tax paid by all employees, pensioners and unemployed receiving unemployment benefits. Contribution of the unemployed not receiving benefits, farmers and veterans is paid by the central budget. The self-employed pay the same contribution (7.5%), but it is levied on a statistically calculated average wage level. There is no financial limit up above which the health insurance fund may not spend its revenues on administrative costs although this issue had been debated before the acceptance of the reform program.

The new health insurance system provides the vast majority of resources to finance health care. In general, financing provision of primary and secondary care is the responsibility of the health funds (that also include drug reimbursement, dental care, rehabilitation and nursing care, but excludes "hotel costs"). Certain specialized procedures, so called tertiary care (e.g. Bone marrow transplants, open-heart surgeries, but also certain drugs on prescription) are financed from the central budget. The central budget is also responsible to finance, among others, the following items: investments, emergency service, blood transfusion, health policy programs, sanitary inspection, occupational medicine, prevention of communicable diseases such as AIDS, and also drug addiction and alcoholism.

In addition, health funds receive money from the central budget as contributions for certain groups of people (e.g. farmers, the unemployed). The territorial health funds and the Branch Fund participate in a revenue equalization process according to an equalization formula which includes two risk factors (age and revenue per capita) in order to flatten the revenue differences between the funds. In the future, other risk factors will be included.

In some cases, the insured are also subject to co-payments. Drugs are subsidized by the HIFs by 50, 70% and 100% (drugs against chronic diseases). If patients choose better standard of services than accepted by the HIF, they have to pay extra. E.g. choosing a hospital for treatment from the list provided by an HIF results in full reimbursement by HIF, but choosing a facility with a higher "reference level" will result in co-payment.

Article 4a of the Act gives the insured the possibility of opting-out, starting 1 January 2002. The premium collected by other institutions than a health fund (most likely the private insurers) will still be offset for tax purposes up 7.5 % of earnings.

There are several cost-containment measures incorporated in the Polish Health Insurance Act. The important ones are:

1. The funds prepare a financial plan that has to be balanced. The plan is submitted to the Supervisory Office by September 30 of the preceding year;
2. Each HIF creates a reserve fund, which can be used only in the cases when spending exceeds revenue; the Supervisory Office has to be notified;
3. There is limited co-payment (mostly stomathological services), thus, its efficiency will probably be limited;
4. The family doctor acts as a „gatekeeper" what is believed to limit the access to specialized care, diagnostic tests, inpatient treatment;
5. The premium may be raised only by the amendment of the Health Act by Parliament;
6. There is wide power of the Supervisory Office to control the financial activities of the health funds.

Despite these measures, it is questionable whether they will be effective. According to international experience, the effective way to constrain inflation in the social insurance model is by the demand-side approach, which is negligible in the Act. The level and scope of co-payments is insufficient. Therefore, due to the increased volume of services expenditure will probably rise. For example, hospital payments based on *per admission* basis will likely increase the total number of admissions (hospitals will be interested in it) and subsequently the expenditure of the health funds on inpatient care will probably grow in absolute terms as well.

7. HEALTH EXPENDITURES AT MACRO LEVEL

The expenditure in the three countries as a proportion of GDP is still below West European levels. However, if the countries' absolute development level is taken into account, the opposite can be said: all three countries spend more on health than the OECD countries used to spend when their per capita GDP was at similar levels. In absolute terms, of course, the three East European countries spend only a fraction of the sums available in more advanced OECD countries (Tables 9.9 and 9.10).

Table 9.9. Developments in health care expenditures as a % of GDP

Country	1990	1991	1992	1993	1994	1995	1996	1997	1998	1999
Poland	4.4	4.7	5.0	4.6	4.6	4.2	4.0	5.3		
Hungary	10.6	10.6	11.2	11.1	11.1	9.7	9.5	8.5	8.2	8.1
Czech R	5.4	5.3	5.4	7.3	7.6	7.5	7.2	7.0		

Source: Authors' estimates based on official national statistics and other information. Individual countries' data can be compared with great deal of caution only. The authors attempted to focus on the consistency of time series for each of the three countries individually.

Table 9.10. Per capita health-care expenditures in US dollars at purchasing power parity (1997 or latest available data)

Turkey	232	Belgium	1747
POLAND	371	Austria	1793
Mexico	391	Australia	1805
Korea	587	Norway	1814
HUNGARY	602	Netherlands	1825
CZECH REPUBLIC	904	Denmark	1848
Greece	974	Iceland	2005
Portugal	1125	France	2051
Spain	1168	Canada	2095
Ireland	1324	Germany	2339
United Kingdom	1347	Luxembourg	2340
New Zealand	1352	Switzerland	2547
Finland	1447	USA	4090
Italy	1589		
Sweden	1728		
Japan	1741	OECD-average	1558

Source: OECD

In Hungary, the National Health Insurance Fund contributes about 70% of the money spent on health care, local and central governments pay 20-25%, while the rest is provided directly by the population. Czech taxpayers (employers, employees and the self-employed) contribute about 75-80% of total health care funding *via* the compulsory health insurance system. State and local government budgets accounted for some 10-15%. The households provide the remaining 10% (as co-payments).

Table 9.11. Total health care expenditures by the source of financing.

Country	Contribution	Budgets	Co-payments
Czech Republic	75%	15%	10%
Hungary	70%	15%	15%
Poland (before 1999)	-	app. 76%	app. 24%

Source: Authors information.

Total expenditures for medicines increased substantially in the Czech Republic and Hungary in the first half of 1990s, chiefly because of the substantial increase in cost of drugs resulting from increased imports.

Table 9.12. Expenditures on drugs as % of GDP

Country	1990	1991	1992	1993	1994	1995	1996
Hungary	1.28	1.78	1.94	2.09	2.2	2.3	2.4
Czech Republic	N/A.	1.05	1.45	1.42	1.86	1.95	1.90

Source: Potucek (1998); Orosz et al (1998); national estimates

8. CONCLUSIONS

From a financial perspective, the reforms of health care brought mixed results. In Hungary, health care expenditures relative to GDP are on the decline. This is explained predominantly by the large-scale evasion of contribution payments. Although the central government, local governments and the patients themselves are forced to put money in the system, this is not enough to compensate for the erosion of contributions. In Hungary, the share of wage earners' contributions fell between 1992 and 1999 from 60 to 51 % in total health expenditures. This gap was filled by direct payments of patients. From an economic point of view, this rising share of "self-financing" is not problematic. The problem is that Hungary was unable to develop alternative insurance mechanisms that would allow its citizens to handle health costs in a fair and efficient manner. This is not a desirable tendency and Poland should make attempts to avoid such a pattern by making private health insurance operate efficiently.

It is possible that Poland will follow the Hungarian or Czech experience, since it is adopting a system where nobody (except for the Ministry of Finance) is interested in containing costs. International experience shows that in order to prepare a system to be financed via social insurance 3-5 years are needed to implement proper infrastructure, information technology, human resources and the legal framework. At the outset of the 1999 reforms, Poland had none of these elements.

The case of the Czech Republic is full of lessons. In that country the health insurance reform and the privatization of a large part of provision were not accompanied by determined cost-containment measures. A fee-for-service system with privatization as it was the case in the Czech Republic was bound to lead to an increase in services and costs. Health care expenditures grew by 2 percentage points of GDP in the first year of the Czech reform! Higher expenditures can be justified, to some extent, by the fact that medical staff's incomes were previously repressed. Capital expenditures on repairs of buildings and purchases of state-of-the-art equipment were also necessary. But a certain part of the increase in costs was unnecessary and detrimental. Equipment and beds are often underused – as compared to virtually *any* West European country.

In the Czech Republic we could observe increased initial spending, but, as the system of contribution collection was more leak-proof than in Hungary, no additional funds from the central budget or from households were necessary. But the situation in the Czech Republic is not without danger, either. Not only leaking generates contribution losses. In the case of Hungary, growing unemployment was part of the problem, or more precisely, the falling level of recorded, official employment. As the job market took a disadvantageous turn in 1992, the social security system was hurt immediately through the loss of contribution revenue. By 1998, the rise in unemployment was arrested but the acceleration of output growth was not reflected in a proportionate rise of official employment. In the Czech Republic unemployment was not a main issue until recently. For the last 2-3 years, however, the rate of unemployed is on the rise.

Sometimes, it is argued that the volume of health care, and thus, the share of health care expenditures, may be overstated, because physicians in the Czech Republic and Hungary regularly issue fraudulent bills. This claim is probably unfounded. Although, the incentive system imbedded in the mechanisms of financing health care institutions is open for such misbehavior, this *cannot* lead to large excess spending at the aggregate level, because cost manipulations affect mostly the division of income among health care providers. Nevertheless, much remains to be done in improving cost control mechanisms and ensuring the quality of care, even if it is clear in advance that there are administrative costs related to the new organizations and bodies supervising them. On the other hand, a closer inspection of the Czech data suggest that the above mentioned changes *did* lead to a comparatively significant relative increase in the remuneration of doctors and nurses – certainly more so than it happened in Hungary or Poland.

In Poland the contribution rate was set at much lower level than for the two other countries. During the legislative process the opposition proposed a 10% rate, which was rejected. Although the 7.5% rate seems low compared to Hungary and the Czech Republic, it nevertheless ensures, that in the first year of the reform (1999) health care spending increased by about 7% in real terms. Whether this is enough or not is too early to tell. Medical staff is underpaid and many facilities are in need for renovation. The "solution" may come in one of two ways - either the rate of contribution will have to increase, or the budget will have to subsidize HIFs with additional transfers. In either case it will put pressure on the population, as it is very unlikely that increased financing will be solely made via increased budget deficits. It is also important to remember that in the case of financial deficiency of the regional health funds, it is possible that local governments, where the health fund operates, may give the health fund a loan (there are no statutory limits here). It is very likely that some NHFs will borrow in order to finance their expenditure increases and probably they will not be able to pay back the loans. So they will argue for contributions increase, which will - at the end of the day - lead to higher public expenditures the health care.

A general problem is the over-capacity on the supply side. In a tax-financed, government controlled system the costs are pretty much under control. In the new social insurance system physician-induced demand may lead to increased spending and there is no proof that the quality of care will be higher. The system can become public and heavily politicized. Thus, it is difficult to point out a player, except for a private insurer or provider, that will be interested in a reliable and effective system of claims' processing or provides competition on quality and price, willingness to sack excessive staff, etc. In Hungary a major accomplishment was the decrease of one quarter in the volume of expensive hospital beds without affecting the quality of care. Regional differences in care also decreased over the past ten years. The number of family practices increased and their equipment improved with the majority of family physicians working in the privatized system offering better incentives. A system of home care and home nursing was also established. The supply side has also decreased in the Czech Republic – since the implementation of the reform the number of hospital beds has decreased by 10%. As the system of providing health is posing severe problems and arguments in developed countries as well, there is no easy path to follow for the three reforming economies.

But there are clear and unquestionable results of the reforms as well. In all three countries, the reform made health care personnel much more sensitive to patients' needs. In the previous system patient's requirements were almost completely ignored. A major accomplishment of the reform is the fact, that consumers can now choose their own physician, treatments and the facilities where they are treated.

There is no proof that the financing of health care based on general tax revenues is better than the one based on social insurance (or vice versa). To a large extent, everything depends on the implementation of the system. In general, social insurance is perceived as more expensive than financing from general tax revenues because of higher administrative costs, moral hazard and supply-induced demand. Technical efficiency can be improved in both systems, e.g. by reducing the doctor/patient ratios, but this works often against the principles of equity. Clearly, there is a trade-off here.

It is also known that the health status of the population depends more on the wealth of the country and its citizens than on total expenditures on health. Healthy life-style, food, sports, everyday comfort usually contribute more than increased health expenditure. In developed market economies the income elasticity of demand for health services is greater than 1, which means that health care has some common characteristics with luxury goods. This general rule, however, may not always hold in the short-term, as the example of Hungary showed.

ENDNOTES

[*] The authors work at the Central European University of Budapest and the Polish Ministry of Finance, respectively. The views presented here are their own and do not imply expression of any opinion on the part of their employers. Authors want to express their special thanks to Maciej Kolodziejczyk and Pawel Sztwiertnia for their help and comments.

[1] As of mid-2000, there were once again rumors of shifting the health insurance system back to the Prime Minister's Office.

[2] Diagnosis-related group. An US-born statistical system of classifying any inpatient stay into groups for the purpose of payment.

[3] Between 2001 and 2002, another 8-9 % reduction is envisaged by the Ministry of Health.

[4] After a few months, however, the change in government led to a change in investment policy priorities. Thus, the X-ray program was slowed down considerably to make room for other ideas.

[5] Until 2000, health care institutions were not allowed to spend a single forint of NHIF money on repairs, let alone capital investments. This separation of funds was abolished at the end of 1999, but there was no extra money earmarked for these types of expenditures.

[6] SIF - Social Insurance Fund (ZUS)

REFERENCES

GUS (1998), *Mały Rocznik Statystyczny (Small Statistical Yearbook) 1998*, GUS, Warsaw

NERA (1998), *Hungary Health Care Study (A Draft Report)*, National Economic Research Associates, London.

Potucek M. (1998), *Health policy reforms in the Czech and Slovak Republics as a political process*, Vienna

OECD (1992), *The Reform of Health Care - A Comparative Analysis of Seven OECD Countries*, Health Policy Studies series, Paris, OECD

OECD (1994), *The Reform of Health Care Systems - A Review of Seventeen OECD Countries*, Health Policy Studies series, Paris, OECD

OECD (1996), *Health Care Reform - The Will to Change*, Health Policy Studies series, Paris, OECD

OECD (1997), *Aging in OECD Countries (A Critical Policy Challenge)*, Social Policy Studies series, Paris, OECD

OECD (1999), *The Health Care System in: Hungary 1999*, OECD Economic Surveys, 1998-1999

Orosz, É., Ellena, G., and Jakab, M.(1998), *Reforming the Health Care System: The Unfinished Agenda*, Bokros, L. and Dethier, J.-J. (eds.): Public Finance Reform during the Transition: The Experience of Hungary, Washington, The World Bank

Reforma (1998), *Reforma służby zdrowia (Reform of health care)*, Centrum Informacyjne Rządu (Government's Information Centre), Warsaw.

WTO (1996), *Health Care Systems in Transition - Czech Republic*, WHO

Index

www.ingramcontent.com/pod-product-compliance
Lightning Source LLC
LaVergne TN
LVHW011755200926
848484LV00003B/708

9780792378280